Decision Making
and Rationality
in the Modern World

....

Upcoming Books in the Fundamentals of Cognition Series

Series Editors
Paul Bloom
Lynn Nadel

Methods in Cognitive Research
Fundamentals of Language
Fundamentals of Perception
Fundamentals of Social Cognition
Fundamentals of Cognitive Development
Fundamentals of Human Memory
Fundamentals of Comparative Cognition

Decision Making and Rationality in the Modern World

....

KEITH E. STANOVICH

University of Toronto

New York   Oxford

OXFORD UNIVERSITY PRESS

2010

Oxford University Press, Inc., publishes works that further Oxford University's
objective of excellence in research, scholarship, and education.

Oxford   New York
Auckland   Cape Town   Dar es Salaam   Hong Kong   Karachi
Kuala Lumpur   Madrid   Melbourne   Mexico City   Nairobi
New Delhi   Shanghai   Taipei   Toronto

With offices in
Argentina   Austria   Brazil   Chile   Czech Republic   France   Greece
Guatemala   Hungary   Italy   Japan   Poland   Portugal   Singapore
South Korea   Switzerland   Thailand   Turkey   Ukraine   Vietnam

Published by Oxford University Press, Inc.
198 Madison Avenue, New York, New York 10016
http://www.oup.com

Oxford is a registered trademark of Oxford University Press

Library of Congress Cataloging-in-Publication Data

Stanovich, Keith E., 1950–
    Decision making and rationality in the modern world/Keith E. Stanovich.
      p. cm.—(Fundamentals of cognition series)
    Includes bibliographical references and index.
    ISBN 978-0-19-532812-7 (alk. paper)
    1. Decision making.   2. Judgment.   3. Reasoning.   I. Title.
    BF448.S72 2009
    153. 8'3—dc22

                                                          2009012876

Printing number: 9 8 7 6 5 4 3 2 1
Printed in the United States of America
on acid-free paper

For Rich,
to commemorate the second stage of our
thirty-year research journey together

CONTENTS

....

Series Introduction   viii
Preface   ix

CHAPTER 1 Rational Thought and Behavior:
Figuring Out What Is True and What to Do   1

CHAPTER 2 Decision Making: Rationality of Action   8

CHAPTER 3 Judgment: Rationality of Belief   51

CHAPTER 4 How Bad Is Our Decision Making?
The Great Rationality Debate   93

CHAPTER 5 Resolving the Debate About the Rationality
of Judgment and Decision Making:
A Dual-Process Account   126

CHAPTER 6 Metarationality: Good Decision-Making Strategies
Are Self-Correcting   143

Bibliography   163
Index   189

SERIES INTRODUCTION

We conceived of the Fundamentals of Cognition series in recognition of an important need: when one teaches an advanced undergraduate course or introductory graduate seminar, there frequently is no suitable book available. Based on our own experience and discussions with our colleagues, we feel that the field needs a series of concise treatments of the fundamentals—primers. These provide state-of-the-art summaries while leaving ample room for additional reading of current material of the instructor's choice.

With this ideal in mind, each book in the Fundamentals of Cognition series has the following in common:

- It is concise
- It is written by a leading scholar in the field, one who has also exhibited an ability to write about complex subjects in an accessible style
- It provides a well-organized and up-to-date survey of our current understanding of the major theories in the discipline

We, in partnership with Oxford University Press, present the Fundamentals of Cognition.

Paul Bloom
Yale University

Lynn Nadel
University of Arizona

PREFACE

....

I accepted Paul Bloom's invitation to participate in this Oxford University Press series because of the opportunity to do a short, conceptually focused introduction to the field of judgment and decision making, as opposed to a comprehensive textbook. Most university-level instructors, as they gain more experience, evolve toward a "less is more" philosophy. This has certainly been true of my own teaching of judgment and decision making. As our field burgeons with more tasks, effects, biases, theories, and applications, teaching it without burying the student in a mass of detail becomes more and more of a challenge. Even more challenging is the attempt to put the field into some sort of context where the conceptual importance of the tasks, effects, and biases is appreciated.

I have taken the opportunity in this short volume to introduce the student to major concepts in judgment and decision making in the context of the Great Rationality Debate in cognitive science—the debate about how much irrationality to attribute to human cognition. Assumptions about human rationality shape how we design society and its institutions, such as the legal system, economic markets, and systems of governance. This is why Tetlock and Mellers (2002) have stressed that "the debate over human rationality is a high-stakes controversy that mixes primordial political and psychological prejudices in combustible combinations" (p. 97). So, although many of the tasks and experiments in the field would, to an outsider, seem to be about minutiae, there are large issues at stake.

In this book, I have tried to give the student a feel for why the experimental demonstrations that they see in their courses and in the laboratory actually speak to deep questions about the nature of mind and behavior. So what this book lacks in comprehensiveness, I hope it makes up for by providing a conceptual framework for the field. How people make decisions and how they form beliefs about the world are essential features of humans that are spoken to directly by the field of judgment and decision making.

I would like to thank my Editor at Oxford University Press, Patrick Lynch for his consistent support; Barbara Mathieu and Jeanne Ford who did great work in manuscript production; the series Editors, Paul Bloom and Lynn Nadel; and Oxford's readers who made very detailed and useful comments on earlier versions of the book: Terry Connolly, University of Arizona; Jonathan St. B. T. Evans, University of Plymouth; Gordon Pitz, University of North Carolina; and David Rettinger, University of Mary Washington. As indicated in my Dedication, my longest-serving reader of all is my friend and colleague Richard West of James Madison University.

Decision Making
and Rationality
in the Modern World

....

CHAPTER 1

....

Rational Thought and Behavior

Figuring Out What Is True and What to Do

Psychologists study rationality because it is one of the most important human values. A person's happiness and well-being can depend upon whether he or she thinks and acts rationally. The high status accorded rationality in this book may seem at odds with other characterizations that deem rationality either trivial (little more than the ability to solve textbook-type logic problems) or in fact antithetical to human fulfillment (as an impairment to an enjoyable emotional life, for instance). These ideas about rationality derive from a restricted and mistaken view of rational thought—one not in accord with the study of rationality in modern cognitive science.

Dictionary definitions of rationality tend to be rather lame and unspecific ("the state or quality of being in accord with reason"), and some critics who wish to downplay the importance of rationality have promulgated a caricature of rationality that involves restricting its definition to the ability to do the syllogistic reasoning problems that are encountered in Philosophy 101. The meaning of rationality in modern cognitive science is, in contrast, much more robust and important.

Cognitive scientists recognize two types of rationality: instrumental and epistemic. The simplest definition of *instrumental rationality,* the one that emphasizes most that it is grounded in the practical world, is the following: behaving in the world so that you get exactly what you most want, given the resources (physical and mental) available to you. Somewhat more technically, we could characterize instrumental rationality as the optimization of the individual's goal fulfillment. In the next chapter we shall see how economists and cognitive scientists have refined the notion of optimization of goal fulfillment into the technical notion of expected utility. The other aspect of rationality studied by cognitive scientists is termed *epistemic rationality*. This aspect of rationality concerns how well beliefs map onto the actual structure of the world. Epistemic rationality is sometimes termed *theoretical rationality* or *evidential rationality* by philosophers. Likewise, instrumental rationality is sometimes termed *practical rationality*. The two types of rationality are related. In order to take actions that fulfill our goals, we need to base those actions on beliefs that are properly calibrated to the world.

Although many people feel (mistakenly or not) that they could do without the ability to solve textbook logic problems (which is why the caricatured view of rationality works to undercut its status), virtually no person wishes to eschew epistemic rationality and instrumental rationality, properly defined. Virtually all people want their beliefs to be in some correspondence with reality, and they also want to act to maximize the achievement of their goals. Psychologist Ken Manktelow (2004) has emphasized the practicality of both types of rationality by noting that they concern two critical things: what is true and what to do. Epistemic rationality is about what is true, and instrumental rationality is about what to do. For our beliefs to be rational they must correspond to the way the world is—they must be true. For our actions to be rational, they must be the best means toward our goals—they must be the best things to do.[1]

Nothing could be more practical or useful for a person's life than the thinking processes that help him or her find out what is true and what

---

1. The student is warned that there are many alternative terms for instrumental and epistemic rationality in the literature (see Audi, 2001; Harman, 1995; Manktelow, 2004; Mele & Rawling, 2004; Nathanson, 1994; Over, 2004). For example, epistemic rationality is sometimes called theoretical rationality or evidential rationality. Instrumental rationality has been variously termed practical, pragmatic, or means/ends rationality in the literature. In the judgment and decision-making literature, the terms correspondence competence and coherence competence are sometimes used (Goldstein, 2004; Hammond, 1996, 2007). Correspondence competence concerns the degree to which beliefs map accurately to the environment and thus reflects what is called epistemic rationality in this book. Coherence competence refers to the ability to follow the consistency axioms of expected utility theory to be discussed in chapter 2. It thus relates to what will be called instrumental rationality in this volume.

is best to do. Such a view of rational thinking—as an eminently practical endeavor—will be the theme of this book. This theme stands in marked contrast to some restricted views of what rationality is (for example, the rationality = logic view that I mentioned earlier). From the viewpoint presented in this book, being rational is not just being logical. Instead, logic (and all other cognitive tools) must prove its worth. It must show that it helps us get at what is true or helps us to figure out what is best to do. My philosophy for the book will echo that of Jonathan Baron (2008), when he argues that

> the best kind of thinking, which we shall call rational thinking, is whatever kind of thinking best helps people achieve their goals. If it should turn out that following the rules of formal logic leads to eternal happiness, then it is rational thinking to follow the laws of logic (assuming that we all want eternal happiness). If it should turn out, on the other hand, that carefully violating the laws of logic at every turn leads to eternal happiness, then it is these violations that we shall call rational. (p. 61)

A similar admonition applies when we think about the relation between emotion and rationality. In folk psychology, emotion is seen as antithetical to rationality. The absence of emotion is seen as purifying thinking into purely rational form. This idea is not consistent with the definition of rationality adopted in this book. Instrumental rationality is behavior consistent with maximizing goal satisfaction, not a particular psychological process. It is perfectly possible for the emotions to facilitate instrumental rationality as well to impede it. In fact, conceptions of emotions in cognitive science stress the adaptive regulatory powers of the emotions. For example, in their discussion of the rationality of emotions, Johnson-Laird and Oatley (1992) conceptualized emotions as interrupt signals supporting goal achievement. Their basic idea is that emotions serve to stop the combinatorial explosion of possibilities that would occur if an intelligent system tried to calculate the utility of all possible future outcomes. Emotions are thought to constrain the possibilities to a manageable number based on similar situations in the past.

In short, emotions get us "in the right ballpark" of the correct response. If more accuracy than that is required, then a more precise type of analytic cognition (discussed in chapter 5) will be required. Of course, we can rely too much on the emotions. We can base responses on a "ball-park" solution in situations that really require a more precise type of analytic thought. More often than not, however, processes of emotional regulation facilitate rational thought and action.

Writer Malcolm Gladwell, in his best-selling book *Blink*, adopts the folk psychological view of the relation between emotion and rationality that is at odds with the way those concepts are discussed in cognitive science. Gladwell discusses the famous case studies of cognitive neuroscientist Antonio Damasio, where damage to the ventromedial prefrontal cortex of these individuals caused nonfunctional behavior without impairing intelligence. Gladwell (2005) argues that "people with damage to their ventromedial area are perfectly rational. They can be highly intelligent and functional, but they lack judgment" (p. 59). But this is not the right way to describe these cases. In the view I will develop in this book, someone who lacks judgment cannot be rational.

Take, for example, Damasio's (1994) description of one of his most famous patients, Elliot. Elliot had had a successful job in a business firm, and was something of a role model for younger colleagues. He had a good marriage and was a good father. Elliot's life was a total success story until one day—Damasio tells us—it began to unravel. Elliot began to have headaches and he lost his focus at work. The headaches had been caused by a brain tumor, which was surgically removed. Subsequent to the surgery, it was determined that Elliot had sustained substantial damage to the ventromedial area of the prefrontal cortex. He had lost a wide range of affective responses.

That was the bad news. The good news was that on an intelligence test given subsequent to the surgery, Elliot scored in the superior range. There was just one little problem here—one little remaining piece of bad news: Elliot's life was a mess. At work subsequent to the surgery Elliot was unable to allocate his time efficiently. He could not prioritize his tasks and received numerous admonitions from supervisors. When he failed to change his work behavior in the face of this feedback, he was fired. Elliot then charged into a variety of business ventures, all of which failed. One of these ventures ended in bankruptcy because Elliot had invested all of his savings in it. His wife divorced him. After this, he had a brief relationship with an inappropriate woman, married her quickly, and then, just as quickly, divorced her. He had just been denied Social Security disability benefits when he landed in Dr. Damasio's office.

This is not a man who is rational according to our definition. Elliot is not a person who is acting optimally in order to maximize his goal satisfaction. According to Gladwell's folk definition, Elliot has lost emotion, so he must be a rational thinker. In the view of modern cognitive science, this is not the case. Elliot is less rational because his processes of emotional regulation—which work in concert with more analytic cognition to support optimal responding—are deficient. As logic itself is a tool of rational thought, so is emotion.

To think rationally means taking the appropriate action given one's goals and beliefs, and holding beliefs that are commensurate with available evidence—but it also means adopting appropriate goals in the first place. Instrumental rationality covers the first of these (taking the appropriate action given one's goals) and epistemic rationality covers the second (holding beliefs that are commensurate with available evidence), but the third factor (adopting appropriate goals in the first place) introduces a new issue. That issue is the distinction between a thin and broad conception of rationality. Political science theorist Jon Elster (1983) deems traditional views of instrumental rationality *thin theories* because individuals' goals and beliefs are accepted as they are, and evaluation centers only on whether individuals are optimally satisfying their desires given their beliefs. Such a view represents a thin theory of rationality because it "leaves unexamined the beliefs and the desires that form the reasons for the action whose rationality we are assessing" (p. 1). It does not subject the desires and goals being maximized to evaluation.

The strengths of the thin theory of instrumental rationality are well known. For example, as we shall see in the next chapter, if the conception of rationality is restricted to a thin theory, many powerful formalisms (such as the axioms of decision theory) are available to serve as normative standards for behavior. The weaknesses of the thin theory are equally well known. In not evaluating desires, a thin theory of rationality would be forced to say that Hitler was a rational person as long as he acted in accordance with the basic axioms of choice as he went about fulfilling his grotesque desires. By failing to evaluate desires, a startlingly broad range of human behavior and cognition escapes the evaluative net of the thin theory. Elster (1983), for one, argues that "we need a broader theory of rationality that goes beyond the exclusively formal considerations...and that allows a scrutiny of the substantive nature of the desires and beliefs in action" (p. 15).

Developing a broad theory of rationality—one that encompasses a substantive critique of desires—has a cost, however. It means taking on some very difficult issues in philosophy and cognitive science. We will nonetheless engage some of these complexities in the final chapter.

However, the field of judgment and decision making in psychology represents largely the study of the thought processes that lead to the rationality of action (taking the appropriate action given one's goals) and to the rationality of belief (holding beliefs that are commensurate with available evidence), respectively. We shall take up the former (instrumental rationality) in chapter 2 and the latter (epistemic rationality) in chapter 3. In those two chapters we will see that humans often display patterns of behavior that depart from those that define both types of rationality. In chapter 4 we will examine the Great Rationality Debate in cognitive science—the debate about just how to interpret the empirical results discussed in chapters 2 and 3. Researchers in the so-called heuristics and biases tradition have interpreted the violations of the rules of good decision making as demonstrations of problematic aspects of human cognition that need to be meliorated. In contrast, evolutionary psychologists and other theorists have emphasized the adaptiveness of some of the responses that people give on judgment and decision-making tasks. In chapter 4 we discuss these alternative interpretations of the empirical literature. In chapter 5, the positions of both sides in the Great Rationality Debate are reconciled within a dual-process theory of human cognition. In chapter 6 we discuss some of the inadequacies of thin theories of rationality and take up some of the broader questions surrounding human judgment and decision making such as the following: When is it rational to be (narrowly) rational? What goals are rational to pursue? What should a person do in situations of coordinate action, where if everyone rationally pursues their own interests, everyone will lose?

Suggestions for Further Reading

Adler, J. E., & Rips, L. J. (2008). *Reasoning: Studies of human inference and its foundations.* New York: Cambridge University Press.

Audi, R. (2001). *The architecture of reason: The structure and substance of rationality.* Oxford: Oxford University Press.

Harman, G. (1995). Rationality. In E. E. Smith & D. N. Osherson (Eds.), *Thinking* (Vol. 3, pp. 175–211). Cambridge, MA: MIT Press.

Manktelow, K. I. (2004). Reasoning and rationality: The pure and the practical. In K. I. Manktelow & M. C. Chung (Eds.), *Psychology of reasoning: Theoretical and historical perspectives* (pp. 157–177). Hove, UK: Psychology Press.

Mele, A. R., & Rawling, P. (Eds.). (2004). *The Oxford handbook of rationality.* Oxford: Oxford University Press.

Nathanson, S. (1994). *The ideal of rationality*. Chicago: Open Court.

Nickerson, R. S. (2008). *Aspects of rationality*. New York: Psychology Press.

Over, D. E. (2004). Rationality and the normative/descriptive distinction. In D. J. Koehler & N. Harvey (Eds.), *Blackwell handbook of judgment and decision making* (pp. 3–18). Malden, MA: Blackwell.

Samuels, R., & Stich, S. P. (2004). Rationality and psychology. In A. R. Mele & P. Rawling (Eds.), *The Oxford handbook of rationality* (pp. 279–300). Oxford: Oxford University Press.

....

CHAPTER 2

Decision Making

Rationality of Action

Good decision making means being instrumentally rational. Instrumental rationality concerns taking action—what to do. It requires you to behave in the world so that you get exactly what you most want, given the resources (physical and mental) available to you. Somewhat more technically, we could characterize instrumental rationality as the optimization of the individual's goal fulfillment. Economists and cognitive scientists have refined the idea of optimization of goal fulfillment into the technical notion of expected utility. The model of rational judgment used by decision scientists is one in which a person chooses options based on which option has the largest expected utility.

Cognitive psychologist Jonathan Baron (2008) has discussed how the term *utility* is a slippery word. It is used technically in decision science in ways that do not map exactly into anything in general discourse. The term as used in cognitive science does not refer to its primary dictionary definition of "usefulness." Instead, in decision theory it means something closer to "goodness." It is important to realize that utility is not the same as pleasure. Instead, utility refers to the good that accrues when people achieve their goals—and a person's goal is not always to maximize pleasure. Utility is thus more closely related to the notions of worth or desirability than it is to pleasure or hedonism. Hastie and Dawes (2001) suggest that it is perhaps best to think of utility as an index of subjective value.

Viewing utility as subjective value provides a nice link to the most basic normative model of optimal decision making: *maximizing expected value*. Before proceeding with a discussion of the expected value model—and its twin, *subjective expected utility*—we need to distinguish a normative from a descriptive model of decision making. A normative model of decision making is different from a descriptive model. Descriptive models are specifications of the response patterns of human beings and theoretical accounts of those observed response patterns in terms of psychological mechanisms. This type of model is the goal of most work in empirical psychology. In contrast, normative models embody *standards* for action and belief—standards that, if met, serve to optimize the accuracy of beliefs and the efficacy of actions. Expected value and subjective expected utility are normative models—they tell us how we *should* make decisions. We will see that a very large literature in cognitive psychology indicates that the descriptive model of how people actually behave deviates from the normative models. In chapter 4 we will discuss alternative interpretations of these behavioral deviations.

In this chapter, we will first consider the simplest of normative models of decision making—expected value—and we will see why it is inadequate. A more encompassing model of optimal choice—subjective expected utility—will then be introduced. Rationality is defined as the maximization of subjective expected utility (SEU). We will then see how the so-called axiomatic approach to SEU provides an easier way of measuring whether people are choosing actions in a rational manner. In that approach, rational choices are defined by consistency relationships among one's actions. The remainder of the chapter will contain a discussion of the empirical evidence indicating that people have been shown to violate many of the axioms of rational choice.

Expected Value and Subjective Expected Utility

Decision situations can be broken down into three components: (a) possible actions, (b) possible events or possible states of the world, and (c) evaluations of the consequences of possible actions in each possible state of the world. Because there are almost always one or more possible future states of world, any action can be viewed as gamble—the consequences of the gamble are unknown because the future state of the world is unknown. Because all of life is a gamble in this respect (we cannot predict consequences for sure because future states of the world cannot be known with certainty), cognitive scientists often study actual gambles to examine how people make decisions and deal with risk.

Consider the following two gambles:

> gamble A: Win $10 if a red card is drawn from a deck of cards; lose
> $6 if a black card is drawn from a deck of cards.
> gamble B: Win $20 if a heart is drawn from a deck of cards; lose $2 if
> a heart is not drawn from a deck of cards.

Gamble A could be represented as follows:

Future state of the world: Red card drawn	Future state of the world: Black card drawn
Outcome: Win $10	Outcome: Lose $6

Likewise, gamble B could be represented as follows:

Future state of the world: Heart drawn	Future state of the world: Heart not drawn
Outcome: Win $20	Outcome: Lose $2

Suppose the decision we faced was whether to choose gamble A or gamble B. Choosing not to gamble is not an option. A choice between two actions must be made. One action is to choose gamble A. The other action is to choose gamble B. One rule to employ here is to choose the action with the highest expected value. But this cannot yet be calculated, because one thing is still missing from our framework. We have not specified the probabilities of the future states of the world. This is easily done if we remember that there are 52 cards in a deck, half are red and half are black, and there are four suits (hearts, diamonds, spades, and clubs) each with 13 cards. The probability of drawing a red card is thus .5 and the probability of drawing a heart is thus .25 (and the probability of drawing a non-heart is thus .75). So the two alternative actions are more completely represented as follows:

Gamble A:

Action:	Future state of the world: Red card (.5 probability)	Future state of the world: Black card (.5 probability)
Choose gamble A	Outcome: Win $10	Outcome: Lose $6

Gamble B:

Action:	Future state of the world: Heart (.25 probability)	Future state of the world: Not Heart (.75 probability)
Choose gamble B	Outcome: Win $20	Outcome: Lose $2

The principle of maximizing expected value says that the action that a rational person should choose is the one with the highest expected value. Expected value is calculated by taking the value of each outcome and multiplying it by the probability of that outcome and then summing those products over all of the possible outcomes. Symbolically, the formula is:

Expected Value = $\Sigma p_i v_i$

where p_i is the probability of each outcome and v_i is the value of each outcome. The symbol Σ is the summation sign, and simply means "add up all of the terms that follow."

For gamble A the expected value is $.5(\$10) + .5(-\$6) = \$5 + (-\$3) = +\$2$

For gamble B the expected value is $.25(\$20) + .75(-\$2) = \$5 + (-\$1.5)$
$$= +\$3.50$$

So on the expected value principle, choosing gamble B is the better action. Of course, there is no guarantee that gamble B will be better in each instance, but over many such similar choices, gamble B will—in the long run—yield $1.50 more per play than will gamble A.

Monetary value is not equal to utility, however. It is easy to think of cases in which one would not want to choose based on maximizing the expected value of the option. Resnik (1987) discussed cases like the following. Imagine you had saved for four years to raise $10,000, which is what you need for a down payment on a home. Two months before you are to make your purchase, someone offers you an investment opportunity. It is one where if you invest your $10,000, in one month you will have an 80% chance of receiving $100,000. However, there is a 20% chance that you will lose all of your money. This gamble is not attractive even though it has an expected value of $80,000 and you must pay only $10,000 to participate. The dollar value here does not translate into utility in a linear fashion. By finding this bet unattractive you are saying that the utility difference between $0 and $10,000 is larger than the utility difference between $10,000 and $100,000 despite the fact that that is not true of the actual dollar amounts.

Things can go in the opposite direction as well in certain special situations. Imagine that you owe $10,000 to a gangster loan shark and must pay it in two hours or get your legs broken. You only have $8,000. Then someone offers you a gamble which you must pay your $8,000 to play. They will flip a coin and if it comes up heads you get $10,000 and if it comes up tails you get nothing. You might find this gamble attractive even though it costs you $8,000 to play and it has an expected value of only $5,000. The reason is that you are in a special situation where the utility difference between $8,000 and $10,000 is larger than the utility difference between $0 and $8,000 despite the fact that that is not true of the actual dollar amounts.

Special situations aside, however, increments in utility for a given monetary value generally decrease as the wealth of the individual increases. As long ago as 1738, mathematician Daniel Bernoulli recognized that the utility of $100 to you if your net worth was $1 million is much less than the utility of $100 to you if your net worth was just $1,000. Or, as Bernoulli (1738/1954) put it at the time, "A gain of one thousand ducats is more significant to a pauper than to a rich man though both gain the same amount."

The more general point here though is that expected value is not the same as the quantity we actually want to estimate: expected utility. Thus, the expected value model must be replaced by an expected utility model, which will add generality as well. The value of winning a kayaking trip in a raffle is measured in its consumption utility, not its monetary value. For someone who has water phobias, its utility might be less than zero.

The expected utility model will allow us to make rational choices in situations like the following: Tomorrow, there are two possible activities on the docket for your family. Either your family can go to the modern art museum or it can go to the beach, but it cannot do both. The first preference of everyone is for the beach, but the Weather Channel says it might rain. Rain would totally ruin the trip to the beach, and you would not have time to backtrack from the coast and go to the museum in the city. The museum trip will not be as good as the beach trip on a good day, but it will be much better than the beach on rainy day. The museum on a rainy day is almost as good as the museum on a day that is not rainy, but not quite. The reason is that there is a neat sculpture garden that would have to be missed if it were raining. Thus, in terms of actions, future states of the world, and outcomes, the decision situation looks like this:

	Future state of the world: It does not rain	Future state of the world: It rains
Action: Go to the beach	Outcome: Most preferred	Outcome: Least preferred
Action: Go to the museum	Outcome: Much preferred to a rainy beach trip	Outcome: Not quite as good as the museum on a nonrainy day

Of course, to subject this situation to a more formal expected utility analysis, we would need a utility estimate for each of the four possible outcomes. But we would need something else as well. We would need to know the probability of it raining tomorrow. In the gambling problems presented earlier, the probability of the future states was known because of the structure of the card deck. In our situation here, the probability that it will rain is not specified *for* the decision maker, but has to be estimated *by* the decision maker. In fact, in most situations in real life the probabilities are not specified by the situation, but have to be subjectively estimated by the decision maker.

Let us assume that the decision maker estimates that the probability of rain is .20. Imagine also that the estimated utilities are as displayed in the table here. Keep in mind that these utility estimates need be relative ones only. If all of these numbers were divided by 10, the calculations that follow would lead to the same decision.

	Future state of the world: It does not rain (probability .80)	Future state of the world: It rains (probability .20)
Action: Go to the beach	Outcome: 100	Outcome: 10
Action: Go to the museum	Outcome: 60	Outcome: 50

We can now apply the maximizing expectation formula as before, except that utilities are substituted for monetary value and subjectively estimated probabilities are substituted for stipulated probabilities:

Subjective Expected Utility (SEU) = $\Sigma p_i u_i$

Where p_i is the subjectively estimated probability of each outcome and u_i is the utility of each outcome.

For the action of going to the beach, the SEU is

$.80(100) + .20(10) = 80 + 2 = 82$

For the action of going to the museum, the SEU is

$.80(60) + .20(50) = 48 + 10 = 58$

Thus, based on an SEU analysis, the action that maximizes expected utility is to go to the beach. This is how an SEU analysis would go in theory. The right action based on an SEU analysis of a person's probabilities and utilities would be compared to the choices that the person actually made. Rationality would be indexed by the closeness of the correspondence. In practice, assessing rationality in this manner can be difficult because eliciting personal probabilities can be tricky. Also, getting measurements of the utilities of various consequences can be experimentally difficult.

The Axiomatic Approach to Expected Utility

Fortunately, there is another useful way to measure the rationality of decisions and deviations from rationality, which is based on one of the fundamental discoveries of modern decision science. It has been proven through several formal analyses that if people's preferences follow certain logical patterns (the so-called *axioms of choice*) then they are behaving as if they are maximizing utility (Dawes, 1998; Edwards, 1954; Jeffrey, 1983; Luce & Raiffa, 1957; Savage, 1954; von Neumann & Morgenstern, 1944). This is the so-called axiomatic approach to whether people are maximizing utility. It is what makes people's degrees of rationality more easily measurable by the experimental methods of cognitive science. The deviation from the optimal choice pattern according to the axioms is a measure (an inverse one) of the degree of rationality.

The axiomatic approach to choice defines instrumental rationality as adherence to certain types of consistency and coherence relationships.[1] For example, one such axiom is that of *transitivity:* If you prefer A to B and B to C, then you should prefer A to C. Violating transitivity is a serious violation of rationality because it could lead to what decision theorists call a "money pump"—a situation where, if you were prepared to act on

---

1. This is the coherence competence that is sometimes discussed in the judgment and decision-making literature (Goldstein, 2004; Hammond, 1996, 2007).

your intransitive preferences, you would be drained of all your wealth. For example, consider three objects that we will arbitrarily label object A, object B, and object C. It is very unwise to prefer object A to B, B to C, and C to A. If you do not think so, I would like to give you—free of charge— object A. That might seem like a nice thing to do. And it is. But because you have intransitive preferences, what I am about to do is not so nice.

I will begin by offering you object C for a little bit of money and for giving me A back. Because you prefer C to A, there must be some finite, if however small, sum of money that you would give me, along with A, to get C. Then, for a little bit of money and object C, I will give you object B (which you say you prefer to C). And, because you gave me A a little while ago, I can now offer it to you in exchange for B (and a little bit of money, of course, because you really prefer A to B). And then I can offer you C....Everyone would probably agree at this point that, basically, this deal stinks! But note that the horribleness of the deal derives from your own preferences—I have only engaged with you in trades in which you agree that you want to trade what you have for what I have. This is why violations of transitivity are such a bad thing, from the standpoint of rationality. No one has to cheat you out of your money because, in a sense, you will cheat yourself out of it!

Of course, at this point, you might be tempted to reply: "But I would not lose money, because I would see what was happening. I would bail out or change my preferences before I started losing." But that, in fact, is just the message carried by the money pump thought experiment. You would view the possibility of a money pump as a clear signal that there might be something wrong with your preference structure.

Following, rather than violating, the principle of transitivity in choice and others like it defines rationality in many disciplines that stress coherence in judgment—that is, that adopt thin theories of rationality as defined in the last chapter. For example, the standard view of so-called "rational man" in economics assumes utility maximization. That is, it is traditionally assumed that people have stable, underlying preferences for each of the options presented in a decision situation. It is assumed that a person's preferences for the options available for choice are complete, well ordered, and well behaved in terms of the axioms of choice (transitivity, and others to be discussed). Economist Gary Becker (1976), for example, states the view of economics as "All human behavior can be viewed as involving participants who maximize their utility from a stable set of preferences" (p. 14).

Irrelevant Context and the Axioms of Choice

All of the axioms of choice, in one way or another, ensure that decisions are not influenced by irrelevant context. If preferences are affected by irrelevant context, then the preferences cannot be stable and we cannot be maximizing utility. It is important to note that what is "irrelevant context" is defined in this literature subjectively—as a contextual feature that people themselves would not want to affect their decision. In the studies that will be discussed in this chapter, the influence of a contextual factor is only deemed irrational if people are overwhelmingly consistent in deeming the contextual factor irrelevant. The difference between an irrelevant contextual feature and a relevant one can be illustrated by comparing transitivity with a well-known example of another axiom of instrumental rationality.

Pretend that Bill prefers, successively, object A to object B in choice 1, B to C in choice 2, and then C to A in choice 3—apparent intransitivity. We might try to absolve Bill of violating transitivity by saying that he was responding to a contextual feature: what objects were involved in the choice just before the one he is making. We could posit that Bill does not view the second alternative in the third choice as simply "A," but, instead, something that he puts a different utility on: "object A offered immediately after a choice involving B." To him, this bizarre entity—"object A offered immediately after a choice involving B"—is not valued the same as the A in choice 1, which he sees as "object A offered in the first choice made." Thus, an "A offered immediately after a choice involving B" might as well be designated D—and there is no inconsistency at all in preferring A to B, B to C, and then C to D. Bill is now no longer intransitive if we deem this contextual feature to be relevant.

Most of us would not find this argument convincing. This kind of contextual difference, most of us feel, should not be affecting a person's choices. But let us consider a different axiom of rational choice in order to see how sometimes we do view a contextual feature as relevant. The principle of *independence of irrelevant alternatives* can be illustrated by the following humorous imaginary situation. A diner is told by a waiter that the two dishes of the day are steak and pork chops. The diner chooses steak. Five minutes later, the waiter returns and says, "Oh, I forgot, we have lamb as well as steak and pork chops." The diner says, "Oh, in that case, I'll have the pork chops." The diner has violated the property of independence of irrelevant alternatives, and we can see why this property is a foundational principle of rational choice by just noting how deeply odd the choices seem. Formally, the diner has chosen x when presented with x and y, but prefers y when presented with x, y, and z. Such a preference reversal is exactly what is prohibited by the principle of irrelevant alternatives.

However, consider an example discussed by Nobel prize–winning economist Amartya Sen (1993). A guest at a party is faced with a bowl with one apple in it. The individual leaves the apple—thus choosing nothing (x) over an apple (y). A few minutes later, the host puts a pear (z) in the bowl. Shortly thereafter, the guest takes the apple. Seemingly, the guest has just done what the diner did in the previous example. The guest has chosen x when presented with x and y, but has chosen y when presented with x, y, and z. Has the independence of irrelevant alternatives been violated? Most will think not. Choice y in the second situation is not the same as choice y in the first—so the equivalency required for a violation of the principle seems not to hold. While choice y in the second situation is simply "taking an apple," choice y in the first is contextualized and probably construed as "taking the last apple in the bowl when I am in public" with all of its associated negative utility inspired by considerations of politeness.

Sen's (1993) example illustrates a situation where it definitely does make sense to contextualize a situation beyond the consumption utilities involved. In contrast, in the dining example, it did not make sense to code the second offer of y to be "pork chops when lamb is on the menu" and the first to be "pork chops without lamb on the menu." A choice comparison between steak and pork should not depend on what else is on the menu. Sometimes though, as in the second example, the context of the situation *is* appropriately integrated with the consumption utility of the object on offer. It makes social sense, when evaluating the utilities involved in the situation, to consider the utility of the first y to be the positive utility of consuming the apple plus the negative utility of the embarrassment of taking the last fruit in the bowl.

Nonetheless, most of the choice situations that have been studied by decision scientists are *not* like the fruit example—they involve contextual factors that most people agree *should* be ignored. Literally dozens of studies throughout the last 30 years have demonstrated that people are systematically influenced by contextual factors that are clearly irrelevant to the decision. These findings have the implication that people are less than rational—that the thinking of most people could be improved so that they acted more optimally to achieve their goals. This is true because the axioms of choice operationalize the idea that an individual has preexisting preferences for all potential options that are complete, well ordered, and stable. When presented with options, the individual simply consults the stable preference ordering and picks the one with the highest personal utility. Because the strength of each preference—the utility of that option—exists in the brain before the option is even presented, nothing about the context of the presentation should affect the preference, unless the individual judges the context to be important (to change the option in some critical way). We will now look at some of the ways in which this general property of rational choice—context independence—is sometimes violated in the actual choices that people make.

In the discussion that follows, we will consider axioms that apply to risky choice as well as those that apply to riskless choice, and some that apply to both. This distinction is made by some theorists and reflects situations where the outcome is unknown versus those where the outcome is known. Riskless choice would, for example, encompass trades with known outcomes (decide whether to trade an apple for a peach; decide whether to trade $5 for a beer; etc.). Risky choice would be represented by the recreation example described previously: Should we go to the beach or the museum on a day when it might or might not rain? Dawes (1998) points out, however, that the distinction is somewhat artificial in that all decisions involve risk—even trades for familiar commodities. He emphasizes that the importance of a commodity resides in its use and the outcome of that use is often uncertain, certainly with complicated commodities such as automobiles. For reasons similar to Dawes's, I will not stress the distinction between risky and riskless choice.

Dominance: The Sure-Thing Principle

There is one particular axiom of choice that is so simple and basic that it is virtually a no-brainer. It is often termed *dominance* (Dawes, 1998), but, in a classic work on the axiomatization of utility theory, was termed the sure-thing principle by Savage (1954). It says the following: Imagine you are choosing between two possible actions with differing anticipated outcomes (call them A and B). Actions and their anticipated outcomes are called prospects by decision researchers. Event X is an event that may or may not occur in the future. If you prefer prospect A to prospect B if event X happens, and you also prefer prospect A to prospect B if event X does not happen, then you definitely prefer A to B. Thus, uncertainty about whether X will occur or not should have no bearing on your preference. The sure-thing principle says that because your preference is in no way changed by knowledge of event X, you should choose A over B whether you know anything about event X or not. In a 1994 article in the journal *Cognition,* cognitive psychologist Eldar Shafir called the sure-thing principle "one of simplest and least controversial principles of rational behavior" (p. 404). Indeed, it is so simple and obvious that it hardly seems worth stating. Yet Shafir, in his article, reviews a host of studies that have demonstrated that people do indeed violate the sure-thing principle.

For example, Tversky and Shafir (1992) created a scenario wherein subjects were asked to imagine that they were students at the end of a term, were tired and run down, and were awaiting the grade in a course that they might fail and thus be forced to retake. Subjects were also told to imagine that they had just been given the opportunity to purchase an extremely attractive vacation package to Hawaii at a very low price. More than half the subjects who had been informed that they had passed the exam chose to buy the vacation package, and an even larger proportion of the group who had been told that they had failed the exam also chose to buy the vacation package. However, only one third of a group who did not know whether they passed or failed the exam chose to purchase the vacation. The implication of this pattern of responses is that at least some subjects were saying "I'll go on the vacation if I pass and I'll go on the vacation if I fail, but I won't go on the vacation if I don't know whether I passed or failed."

Shafir (1994) describes a host of decision situations where this outcome obtains. Subjects made one decision when event X obtained, made the same decision when event X did not obtain, but made a different decision when they were uncertain about event X—a clear violation of the sure-thing principle. Shafir, Simonson, and Tversky (1993) show how a tendency to choose options that can be justified with reasons can lead to violations of the sure-thing principle. They describe an experiment in which subjects were to decide whether they would accept a bet where they would win $200 if heads came up on a coin toss and lose $100 if tails came up. After being told to imagine that they had already played once and won, 69% of the subjects said they would accept the bet and play again. In another situation later in the experimental session, the subjects were told to imagine that they had already played once and lost; in this case, 59% of the subjects said they would accept the bet and play again. In a final situation in the experimental session, the subjects were told to imagine that they had already played once but did not know whether they had won or lost. Under this condition, only 36% of the subjects said they would accept the bet and play again.

In short, a majority would accept the bet if they knew they had previously won, a majority would play the game again if they knew they had previously lost, but only a minority would play if they did not know the outcome of the previous play. This violation of the sure-thing principle is apparent in the response patterns of individual subjects. Shafir et al. (1993) found that of the subgroup of people who accepted the bet after either a win or a loss, fully 65% rejected the bet under conditions of uncertainty about the previous outcome. In short, many people chose A (accept the bet) over B (reject the bet) if event X (a win) had occurred and chose A (accept the bet) over B (reject the bet) if X had not occurred (a loss), but when they did not know the outcome of the previous play, they chose B (reject the bet) over A (accept the bet). Shafir et al. (1993) explain this violation of the sure-thing principle in terms of an uncritical reliance on an automatic search-for-reasons heuristic. When subjects are told that they had won the first bet there is a reason to play again. They are up $200 and cannot possibly lose money even if they lose the second bet. When subjects are told that they had lost the first bet there is again reason to play—there is a chance to end up ahead even though now they are down $100. However, when subjects do not know the previous outcome, no immediate reason to play comes to mind. They do not realize that they would have a reason no matter what happened. Because no immediate reason for playing again is generated, playing again seems less attractive.

Violations of the sure-thing principle are not limited to make-believe problems or laboratory situations. Shafir (1994) discussed some real-life examples, one involving the stock market just prior to the 1988 U.S. presidential election between George H. W. Bush and Michael Dukakis. Market analysts were near unanimous in their opinion that Wall Street preferred Bush to Dukakis. Yet subsequent to Bush's election, stock and bond prices declined and the dollar plunged to its lowest level in 10 months. Interestingly though, analysts agreed that the outcome would have been worse had Dukakis been elected. Yet if the market was going to decline subsequent to the election of Bush and was going to decline even further subsequent to the election of Dukakis, then why didn't it go down before the election due to the absolute certainty that whatever happened (Bush or Dukakis), the outcome was bad for the market? The market seems to have violated the sure-thing principle. Violations of the sure-thing principle occur in examples such as these because people are reluctant to engage in fully disjunctive reasoning. Fully disjunctive reasoning involves considering all possible states of the world when deciding among options—checking out all of the possibilities.

Precluding Context Effects: The Independence Axiom

In our discussion of transitivity, we saw an example of inappropriate contextualization. Many other axioms of rational choice have the same implication—that choices should be not be inappropriately contextualized (see Broome, 1990; Reyna, 2004; Schick, 1987; Tan & Yates, 1995; Tversky, 1975). Consider another axiom from the theory of utility maximization under conditions of risk, the so-called *independence axiom* (a different axiom from the independence of irrelevant alternatives, and sometimes termed *substitutability* or *cancellation*; see Baron, 1993; Broome, 1991; Luce & Raiffa, 1957; Neumann & Politser, 1992; Shafer, 1988; Tversky & Kahneman, 1986). The axiom states that if the outcome in some state of the world is the same across options, then that state of the world should be ignored. Again, the axiom dictates a particular way in which context should be ignored. As in the independence of irrelevant alternatives example, humans sometimes violate the independence axiom because their psychological states are affected by just the contextual feature that the axiom says should not be coded into their evaluation of the options. The famous Allais (1953) paradox provides one such example. Allais proposed the following two choice problems:

Problem 1. Choose between:

    A. $1 million for sure

    B. .89 probability of $1 million
       .10 probability of $5 million
       .01 probability of nothing

Problem 2. Choose between:

    C. .11 probability of $1 million
       .89 probability of nothing

    D. .10 probability of $5 million
       .90 probability of nothing

Many people find option A in problem 1 and option D in problem 2 to be the most attractive, but these choices violate the independence axiom. To see this, we need to understand that .89 of the probability is the same in both sets of choices (Savage, 1954; Slovic & Tversky, 1974). In both problem 1 and problem 2, in purely numerical terms, the subject is essentially faced with a choice between .11 probability of $1 million versus .10 probability of $5 million. If you chose the first option (A) in problem 1 you should choose the first one (C) in problem 2. Here is why.

The preference for A in the first choice means that the utility of $1 million is greater than the utility of a .89 probability of $1 million plus the utility of a .10 probability of $5 million. Symbolically, we could write it this way:

$$u(\$1,000,000) > .89u(\$1,000,000) + .10u(\$5,000,000)$$

subtracting .89u($1,000,000) from both sides, we get:

$$.11u(\$1,000,000) > .10u(\$5,000,000)$$

But looking at the second choice, we can see that this is exactly what is offered in the choice between C and D, and many people chose D, thus indicating, in complete contradiction to the first choice, that:

$$.10u(\$5,000,000) > .11u(\$1,000,000)$$

Many theorists have analyzed why individuals finding D attractive might nonetheless be drawn to option A in the first problem (Bell, 1982; Loomes & Sugden, 1982; Maher, 1993; Schick, 1987; Slovic & Tversky, 1974). Most explanations involve the assumption that the individual incorporates psychological factors such as regret into their construal of the options. But the psychological state of regret derives from the part of the option that is constant and thus, according to the axiom, should not be part of the context taken into account. For example, the zero-money outcome of option B might well be coded as something like "getting nothing when you passed up a sure chance of a million dollars!" The equivalent .01 slice of probability in option D is folded into the .90 and is not psychologically coded in the same way. Whether this contextualization based on regret is a justified contextualization has been the subject of intense debate (Broome, 1991; Maher, 1993; Schick, 1987; Tversky, 1975).

Framing Effects: Failures of Descriptive Invariance

The standard view of so-called "rational man" in economics and decision theory traditionally assumes that people have stable, underlying preferences for each of the options presented in a decision situation. That is, a person's preferences for the options available for choice are assumed to be complete, well ordered, and well behaved in terms of the axioms of choice mentioned previously (transitivity, etc.). Well-behaved internal preferences have the implication that a person is a utility maximizer, acting to get what he or she most wants. Thus, "rational, economic man" maximizes utility in choice by having previously existing, well-ordered preferences that reliably determine choices when the person has to act on the preferences.

The main problem with this conception is that three decades of work by Kahneman and Tversky (2000) and a host of other cognitive and decision scientists (Dawes, 1998; Fischhoff, 1991; Gilovich, Griffin, & Kahneman, 2002; Lichtenstein & Slovic, 1971, 2006; Shafer, 1988; Shafir & LaBoeuf, 2002; Shafir & Tversky, 1995; Slovic, 1995) have brought the view of rational man with well-ordered preference sets into question. What this work has shown is that people's choices—sometimes choices about very important things—can be altered by irrelevant changes in how the alternatives are presented to them. How the problem is framed affects what they choose. There are dozens of such demonstrations of framing effects in the research literature, but one of the most compelling is from the early work of Tversky and Kahneman (1981). Give your own reaction to decision 1 in the following paragraph.

Decision 1. Imagine that the United States is preparing for the outbreak of an unusual disease, which is expected to kill 600 people. Two alternative programs to combat the disease have been proposed. Assume that the exact scientific estimates of the consequences of the programs are as follows: If program A is adopted, 200 people will be saved. If program B is adopted, there is a one-third probability that 600 people will be saved and a two-thirds probability that no people will be saved. Which of the two programs would you favor, program A or program B?

Most people when given this problem prefer program A—the one that saves 200 lives for sure. There is nothing wrong with this choice taken alone. It is only in connection with the responses to another problem that things really become strange. The experimental subjects (sometimes the same group, sometimes a different group—the effect obtains either way) are given an additional problem. Again, give your own immediate reaction to Decision 2 in the next paragraph.

Decision 2. Imagine that the United States is preparing for the outbreak of an unusual disease, which is expected to kill 600 people. Two alternative programs to combat the disease have been proposed. Assume that the exact scientific estimates of the consequences of the programs are as follows: If program C is adopted, 400 people will die. If program D is adopted, there is a one-third probability that nobody will die and a two-thirds probability that 600 people will die. Which of the two programs would you favor, program C or program D?

Most subjects when presented with decision 2 prefer program D. Thus, across the two problems, the most popular choices are program A and program D. The only problem here is that decision 1 and decision 2 are really the same decision—they are merely redescriptions of the same situation. Program A and C are the same. That 400 will die in program C implies that 200 will be saved—precisely the same number saved (200) in program A. Likewise, the two-thirds chance that 600 will die in program D is the same two-thirds chance that 600 will die ("no people will be saved") in program B. If you preferred program A in decision 1 you should have preferred program C in decision 2. The results of many experiments have indicated that groups of people show inconsistent response patterns on these problems.

Here a brief word about research methodology is needed. Framing experiments—and most other experiments on decision making—can be run either between subjects or within subjects. For example, in a between-subjects design, one group of subjects would be presented with gain version ("200 will be saved") and a different group of subjects would be presented with the loss version ("400 will die"). Random assignment of subjects to conditions ensures that the two groups are roughly equivalent and that the response patterns obtained from them are comparable. In contrast, in a within-subjects design, each subject responds to both versions of the problem. Usually the two versions are separated in time (by interpolating other unrelated experimental tasks) so that the relation between the problems is not completely transparent. Of course, in within-subjects experiments the two versions are counterbalanced—one half of the subjects receives the gain version first and the other half of the subjects receives the loss version first.

Not surprisingly, between-subjects experiments show larger framing effects because this design contains no cue that there is an issue of consistency at stake. Nonetheless, even in within-subjects designs, inconsistent responses are also obtained: Many subjects switch their preferences depending on the phrasing of the question. It is important to note that the subjects themselves—when presented with both versions of the problem next to each other—tend to agree that the problems are identical and that the alternative phrasing should not have made a difference.

The inconsistency displayed in the Disease problem is a violation of a very basic axiom of rational decision, the so-called property of descriptive invariance (Kahneman & Tversky, 1984, 2000; Tversky & Kahneman, 1981). If choices flip-flop based on problem characteristics that the subjects themselves view as irrelevant, then subjects can be said to have no stable, well-ordered preferences at all. If preferences reverse based on inconsequential aspects of how the problem is phrased, people cannot possibly be maximizing expected utility. Such failures of descriptive invariance have quite serious implications for our view of whether or not people are rational, yet such failures are not difficult to generate. The decision-making literature is full of them. Consider the following two problems (from Tversky & Kahneman, 1986) framed in a gambling context commonly used in the decision theory literature:

Decision 3. Imagine that, in addition to whatever else you have, you have been given a cash gift of $300. You are now asked to choose between two options:

A. a sure gain of $100
B. a 50% chance of winning $200 and a 50% chance of winning nothing

Decision 4. Imagine that, in addition to whatever else you have, you have been given a cash gift of $500. You are now asked to choose between two options:

C. a sure loss of $100, and
D. a 50% chance of losing $200 and a 50% chance of losing nothing.

Tversky and Kahneman (1986) found that 72% of their sample preferred option A over B and that 64% of their sample preferred option D over option C. Again, though, just as in the disease example, the two decisions reflect comparisons of exactly the same outcomes. If someone preferred A to B, then that person should prefer C to D. The sure gain of $100 in option A when added to the starting sum of $300 means ending up with $400—just as the sure loss on option C means ending up with $400 in decision 4. Option B means a 50% chance of ending up with $500 ($300 plus winning $200) and a 50% chance of ending up with $300 ($300 plus winning nothing)—just as does option D in decision 4 (50% chance of $500 minus $200 and a 50% chance of $500 minus nothing).

The theory of why these failures of descriptive invariance occur was termed prospect theory by Kahneman and Tversky (1979; Tversky & Kahneman, 1986). What the examples have in common is that in both cases subjects were risk averse in the context of gains and risk seeking in the context of losses. They found the sure gain of 200 lives attractive in decision 1 over a gamble of equal expected value, and in decision 3 they found the sure $100 gain attractive over a gamble of equal expected value. In contrast, in decision 2 the sure loss of 400 lives was unattractive compared with the gamble of equal expected value. Of course, the "sure loss" of 400 here that subjects found so unattractive is exactly the same outcome as the "sure gain" of 200 that subjects found so attractive in decision 1!

Similarly, the "sure loss" in option C of decision 4 was seen as unattractive compared to a gamble of equal expected value. In both of these problems, subjects did not take total wealth into account but instead coded outcomes in terms of contrasts from current wealth—as gains and losses from a zero point. This is one of the key assumptions of Kahneman and Tversky's (1979) prospect theory (see also, Markowitz, 1952). How this assumption—that prospects are coded as gains and losses from a zero point—leads people to be risk averse for gains and risk seeking for losses is illustrated in Figure 2.1. This figure depicts the utility function as it departs from zero in both the positive and negative directions. The solid curve, representing the utility function, is negatively accelerated in both directions. Point A indicates the utility of a gain of $200 on the function and point B indicates the (negative) utility of a $200 loss. Now imagine that a sure gain of $200 was being considered against a .50 chance of winning $400 and a .50 chance of winning nothing. The utility of the 50/50 prospect would be represented by the average of the utility of −$400 and $0. That utility is indicated in Figure 2.1, and it is immediately apparent that it is a lower utility than that represented by the sure-thing prospect of $200. The reason is because of the negatively accelerated nature of the function. Thus, people are risk averse for gains.

But this aspect of the function (its negative acceleration) also means that people will be risk seeking for losses. Imagine that a sure loss of $200 was being considered against a .50 chance of losing $400 and a .50 chance of losing nothing. The utility of the 50/50 prospect would be represented by the average of the utility of −$400 and $0. That utility is indicated in Figure 2.1, and it is immediately apparent that it is a higher utility than that represented by the sure-thing prospect of losing $200 (point B).

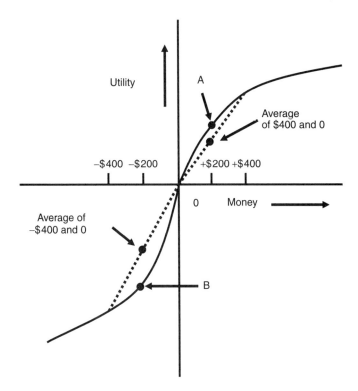

FIGURE **2.1**

Thus, the 50/50 gamble has less negative utility. Therefore, people will be risk seeking for losses.

One of the other key assumptions of prospect theory is that the utility function is steeper (in the negative direction) for losses than for gains. This is why people are often risk averse even for gambles with positive expected values. Would you flip a coin with me—heads you give me $500, tails I give you $505? Most people refuse such favorable bets because the potential loss, although nominally smaller than the potential gain, looms larger psychologically. Figure 2.2 presents an example of the utility function of prospect theory that displays this feature—the function declines more steeply in the negative direction than it rises in the positive direction.

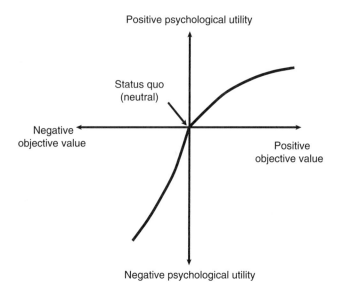

Figure 2.2

These two aspects of how people approach decisions—the differential steepness of the utility function and the recoding of options as being from a zero reference point of the current status quo (in terms of wealth, lives, or whatever is at issue)—appear to be automatic defaults in dealing with information in decision situations. They cannot be turned off, but they can be overridden (for example, by analytic strategies to make sure that one's preferences are invariant under different representations of the problem). That these two characteristics of the way we code decision information can cause an outright reversal of preferences if not overridden is a somewhat frightening implication. Latent here is the unsettling idea that people's preferences come from the outside (from whoever has the power to shape the environment and determine how questions are phrased) rather than from their unique psychological makeup. Since most situations can be reframed either way, this means that rather than having stable preferences that are just elicited in different ways, the elicitation process itself can totally determine what the preference will be! Framing effects have potent social implications (Baron, Bazerman, & Shonk, 2006; Thaler & Sunstein, 2008). As Kahneman (1994) has pointed out, the assumption of stable, rational, well-ordered preferences has been used to "support the position that it is unnecessary to protect people against the consequences of their choices" (p. 18).

There are also many important practical consequences of the demonstrations of framing effects. For example, in the important area of medical treatment, outcome information can often be represented in terms of either losses or gains. Work by McNeil, Pauker, Sox, and Tversky (1982) has shown that—as in the earlier examples—alternative phrasings of the same outcome can lead to different treatment choices. Respondents chose between two treatments for lung cancer (surgery or radiation therapy), and the outcome was presented to one group in terms of a survival frame and to the other in terms of a mortality frame. The percentage of respondents preferring each of the treatments is shown in parentheses:

Survival Frame

Surgery: Of 100 people having surgery, 90 live through the postoperative period, 68 are alive at the end of the first year, and 34 are alive at the end of 5 years (preferred by 82% of respondents)

Radiation Therapy: Of 100 people having radiation therapy, 100 live through the treatment, 77 are alive at the end of the first year, and 22 are alive at the end of 5 years (preferred by 18% of respondents)

Mortality Frame

Surgery: Of 100 people having surgery, 10 die during surgery or postoperative period, 32 die by the end of the first year, and 66 die by the end of 5 years (preferred by 56% of respondents)

Radiation Therapy: Of 100 people having radiation therapy, none die during treatment, 23 die by the end of the first year, and 78 die by the end of 5 years (preferred by 44% of respondents)

The radiation therapy was more attractive in the mortality frame than in the survival frame because, as predicted by prospect theory, its positive feature (the better immediate outcome) loomed larger as a loss avoidance (going from 10 to 0) than as gain enhancer (going from 90 to 100). Of course, it's the same 10% no matter how you look at it! Thus, this is another example of a failure of descriptive invariance in people's judgment and decision making. McNeil et al. (1982) found that the framing effect was just as large for physicians and those with statistical training as it was for clinic patients. Note that it is a bit scary that preferences for something as important as treatment for lung cancer can reverse based on a rephrasing of the outcomes that conveys no differential information about the treatments and that changes nothing about the outcomes themselves.

The key feature in all of these problems is that subjects appear to accept whatever framing is given in the problem as set—without trying alternative ones to see if inconsistencies might result. Kahneman (2003) notes that "the basic principle of framing is the passive acceptance of the formulation given" (p. 703). The frame presented to the subject is taken as focal, and all subsequent thought derives from it rather than from alternative framings because the latter would more require thought.

Framing effects can be so potent that they lead people into choices that—upon reflection—they would see as deeply embarrassing. To demonstrate this, try responding to some additional problems (taken from Tversky & Kahneman, 1986):

Decision 5. Which of the following options do you prefer (choose one)?

A. A sure gain of $240
B. 25% chance to gain $1,000 and 75% chance to gain nothing

Decision 6. Consider the following two lotteries, described by the percentage of marbles of different colors in each box and the amount of money you win or lose depending on the color of a randomly drawn marble. Which lottery do you prefer?

Lottery C			
90% White	6% Red	1% Green	3% Yellow
$0	win $45	win $30	lose $15
Lottery D			
90% White	7% Red	1% Green	2% Yellow
$0	win $45	lose $10	lose $15

Decision 7. Which of the following options do you prefer (choose one)?

E. A sure loss of $750
F. 75% chance to lose $1,000 and 25% chance to lose nothing

I have used these examples to illustrate a principle of rational choice that is one of the most obvious principles of decision theory. It is so obvious that the lay reader will probably even wonder why it needs stating. It is another version of the no-brainer discussed earlier in this chapter—the sure-thing principle, which is often termed the dominance principle. It states, roughly (see Dawes, 1998; Shafer, 1988; Tversky & Kahneman, 1986), that if you prefer the outcome of action A to the outcome of action B no matter what happens (that is, no matter what currently unknown state of the world occurs), then you should take action A. Imagine two payoff schemes for the flip of a coin, scheme A and scheme B. For scheme A you get $8 if the coin comes up heads and $3 if it comes up tails. For payoff scheme B you get $5 if it comes up heads and $2 if it comes up tails. Scheme A is better no matter what happens. It is the dominating choice and thus is the obvious one to pick.

Of course, no one would ever violate the dominance principle if it were as obvious as this. But what Tversky and Kahneman (1986) and other researchers have found is that framing effects can cause people to violate dominance. Violations of something so basic are actually a very good way of highlighting why inconsistent choices based on irrelevant framing effects should be avoided. Recall that failures of descriptive invariance occur in situations that the decision maker judges to be similar. There are certain aspects of the context of the problem that should not make a difference—*should not* by the decision maker's own judgment. Thus, it is a form of what Wilson and Brekke (1994) call *mental contamination*—our behavior is affected by factors that we wish not to be implicated in our decisions. This is why such inconsistencies in our behavior should be alarming. They mean that our behavior is being contaminated by features that prevent us from maximizing our satisfaction—that we are not being instrumentally rational. For you to violate the dominance principle would be alarming because you do not really want to pick an option that is worse than another option no matter what happens, do you? Of course not. Nonetheless, you probably just did.

First, consider another problem in which you probably will not violate a dominance relationship:

Decision 8. Which of the following options do you prefer? (Choose one.)

G. a 25% chance to win $240 and a 75% chance to lose $760
H. a 25% chance to win $250 and a 75% chance to lose $750

Here the decision is easy. It is clear that H is better, and you knew that even without knowing the term for it (dominance). H is dominant because, if you win, you win more with H and, if you lose, you lose less—and the probabilities of winning and losing are the same. Nevertheless, if you responded to the previous problems like most people tend to, you probably did implicitly choose G over H. Refer to the earlier decisions you made on decisions 5 and 7. In decision 5, most people (see Tversky & Kahneman, 1986) prefer option A because again, consistent with prospect theory, most people are risk averse for gains—even when the gamble has a slightly higher expected value (as is the case here). In decision 7, most people are risk seeking for losses and thus prefer option F (because here they like the idea of a chance to avoid a loss entirely). Most individuals thus choose options A and F.

Imagine that we were simultaneously executing these two decisions (that is, A and F). Due to choosing option A in decision 5, the person would receive a sure $240 and then play the gamble in F, thus ending up with a 75% chance of losing $760 (the $1,000 lost minus the $240 gained) and a 25% chance of winning $240 (the $240 gained from taking option A plus the 25% chance of losing nothing further). But this outcome is exactly option G in decision 8. Similarly the choice of B and E in decisions 5 and 7 (the choices that most people do not like) combine to make the dominant alternative H in decision 8—clearly the better choice. Due to choosing option E in decision 7, the person would receive a sure loss of $750 and also play the gamble in B, thus ending up with a 25% chance of winning $250 (the sure loss of $750 in E added to the 25% chance of gaining $1,000) in B and a 75% chance of losing $750 (the 75% chance of losing nothing in B added to the sure loss of $750 in E).

Finally, what about decision 6? Well, if you were like most people, you did it again—you violated dominance. Tversky and Kahneman (1986) found that 58% of the subjects in their study preferred lottery C even though it is dominated by lottery D. Do a simple cancellation exercise to see this. This is made easier by looking at the matched layout in the table that follows. The 90% white win in both lotteries obviously cancel—as does the 6% red win of $45. But the latter cancellation leaves a 1% red win of $45 in lottery D, and that is preferred to the 1% green win of $30 in lottery C. Finally, the 1% green loss of $10 in lottery D should be preferred to the extra 1% yellow loss of $15 in lottery C.

In short, lottery D is either equal to or superior to lottery C in every single component; it is a dominating choice, yet only 42% of Tversky and Kahneman's (1986) subjects recognized this fact. Instead, attention is drawn to the extra "win" category in lottery C, and some people never do a numerical analysis of the exact distribution of the probabilities. Thus, choices can violate the basic principle of dominance when the dominance relationship is less than obvious. More importantly, such violations of descriptive invariance mean that people cannot be expected utility maximizers.

Lottery C				
90% White	6% Red	1% Green	3% Yellow	
$0	win $45	win $30	lose $15	
Lottery D				
90% White	7% Red	1% Green	2% Yellow	
$0	win $45	lose $10	lose $15	
		Matched Layout		
Lottery C				
90% White	6% Red	1% Green	2% Yellow	1% Yellow
$0	win $45	win $30	lose $15	lose $15
Lottery D				
90% White	6% Red	1% Red	2% Yellow	1% Green
$0	win $45	win $45	lose $15	lose $10

The examples discussed here are not atypical. Instead, they represent just the tip of the iceberg of a large literature on anomalies in preference judgments (Kahneman & Tversky, 2000; Lichtenstein & Slovic, 2006). That human choices are so easily altered by framing has potent social and economic implications. Thaler (1980) describes how years ago the credit card industry lobbied intensely for any differential charges between credit cards and cash to be labeled as a discount for using cash rather than a surcharge for using the credit card. They were implicitly aware of an assumption of Kahneman and Tversky's (1979) prospect theory—that any surcharge would be psychologically coded as a loss and weighted highly in negative utility (see Figure 2.2). The discount, in contrast, would be coded as a gain. Because the utility function is shallower for gains than for losses, forgoing the discount would be psychologically easier than accepting the surcharge. Of course, the two represent exactly the same economic consequence. The industry, merely by getting people to accept the higher price as normal, framed the issue so that credit card charges were more acceptable to people.

Humans appear to be without an abstraction device that puts decisions in a common format. Language, for example, is a potent decontextualizing device in that it supports abstraction (the process of abstracting away irrelevant detail; see Adler, 1984). By coding as equivalent the deep structures underlying "the cat chased the boy" and "the boy was chased by the cat," language abstracts away specifics not relevant to the communication. We lack such a feature in other domains, and, as a result, are led into the unwanted framing effects that signal the violation of the axioms of rational choice. For example, Thaler (1980) describes research in which many people choose to travel 20 minutes to another branch of a store to save $5 on a $15 calculator but would not make the same trip to save $5 on a $125 calculator. The standard economic analysis views these two situations as equivalent (in each case the person has the choice between the status quo and driving to save $5), and any failure to respond the same as a violation of economic rationality. Many people show framing effects in such situations (responding to the ratio of price to savings) because their decision-making apparatus has no way of representing decisions in a canonical form—no parallel to the way language automatically transforms the structure of "the cat chased the boy" into an underlying representation that matches that of "the boy was chased by the cat."

Recall the research of Shafir et al. (1993) discussed earlier in this chapter, which found that people are drawn to decisions that can be justified with reasons. Shafir and colleagues demonstrate how an unreflective use of this strategy can lead to irrational framing effects. In one experiment, subjects were told that they were to simulate being a jury member on an only-child sole-custody case following a messy divorce. The facts of the case are complicated by numerous factors and the subjects are told to base their decision on the following characteristics of the two parents:

Parent A:
>average income
>average health
>average working hours
>reasonable rapport with the child
>relatively stable social life

Parent B:
>above-average income
>very close relationship with the child
>extremely active social life
>lots of work-related travel
>minor health problems

One group of subjects was asked which parent they would award custody to, and 64% chose parent B. However, another group of subjects was given the same factors and asked the question to which parent they would *deny* access. Of this group, 55% decided to deny access to parent B. Thus, a majority thought that parent B should be *given* access and a majority thought that parent B should be *denied* access—a clear inconsistency and another example of a framing effect. There are more positive features that serve as reasons for awarding parent B custody, but there are also more negative features that can serve as reasons for denying parent B. Shafir et al. (1993) discuss how this framing effect results from an unreflective search for reasons without a more analytic integration of the weight of the evidence provided by each reason.

One type of framing manipulation that is very potent involves presenting the options in a way that designates one option as a natural default. When over-used, this so-called default heuristic (Todd & Gigerenzer, 2007) can rob us of personal autonomy. This heuristic operates via a simple rule: If you have been given a default choice, stick with it. That humans have such a heuristic is suggested by two decades of work on status quo biases in decision making (Frederick, 2002; Kahneman, Knetsch, & Thaler, 1991; Thaler, 1980). That humans overuse the default heuristic to the point of failing to maximally achieve their goals is also demonstrated in this same two decades of research. People who overuse the default heuristic give up their autonomy by ceding control of their lives to those with the power to set the defaults.

The default tendency can easily be exploited to create alternative framings. Whoever controls the default will in effect determine what people "want." The reason for the scare-quotes is obvious. Such "wants" or "choices" are not some preexisting preferences, autonomously preserved in people's brains, waiting to be emitted. They are wants and choices determined by context—by whoever set the default. Consider a real-life example. In the 1980s, both New Jersey and Pennsylvania attempted to reduce the cost of insurance by introducing the consumer choice of a reduced right to sue in order to receive a concomitant lower rate (see Johnson, Hershey, Meszaros, & Kunreuther, 2000). However, it was implemented differently in the two states. In New Jersey, the status quo was reduced rates and a limited right to sue. To gain the full right to sue, consumers had to agree to pay a higher rate for their insurance. In contrast, in Pennsylvania, the status quo was the full right to sue. In order to pay a lower rate the consumer had to agree to a reduced right to sue. In New Jersey, only 20% of drivers chose to acquire the full right to sue (by agreeing to pay the higher rate), but in Pennsylvania, where full right to sue was already in place, 75% of the drivers chose to retain it (thus forgoing a reduced rate). The default heuristic froze these consumers into their current situation by framing as "normal" the insurance features the consumer already had. The reality is that, in Pennsylvania, reversing the status quo in the wording of the legislation could have saved consumers approximately $200 million.

The Curious Attraction of the Status Quo: The Endowment Effect

Framing effects caused by changes in what is presented as the status quo are potent because two decades of work on decision making have indicated that people have a strong bias toward the status quo: They overvalue what they already have. This is sometimes termed *the endowment effect* in the literature, and it follows from the shape of the utility function in prospect theory, as discussed previously. Giving up something that is owned is seen as incurring a loss, and thus it has a large negative utility. Therefore, people require a relatively large amount of money to give up an article they already own. In contrast, the idea of the same article not yet owned is viewed as a gain. The positive utility of this gain is less in absolute magnitude than the negative utility of losing the same article once it is owned. Thus, people tend to require a much higher payment to give up an article than they would spend to buy the same article if they did not already own it.

Thaler (1980) illustrated the endowment effect with a humorous example: Mr. R bought a case of good wine in the late 1950s for about $5 a bottle. A few years later his wine merchant offered to buy the wine back for $100 a bottle. He refused, although he has never paid more than $35 for a bottle of wine.

In this example, we see that Mr. R would not pay more than $35 for (presumably) the same bottle that he would require more than $100 to give up. If Mr. R did not own the bottle and was given a choice between the bottle and $37, from his past behavior we can infer that he would take the $37. He would by this behavior be showing that the bottle is worth less than $37 to him. But when he owns the bottle, he says that it is worth more than $100!

Endowment effects result from loss aversion and are a special case of even more generic status quo biases, where the disadvantages of giving up a situation are valued more highly than the advantages of an alternative situation. Such status quo biases show up in many real-life situations of practical import. For example, Samuelson and Zeckhauser (1988) did some of the classic work on the status quo bias by having subjects play the role of someone receiving an inheritance from an uncle. The subjects were given information on a variety of investment vehicles that were said to be open to them: a moderate-risk company stock, a high-risk company stock, treasury bills, municipal bonds, and so forth. Subjects were then supposed to allocate the cash received from their uncle to the various investment choices (subjects were told that the tax and commission consequences of any of their choices were trivial). This condition established the baseline—how a group of subjects such as those in the study would allocate assets without knowledge of a default.

In the other conditions of the experiment, the subjects allocated the money with a default available. This was done by changing the key sentence in the control condition ("you inherited a large sum of money from your uncle") to "you inherited a large sum of cash and securities from your uncle." In various conditions of the experiment, the bulk of the money was said to be already invested, respectively, in the moderate-risk company, the treasury bills, and so on. There was a strong tendency on the part of subjects to leave the money as it had already been invested, even though this was not what the subject would have invested in had that investment vehicle not been the default.

Status quo biases operate in many real-life contexts of economic and public policy choice. Hartman, Doane, and Woo (1991) describe a survey conducted by Pacific Gas and Electric in the 1980s. Because of various geographic factors (urban-rural, etc.), service reliability varied in their service area. Some of their customers suffered more outages than others. Customers with unreliable service were asked whether they would be willing to pay for more reliable service and, if so, whether they would accept increases of various percentages. Customers with reliable service were asked if they would be willing to accept somewhat less reliable service and receive a discount on their bills of a certain percentage (in fact, the same percentages as the other group, only a decrease instead of an increase). Although there were not income differences between these groups of customers, neither group wanted to change. People overwhelmingly wanted to stay with whatever their status quo was. The service difference between the two groups was large. The unreliable service group suffered 15 outages per year of 4 hours' average duration, and the reliable service group suffered 3 outages per year of 2 hours' average duration, yet very few customers wanted to switch!

More Anomalies: Preference Reversals and Procedural Invariance

Descriptive invariance is an important property of rational choice and, as we have just seen, it is violated in a host of choice situations. There is a related principle—procedural invariance—that is equally basic and equally problematic for human decision making. Procedural invariance is one of the most basic assumptions that lies behind the standard model of rational choice (Kahneman & Tversky, 2000; Slovic, 1995; Tversky & Kahneman, 1986). It is the principle that choices should not depend on the way that the preferences are elicited. However, although this assumption is indeed basic to the notion of "rational economic man," the evidence has accumulated over the past 30 years that irrational sets of preferences often result because procedural invariance is violated.

Lichtenstein and Slovic (1971, 2006; see also Slovic, 1995) were the first to demonstrate so-called *preference reversals,* in which preferences changed based on the mode of elicitation. Subjects were asked which of the following two gambles they preferred:

gamble A: 11/12 chance to win $12 and 1/12 chance to lose $24
gamble B: 2/12 chance to win $79 and 10/12 chance to lose $5

The majority of subjects preferred gamble A (with the high probability of winning). However, in a separate session, subjects were asked to price each of the gambles—that is, they were asked to imagine that they owned each of the gambles and to state a minimum price at which they would sell them. Most subjects put a higher selling price on gamble B. In fact, 87% of those who chose gamble A put a higher price on B. This is a profound violation of the strictures of rational choice, because it leads to an intransitivity. Presumably there is an amount of money (M) that could lead to the following set of preferences: B is preferred to M, M is preferred to A, but nonetheless A is preferred to B.

Or, if that is not clear, demonstrate to yourself the money pump implications of that set of preferences. Imagine you prefer gamble A to gamble B in a direct comparison, but price gamble A at $4 and gamble B at $5. Imagine that I give you—free of charge—A and B. Now that seems nice.

But, as in our previous money pump example, what comes next is not so nice. I will buy A from you for $4.25 (you will sell, because you value it at only $4). Then I will give you A and take B (you will agree to exchange, because you prefer A to B in a direct comparison). Now, since I am holding B I will sell you B for $4.75 (you will buy it because you think it is worth $5). Now you are back where you started, holding both A and B—but you have bought for $4.75 and sold for $4.25. You are down $.50 and we are back where we started—and could do the whole sequence over and over again if you really had those preferences. This type of outcome is of course why decision theorists view sets of preferences that lead to money pumps as fundamentally irrational. Violations of consistency requirements such as procedural invariance lead to implications that even people committing the violations would admit that they would want to avoid.

Nevertheless, despite the fact that they are so clearly an indication of an irrational set of preferences, preference reversals have been demonstrated with a variety of paradigms. For example, they are not confined to choices involving probabilities. Consider the following two contracts:

contract A: You receive $2,500 five years from now.
contract B: You receive $1,600 in one and a half years.

Tversky, Slovic, and Kahneman (1990) found that three quarters of their subjects preferred contract B, but when asked what was the smallest amount they would sell each of the contracts for if they owned it, three quarters of their subjects set a higher price on contract A. This set of responses again leads to a disastrous money pump.

Cognitive scientists have uncovered some of the reasons why these violations of procedural invariance occur (see Lichtenstein & Slovic, 2006; Slovic, 1995). For example, one reason is due to so-called *compatibility effects*. This refers to the compatibility, or similarity, between the mode of response and aspects of the alternatives being evaluated. When the response mode is pricing, this means that the monetary outcomes in the contracts will be given more weight than they are in the choice situation. In the preceding example, the $2,500 is weighted more highly in a pricing decision than in a choice decision.

The Regularity Principle

The principle of independence of irrelevant alternatives tells us that the relative preference for X over Y in a choice situation cannot be changed by the introduction of a third alternative, Z. If alternative Z is unattractive and is the least favored of the three, X should still be preferred to Y to the same relative degree. Even in cases where Z is attractive and is the preferred alternative of the three, when asked to evaluate the remaining alternatives, people should still prefer X to Y and by exactly the same degree. The regularity principle is a special case of independence of irrelevant alternatives. Violation of regularity seems an even more bizarre violation of rational strictures than we have discussed thus far. Imagine a two-choice situation involving option A and option B, and that option A is chosen x% of the time. The regularity principle states that, when we add a third option C to turn this into a three-choice situation, x *cannot* go up: That is, an option cannot become *more* attractive (in an *absolute* sense) when more options are added.

Here is a humorous example of the violation of regularity. In one of their research articles, professor of medicine Donald Redelmeier and cognitive psychologist Eldar Shafir (Redelmeier & Shafir, 1995) described economist Thomas Schelling's anecdote about going to a bookstore to buy an encyclopedia. When Schelling got to the bookstore, he found that two different encyclopedias were on special sale that day. He walked out without purchasing either. However, he thought that it was probably true that either one would have been satisfactory had he evaluated it in isolation! This seems deeply irrational. Here is a way to think about it. Had there been one encyclopedia on offer, not purchasing one at all would have had a certain level of attractiveness (high or low—the absolute level does not matter) as an option. Now a second encyclopedia becomes an option too, and the attractiveness of not purchasing one goes up! This just seems crazy. But we can see how it derives from a tendency not to make decisions. The choice between the two encyclopedias seems hard, and in order to avoid it we opt for not purchasing either one (on the difficulties that people have with too many choices, see Schwartz, 2004).

There are two things to understand about the Schelling anecdote told by Redelmeier and Shafir (1995). First, it is a very fundamental violation of the principles of rational choice. Second, it represents not just an error in a meaningless anecdote but a thinking problem in real life. Work by Shafir et al. (1993), discussed previously, and others (see Huber & Puto, 1983; Tentori, Osherson, Hasher, & May, 2001; Tversky & Simonson, 1993) has demonstrated how a focus on unanalyzed reasons can result in suboptimal choices. They describe a consumer choice experiment in which one group of subjects had to choose between two microwave ovens: an Emerson-brand model originally priced at $110 but being offered at a 33% discount and a Panasonic model originally priced at $180 but also being offered at a 33% discount. Given this choice, 57% of the subjects chose the Emerson and 43% chose the Panasonic. Another group was given these two choices, along with a third: a $200 Panasonic model at a 10% discount. This last alternative was fairly unpopular, being preferred by only 13% of the subjects, whereas 27% of this second group preferred the Emerson and 60% preferred the $180 Panasonic. But if we look closely we can see that the regularity principle has been violated by this pattern of choices. When the Emerson was the only other choice, the $180 Panasonic was preferred by 43% of the consumers. However, when the Emerson and a $200 Panasonic were the alternatives, the number wanting the $180 Panasonic went up (to 60%) instead of down, thus violating a very basic premise of rational consumer behavior.

Shafir et al. (1993) explain this effect in terms of the differential reasons that were available for choice. The choice between the $110 Emerson and $180 Panasonic was a difficult one because there were equal numbers of reasons for both alternatives. When the $200 Panasonic is introduced, it is most easily comparable to the $180 Panasonic and there are more reasons to buy the latter (there are not many differences in the features of the two and the 33% discount on the $180 model makes it considerably cheaper, etc.). Of course, the reasons to choose the one Panasonic over the other do not bear at all on the Emerson, but an unreflective "count up the reasons" heuristic does not take this into account and instead registers that there have been many reasons brought to mind in favor of the $180 Panasonic.

Redelmeier and Shafir (1995) found that regularity violations can occur in the medical decision making of actual physicians. They examined the decision making of two groups of physicians—a sample from the Ontario College of Family Physicians, and a sample of neurologists and neurosurgeons. One group of physicians were to evaluate the following scenario: The patient is a 67-year-old farmer with chronic right hip pain. The diagnosis is osteoarthritis. You have tried several nonsteroidal anti-inflammatory agents (for example, aspirin, naproxen, and ketoprofen) and have stopped them because of either adverse effects or lack of efficacy. You decide to refer him to an orthopedic consultant for consideration for hip replacement surgery. The patient agrees to this plan. Before sending him away, however, you check the drug formulary and find that there is one nonsteroidal medication that this patient has not tried (ibuprofen). What do you do?

The physician's task was to choose between two alternatives: "refer to orthopedics and also start ibuprofen" and "refer to orthopedics and do not start any new medication."

The second group of physicians had the same scenario except for the ending, which offered the choice of two nonsteroidal medications. The end of the scenario read: "Before sending him away, however, you check the drug formulary and find that there are two nonsteroidal medications that this patient has not tried (ibuprofen and piroxicam). What do you do?"

The physician's task in scenario 2 was to choose between three alternatives: "refer to orthopedics and also start ibuprofen," "refer to orthopedics and also start piroxicam," and "refer to orthopedics and do not start any new medication."

Of the first group of physicians, who had only one medication choice, 53% decided to refer without starting new medication. In contrast, in the second group—who had two medication alternatives—a larger percentage (72%) decided to refer without starting new medication. This of course is a violation of regularity because an alternative became more popular as more alternatives were added. The reason for this is that this medical decision-making example is mirroring the logic of the encyclopedia example—the added alternatives are encouraging the lazy decision maker to avoid choosing between the medications (which adds to the cognitive load).

The Constructed Preference View of Choice

The model of "rational economic man" upon which much economics is based may well be an appropriate ideal theory for behavior, but it is not descriptively accurate. This descriptive inaccuracy has some profound implications, as was recognized by economists who first tested some of the findings of preference reversals obtained in psychological laboratories. Grether and Plott (1979) pointed out in an economic journal that the experimental findings of preference reversals "suggest that no optimization principles of any sort lie behind even the simplest of human choices" (p. 623). Precisely because of the profound implications for models of rational behavior commonly used in economics, Grether and Plott

(1979) conducted an extensive series of studies to ascertain whether the initial results of Lichtenstein and Slovic (1971, 1973) were replicable and found that they were. It is important to understand that the preference reversal finding is a central, not a peripheral, feature of studies of human choice. Shafer (1988) has noted that perhaps the most critical finding in three decades of research in decision science is that people's preferences are variable under different, but equivalent, descriptions.

What is it about the structure of human cognition that leads to deviations from rational prescriptions—deviations that mean that people are not reaching their goals as easily as they could? Why do people violate the regularity principle, independence of irrelevant alternatives, descriptive invariance, procedural invariance, and other axioms of rational choice? In part, the answer is provided by the dominant model of preference reversals in cognitive science: the so-called *constructed preference view* (Fischhoff, 1991; Kahneman, 1991; Kahneman & Tversky, 2000; Payne, Bettman, & Johnson, 1992; Shafer, 1988; Shafir & Tversky, 1995; Slovic, 1995). Instead of assuming a set of preferences that exist prior to the choice situation in a stable, well-ordered form, the contemporary view is that preferences are constructed online—in direct response to the probe for a decision. Importantly, the preferences are constructed in part by using cues in the elicitation situation to help access decision-relevant information in memory.

Under the present conception, it might then be a little misleading to say, as does the currently popular view in decision science, that preferences are "constructed" (which implies, wrongly, that they must be built from scratch). Instead, it might be more accurate for decision science to move to the phrasing "preferences result from sampling based on decision-relevant retrieval cues." Just as it was not correct for the classical model to assume the existence of well-ordered, easily retrievable preferences that only had to be called up by any choice situation, it is probably a mistake to say that failure to adhere to the axioms that follow from such an assumption necessarily means that there are no such things as preferences. It may be premature to conclude that "if different elicitation procedures produce different orderings of options, how can preferences be defined and in what sense do they exist?" (Slovic, 1995, p. 364) or that "perhaps... there exists nothing to be maximized" (Krantz, 1991, p. 34).

It is true that there seems not to be one set of preexisting preferences (as is posited in the "rational economic man" assumption of economics) sitting there in our brains, ready to be "read off." Instead, preference is in some sense distributed throughout the brain and is determined in a particular situation by a sampling process that is very labile and subject to producing differing outputs. Despite the inherent lability in our preference judgments, we can work to structure our decisions so that we show greater instrumental rationality. First, we can learn to carry out varied and more exhaustive samplings of the information relevant to the decision. With explicit knowledge of the effect of framing on decisions, we can teach ourselves to deliberately reframe problems to make sure that our choices are invariant. Second, we can learn rules—the rules of logic, decision theory, and evidence evaluation discussed in this book—that, if applied uniformly, can lend stability to our judgments and remove some inconsistencies from our actions. In short, we can acquire the cultural tools that aid in rational judgment.

Finally, it should be noted that the principles of choice being violated in these examples are relatively uncontroversial. When presented with a rational choice axiom that they have just violated (the sure-thing principle, transitivity, descriptive invariance, procedural invariance, etc.) in a choice situation, most subjects will actually endorse the axiom. As Shafir and Tversky (1995) describe it: "When confronted with the fact that their choices violate dominance or descriptive invariance, people typically wish to modify their behavior to conform with these principles of rationality.... People tend to accept the normative force of dominance and descriptive invariance, even though these are often violated in their actual choices" (p. 97). That subjects endorse the strictures of rationality when presented with them explicitly (Stanovich & West, 1999) suggests that most subjects' cognitive abilities are such that they can appreciate the force of the axioms of rational choice.

Outcome Bias

It is important to be able to objectively judge whether the decisions of others are correct. Juries must do this. Likewise, the actions of various professionals—doctors, teachers, politicians, coaches, and so on—are subject, more or less, to review and critique. We adjust our faith in others, as well as administer rewards and punishments, based on an evaluation of the quality of their decisions. But there is a particular bias operating when we make such evaluations. Sometimes when we have difficulty judging whether a decision was good or not it is because certain cognitive biases are operating. For instance, we often show *outcome bias*, which is demonstrated when subjects rate a decision with a positive outcome as superior to a decision with a negative outcome even when the information available to the decision maker was the same in both cases. In short, we do not take into account the good luck or bad luck that contributed to an outcome independent of how well chosen the action was.

Baron and Hershey (1988) studied outcome bias using a paradigm that was adapted by my own research group (Stanovich & West, 1998c). One group of subjects evaluated the following scenario, form A (the positive outcome scenario):

A 55-year-old man had a heart condition. He had to stop working because of chest pain. He enjoyed his work and did not want to stop. His pain also interfered with other things, such as travel and recreation. A successful bypass operation would relieve his pain and increase his life expectancy from age 65 to age 70. However, 8% of the people who have this operation die as a result of the operation itself. His physician decided to go ahead with the operation. The operation succeeded. Evaluate the physician's decision to go ahead with the operation on the following scale:

1. incorrect, a very bad decision
2. incorrect, all things considered
3. incorrect, but not unreasonable
4. the decision and its opposite are equally good
5. correct, but the opposite would be reasonable too
6. correct, all things considered
7. clearly correct, an excellent decision

A second group of subjects received form B, in which they evaluated a medical decision that was designed to be objectively better than the first: a 2% chance of death rather than 8%; a 10-year increase in life expectancy versus a 5-year increase, and so forth. However, it had an unfortunate negative outcome—the death of the patient.

Baron and Hershey (1988) found, as did my own research group, that the decision with the positive outcome was rated as a better decision than the decision with the negative outcome, despite the fact that the latter was objectively better. Subjects could not separate the objective factors that determined decision quality from the good luck or bad luck that contributed to the outcome. Such an outcome bias in human judgment interferes with our ability to evaluate the quality of decisions. Nevertheless, people find it hard to evaluate the quality of a decision prior to the outcome when they are given the outcome as part of the context.

Summary and Implications

Good decisions are those that fulfill a person's goals as efficiently as possible. That is the definition of instrumental rationality—the rationality of action—and cognitive scientists have refined the definition of this type of rationality into the quantitative concept of maximizing subjectively expected utility. The axiomatic approach to expected utility allows us to assess rationality without measuring utilities directly. It has been demonstrated that if people follow certain rational principles, then we can be assured that they are maximizing utility, without our measuring utility values directly.

The principles of the axiomatic approach collectively prohibit various types of irrelevant context from affecting choices. To the extent that the contextual factors specified by the axioms affect human choice, then the decisions we make are less than rational. In this chapter, we have seen that people are subject to a variety of context effects that are prohibited if the individuals are to considered instrumentally rational. This is something to be concerned about. Whether or not people are rational is not just an abstract issue for discussion in university philosophy classes. The conclusion that people are less than rational has many important implications.

The thinking biases described in this chapter have very practical import: They contribute to some serious social and personal problems. Because of inadequately developed rational thinking abilities—specifically, because of some of the contextual errors described in this chapter—physicians choose less effective medical treatments; people fail to accurately assess risks in their environment; information is misused in legal proceedings; millions of dollars are spent on unneeded projects by government and private industry; parents fail to vaccinate their children; unnecessary surgery is performed; animals are hunted to extinction; billions of dollars are wasted on quack medical remedies; and costly financial misjudgments are made (Baron et al., 2006; Camerer, 2000; Gilovich, 1991; Groopman, 2007; Hilton, 2003; Sunstein, 2002; Thaler & Sunstein, 2008).

Perhaps even more important than these practical implications, however, is the nature of the relation between rationality and personal autonomy. Being rational means being unaffected by contextual factors that we deem irrelevant to the decision. If these contextual factors come to affect our decision, then it means that we lose personal autonomy to those who control those very factors. We give up our thinking to those who manipulate our environments, and we let our actions be determined by those who can create the stimuli that best trigger our shallow automatic processing tendencies. We make the direction of our lives vulnerable to deflection by others who control our symbolic environment—to those who control which frame we are presented with; to those who control what is in the choice set and in what order the alternatives are presented to us; and to those who control what we should consider the status quo.

Epley, Mak, and Chen Idson (2006) provide a telling example of how our behavior can be manipulated by those able to control the frame. They ran a study in which subjects were greeted at the laboratory and given a $50 check. During the explanation of why they were receiving the check, one group of subjects heard the check described as a "bonus" and another group of subjects heard it described as a "tuition rebate." Epley and colleagues conjectured that the bonus would be mentally coded as a positive change from the status quo, whereas the rebate would be coded as a return to a previous wealth state. They thought that the bonus framing would lead to more immediate spending than the rebate framing, because spending from the status quo is more easily coded as a relative loss. This is exactly what happened. In one experiment, when the subjects were contacted 1 week later, the bonus group had spent more of the money. In another experiment, subjects were allowed to buy items from the university bookstore (including snack foods) at a good discount. Again, the subjects from the bonus group spent more in the laboratory discount store.

Epley (2008) demonstrated the relevance of these findings in an Op-Ed piece in the *The New York Times* of January 31, 2008. Subsequent to the subprime mortgage crisis of 2007–2008, Congress and the president were considering mechanisms to stimulate a faltering economy. Tax rebates were being considered in order to get people to spend more (such tax rebates had been used in 2001, also as a stimulative mechanism). Epley pointed out in his Op-Ed piece that if the goal was to get people to spend their checks, then the money would be best labeled as a tax bonus rather than a tax rebate. The term *rebate* implies that money that is yours is being returned—that you are being restored to some status quo. Prospect theory predicts that you will be less likely to spend from the status quo position. However, describing the check as a tax bonus suggests that this money is "extra"—an increase from the status quo. People will be much more likely to spend such a "bonus." Studies of the 2001 program indicated that only 28% of the money was spent, a low rate perhaps in part caused by its unfortunate description as a "rebate."

Epley's point illustrates that policy analysts need to become more familiar with framing issues. In contrast, advertisers are extremely knowledgeable about the importance of framing. You can bet that a product will be advertised as "95% fat free" rather than "contains 5% fat." The providers of frames well know their value. The issue is whether you, the consumer of frames, will come to understand their importance and thus transform yourself into a more autonomous decision maker.

If decision makers are not sensitive to how choices are framed and contextualized in other ways, then their choices will be determined by whoever in their world has the power to determine these things. Phrased in this manner, the state of affairs seems somewhat ominous. But maybe there is an upside here. Yes, a malicious controller of our environment might choose to exploit us. But perhaps a benevolent controller of our environment could help us—could save us from our irrational acts without our having to change basic aspects of our cognition. The upside is that for certain cognitive problems it might be easier to change the environment than to change people. Because in a democracy we in part control our own environment, as a society we could decide to restructure the world so that it helped people to be more rational.

For example, in a cross-national study of organ donation rates, Johnson and Goldstein (2006) found that 85.9% of individuals in Sweden had agreed to be organ donors. However, the rate in the United Kingdom was only 17.2%. In the United States it is roughly 28%, more similar to that in the United Kingdom than to that in Sweden. The differences between Sweden, the United Kingdom, and the United States have nothing to do with attitudes toward organ donation. The difference is due to a contrast in the public policy about becoming an organ donor in these different countries. In Sweden—like Belgium, France, Poland, and Hungary, where agreement to organ donorship is over 95%—the default value on organ donorship is presumed consent. In countries with this public policy, people are assumed to have allowed their organs to be harvested, but can opt out by taking an action (usually by getting a notation on their driver's licenses). In contrast, the United States and the United Kingdom—like Germany, Denmark, and the Netherlands, where agreement to organ donorship is less than 30%—the default value is no donation, with explicit action required to opt for organ donation.

The citizens of *all* of these countries are having their behavior affected greatly by the status quo in their local environments. It is just that the local environment is structured much more optimally in some cases than in others. Johnson and Goldstein (2006) determined that when people really think about this issue without a default being given to them, roughly 80% (much closer to the percentage in Sweden and other opt-out countries) prefer to be organ donors. Since 1995, over 45,000 people have died while on waiting lists for an organ in the United States. A very small change in the donor decision-making environment that hurts no one (since an opt-out procedure is allowed in all countries with presumed consent) could save the lives of thousands of people.

Examples such as organ donation are what led economist Richard Thaler and legal theorist Cass Sunstein (Thaler & Sunstein, 2008) to advocate a policy of what they call *libertarian paternalism*. The paternalistic part of their philosophy is the acknowledgment that government should try to steer the choices of people toward actions that will be good for them. The libertarian part of their philosophy is the guarantee that any policy changes preserve complete freedom of choice. How is it possible to steer people's choices without interfering with freedom of choice? The answer is to exploit the extreme sensitivity of the decision maker to context. Specifically, this often means controlling the aspects of the environment that (indirectly) control the behavior of the decision maker—default values, framings, choice sets, designated status quos, choice procedures, and choice descriptions. Our natural tendency as humans is to be influenced by irrelevant aspects of our choice environments. This leads us into choices that are less than rational. But our collective intelligence, in the form of democratic decisions about what Thaler and Sunstein (2008) term "choice architectures," could help us to design environments that serve the public good and that result in more rational actions on our part.

Suggestions for Further Readings

Ariely, D. (2008). *Predictably irrational.* New York: HarperCollins.

Baron, J. (2008). *Thinking and deciding* (4th ed.). New York: Cambridge University Press.

Dawes, R. M. (1998). Behavioral decision making and judgment. In D. T. Gilbert, S. T. Fiske, & G. Lindzey (Eds.), *The handbook of social psychology* (Vol. 1, pp. 497–548). Boston: McGraw-Hill.

Dawes, R. M. (2001). *Everyday irrationality: How pseudo-scientists, lunatics, and the rest of us systematically fail to think rationally.* Boulder, CO: Westview Press.

Edwards, W. (1954). The theory of decision making. *Psychological Bulletin, 51,* 380–417.

Hastie, R., & Dawes, R. M. (2001). *Rational choice in an uncertain world.* Thousand Oaks, CA: Sage.

Kahneman, D., & Tversky, A. (Eds.). (2000). *Choices, values, and frames.* New York: Cambridge University Press.

Koehler, D. J., & Harvey, N. (Eds.). (2004). *Blackwell handbook of judgment and decision making.* Oxford: Blackwell.

Lichtenstein, S., & Slovic, P. (Eds.). (2006). *The construction of preference.* New York: Cambridge University Press.

Luce, R. D., & Raiffa, H. (1957). *Games and decisions.* New York: Wiley.

von Neumann, J., & Morgenstern, O. (1944). *The theory of games and economic behavior.* Princeton, NJ: Princeton University Press.

CHAPTER 3

Judgment

Rationality of Belief

The expected utility of an action involves multiplying the probability of an outcome by its utility (and summing across possible outcomes). Thus, determining the best action involves estimating the probabilities of various outcomes. These probabilities are not conscious calculations, of course—they are one's confidence estimates about states of the world. They are one's beliefs and the confidence that one has in them. If these beliefs are wrong, decision making will be poor. If our probabilistic judgments about the states of the world are wrong, decision making will not maximize one's utility—our actions will not result in our getting what we most want. Thus, if we are to determine what to do, we need to make sure that our actions are based on what is true. It is in this sense that rationality of belief—epistemic rationality—is one of the foundations for rationality of action.

Probabilistic judgment is the field that studies whether a person's beliefs are well calibrated—whether they map the world appropriately. There are many rules of probabilistic judgment that must be followed if our beliefs are to be epistemically rational, if they are to be a good measure of what is true. Rationality of belief is assessed by looking at a variety of probabilistic reasoning skills, evidence evaluation skills, and hypothesis testing skills—many of which will be discussed in this chapter.

To calibrate one's beliefs rationally, it is not necessary to be a calculating genius but, as with axiomatic utility theory, there are a few qualitative principles that must be adhered to if epistemic rationality is to be achieved. One must follow some very basic rules for dealing with probabilities and for updating beliefs based on evidence. But, in parallel to the discussion in the last chapter, there is an important research tradition indicating that people violate many of these principles of rational belief.

In 2002, cognitive scientist Daniel Kahneman of Princeton University won the Nobel Prize in Economics for work done with his longtime collaborator Amos Tversky (who died in 1996). The press release for the award drew attention to the roots of the award-winning work in "the analysis of human judgment and decision-making by cognitive psychologists" (Royal Swedish Academy of Sciences, 2002). Kahneman was cited for discovering "how human judgment may take heuristic shortcuts that systematically depart from basic principles of probability. His work has inspired a new generation of researchers in economics and finance to enrich economic theory using insights from cognitive psychology into intrinsic human motivation." In short, Kahneman and Tversky's work was about how humans make choices and assess probabilities (see Kahneman & Tversky, 2000). It dealt with both instrumental rationality (chapter 2) and epistemic rationality (this chapter)—with whether people take appropriate actions and have beliefs appropriately calibrated to evidence. The research program inaugurated by Kahneman and Tversky in the early 1970s (Kahneman & Tversky, 1972, 1973; Tversky & Kahneman, 1974) has been termed the *heuristics and biases research program*. The term *biases* refers to the systematic errors that people make in choosing actions and in estimating probabilities, and the term *heuristic* refers to *why* people often make these errors—because they use mental shortcuts (heuristics) to solve many problems. We shall discuss the psychological theory of these mental shortcuts in chapter 5 and alternative interpretations of these findings in chapter 4. In this chapter, we will discuss the requirements of epistemic rationality and how people sometimes fall short of these requirements. Many of the requirements of epistemic rationality concern reasoning about probabilities, so that will be a particular focus of this chapter.

Bayes' Theorem

To attain epistemic rationality, a person must have beliefs probabilistically calibrated to evidence in the right way. One normative model of probabilistic reasoning of this type is the so-called *probability calculus*. Mathematically, probability values follow certain rules. These rules form one of the most important normative models for subjective probability estimates. Thus, in order for us to be epistemically rational, our probability estimates must follow the rules of objective probabilities. Most of these rules are quite intuitive. Here are a few of the most important:

Probabilities vary between 0 and 1. So $0 \leq P(A) \leq 1$; where $P(A)$ is the probability of event A.

If an event is certain to happen, then its probability is 1.0. So $P(A) = 1$, when A is certain.

If an event is certain *not* to happen, then its probability is 0. So $P(A) = 0$, when A is certain not to happen.

If event A and event B cannot *both* happen, they are said to be mutually exclusive. When event A and event B are mutually exclusive, then the probability of one *or* the other occurring is the probability of each added together:

$$P(A \text{ or } B) = P(A) + P(B)$$

Conditional probabilities concern the probability of one event given that another has occurred. They are written as follows: $P(A/B)$, which can be stated in a variety of ways, including "the probability of A given B," "the probability of A conditional on the occurrence of B," and "the probability of A happening given that B has occurred."

When A and B are mutually exclusive, then $P(A/B) = 0$, because if B has occurred, A cannot. However, when A and B are not mutually exclusive the formula for the conditional probability is

$$P(A / B) = P(A \text{ and } B) / P(B)$$

Note that, in general, $P(A/B)$ is not necessarily the same as $P(B/A)$, because the formula for the latter has a different denominator:

$$P(B/A) = P(A \text{ and } B) / P(A)$$

We can, however, write one of the conditional probabilities in terms of the other. When we do, after a little simple algebra we come to one of the most famous theorems in decision theory, Bayes' theorem, sometimes called Bayes' rule. But before we do, I need to pause and say a few words about the symbols to come. First, what follows in the next few pages is the most mathematical and technical part of this book. However, it is not the math but the *concepts* that are important, and they should be clear throughout the discussion even if you are math-phobic and wish to ignore the numbers and formulas. This is a key point. You need not learn anything more than a way of thinking—some verbal rules—in order to be a Bayesian thinker. Formal Bayesian statistics involve calculation, to be sure, but to escape the thinking errors surrounding probability you only need to have learned the *conceptual* logic of how correct thinking about probabilities works.

With that said, here is Bayes' rule:

$$P\left(A/B\right) = \frac{P(A)*P\left(B/A\right)}{P(A)*P\left(B/A\right)+P(\sim A)*P\left(B/\sim A\right)}$$

The rule has only one term we have not seen before, $\sim$A, which means "not A." Thus, $P(\sim A)$ is the probability of some event *other* than A occurring.

Decision theorists have shown that there are certain untoward consequences (similar to the money pump that we discussed in the previous chapter) if our probability judgments do not follow the simple rules of probability just outlined. If you feel that the probability that the New England Patriots will win the next Super Bowl is .25 and that the Chicago Bears will win the next Super Bowl is .10, then you had better think that the probability of the Patriots *or* the Bears winning is .35. [Recall the previous equation indicating that P(A or B) = P(A) + P(B).] If you violate this stricture you will not be epistemically rational, and any action that you take on the basis of these probabilities will be suboptimal—it will not maximize your expected utility.

All of the rules of probability are important, but for judgment and decision making Bayes' rule has special salience. Discovered by the Reverend Thomas Bayes of Tunbridge Wells, England, in the 18th century (Stigler, 1983, 1986), the formula is used for more than just the mundane task of turning one conditional probability, $P(B/A)$, into another, $P(A/B)$. The formula is also used as the formal standard for the important task of belief updating—how the belief in a particular hypothesis should be updated based on the receipt of new evidence that is relevant to the hypothesis. All we have to do is substitute the A and B in the formula with two fundamental concepts: the focal hypothesis under investigation (labeled H) and a set of data that is collected, relevant to the hypothesis (labeled D).

$$P\left(H/D\right) = \frac{P(H)*P\left(D/H\right)}{P(H)*P\left(D/H\right)+P(\sim H)*P\left(D/\sim H\right)}$$

In the formula you see an additional symbol, ~H (not H). This simply refers to the alternative hypothesis: the mutually exclusive alternative that must be correct if the focal hypothesis, H, is false. Thus, by convention, the probability of the alternative hypothesis, ~H, is 1 minus the probability of the focal hypothesis, H. For example, if I think the probability that the fish at the end of my line is a trout is .60, then that is the equivalent of saying that the probability that the fish at the end of my line is not a trout is .40.

The formula tells us how to update our prior belief in a hypothesis after the receipt of new data. In the formula, P(H) is the probability estimate that the focal hypothesis is true *prior* to collecting the data, and P(~H) is the probability estimate that the alternative hypothesis is true *prior* to collecting the data. Additionally, a number of conditional probabilities come into play. For example, P(H/D) represents the probability that the focal hypothesis is true *subsequent* to the data pattern actually observed (this is sometimes termed the *posterior* probability). P(D/H) is the probability of observing that particular data pattern given that the focal hypothesis is true, and P(D/~H) (as we shall see later, a very important quantity) is the probability of observing that particular data pattern given that the alternative hypothesis is true. It is important to realize that P(D/H) and P(D/~H) are *not* complements (they do not add to 1.0). The data might be likely given both the focal and alternative hypothesis or unlikely given both the focal and alternative hypotheses.

People often have trouble following the strictures of Bayes' rule when updating belief, and we shall see several examples of this in the remainder of this chapter. Again, however, I would emphasize the point that getting the numbers precisely correct is not what we will be stressing in this chapter, but instead getting in the right conceptual ballpark of the correct estimate. It is not correct calculation we are after, but instead getting a feel for Bayesian thinking.

Problems with Probabilities: Base Rate Neglect

The difficulties that people have with probabilistic information is illustrated in two examples of problems that have been the subject of much research. The first is the so-called cabs problem (Bar-Hillel, 1980; Koehler, 1996; Lyon & Slovic, 1976; Macchi, 1995; Tversky & Kahneman, 1982), and it has been the subject of over two decades of research:

A cab was involved in a hit-and-run accident at night. Two cab companies, the Green and the Blue, operate in the city in which the accident occurred. You are given the following facts: 85% of the cabs in the city are Green and 15% are Blue. A witness reported that the cab in the accident was Blue. The court tested the reliability of the witness under the same circumstances that existed on the night of the accident and concluded that the witness correctly identified each of the two colors 80% of the time. What is the probability (expressed as a percentage ranging from 0% to 100%) that the cab involved in the accident was Blue?

Try one more problem before I explain the logic behind the right answer. The next problem shares the logic of the cabs problem but is more relevant to everyday life. It concerns the estimation of medical risk, and it too has been the focus of considerable research (Casscells, Schoenberger, & Graboys, 1978; Cosmides & Tooby, 1996; Sloman, Over, Slovak, & Stibel, 2003; Stanovich & West, 1999), including some involving medical personnel:

Imagine that the XYZ virus causes a serious disease that occurs in 1 in every 1,000 people. Imagine also that there is a test to diagnose the disease that always indicates correctly that a person who has the XYZ virus actually has it. Finally, imagine that the test has a false-positive rate of 5 percent. This means that the test wrongly indicates that the XYZ virus is present in 5% of the cases where the person does not have the virus. Imagine that we choose a person randomly and administer the test, and that it yields a positive result (indicates that the person is XYZ-positive). What is the probability (expressed as a percentage ranging from 0% to 100%) that the individual actually has the XYZ virus, assuming that we know nothing else about the individual's personal or medical history?

Do not read on until you have taken a stab at both problems. Do not feel that you must calculate the answer precisely (although if you think you can, go ahead). Just give your best guesstimate. The point is not to get the precise answer so much as to see whether you are in the right ballpark. The answers of many people are not.

We will start with the cabs problem. Bayes' theorem dictates how the probability assessment in such a question is to be calculated. The theorem provides the optimal way of combining the two pieces of information that have been given:

1. That, overall, 15% of the cabs are Blue.
2. That a witness whose identification accuracy is 80% identified the cab in question as Blue.

Most people do not naturally combine the two pieces of information optimally. In fact, many people are surprised to learn that the probability that the cab is Blue is .41, and that, despite the witness's identification, it is still more likely that the cab involved in the accident was Green (.59) rather than Blue (.41). The reason is that the general or prior probability that the cab is Green (85%) is higher than the credibility of the witness's identification of Blue (80%). Without using the formula, we can see how the probability of .41 is arrived at. In 100 accidents of this type, 15 of the cabs will be Blue and the witness will identify 80% of them (12) as Blue. Furthermore, out of 100 accidents of this type, 85 of the cabs will be Green and the witness will identify 20% percent of them (17) as Blue. Thus, 29 cabs will be identified as Blue, but only 12 of them will actually be Blue. The proportion of cabs identified as Blue that actually are Blue is 12 out of 29, or 41%.

The following table is another way of displaying the state of affairs. From the top to the bottom, we can see that of 100 accidents of this type, 85 will involve Green cabs and 15 will involve Blue cabs. One row down, we can see that of the 85 Green cabs involved in accidents, the witness identifies 68 as Green and 17 as Blue. Of the 15 Blue cabs involved in accidents, the witness identifies 12 as Blue and 3 as Green. In the bottom row we can see that a total of 29 cabs are identified as Blue but only 12 actually are Blue.

100 Cab Accidents			
85 involve Green Cabs		15 involve Blue Cabs	
Witness identifies 68 of these as Green	Witness identifies 17 of these as Blue	Witness identifies 12 of these as Blue	Witness identifies 3 of these as Green
	29 cabs are identified as Blue but only 12 actually are		

In terms of Bayes' rule, here is how the calculation goes:

$$P(H/D) = P(H)P(D/H)/[P(H)P(D/H) + P(\sim H)P(D/\sim H)]$$

$$P(H/D) = (.15)(.80)/[(.15)(.80) + (.85)(.20)] = .41$$

Less than half of the subjects given this problem give answers between .20 and .70. Most answer around .80. In short, they answer with the figure indicating the witness's accuracy without discounting this figure (as they should) because the prior probability (.15) is quite low. That is, most people greatly overestimate the probability that the cab is Blue.

They overweight the witness's identification and underweight the *base rate*, or prior probability, that the cab is Blue. This is an example of a tendency to overweight concrete and vivid single-case information when it must be combined with more abstract probabilistic information.

A similar tendency to underweight prior probabilities in the form of base rate information has been demonstrated with the XYZ virus problem presented earlier. The most common answer is 95%. The correct answer is approximately 2%! People vastly overestimate the probability that a positive result truly indicates the XYZ virus because of the same tendency to overweight the case information and underweight the base rate information that we saw in the cabs problem. Although the correct answer to this problem can again be calculated by means of Bayes' rule, a little logical reasoning can help to illustrate the profound effect that base rates have on probabilities. We were given the information that out of 1,000 people, just 1 will actually be XYZ-positive. If the other 999 (who do not have the disease) are tested, the test will indicate incorrectly that approximately 50 of them have the virus (.05 multiplied by 999) because of the 5 percent false-positive rate. Thus, of the 51 patients testing positive, only 1 (approximately 2%) will actually be XYZ-positive. In short, the base rate is such that the vast majority of people do not have the virus. This fact, combined with a substantial false-positive rate, ensures that, in absolute numbers, the majority of positive tests will be of people who do not have the virus.

In terms of Bayes' rule, here is how the calculation goes:

$$P(H/D) = P(H)P(D/H)/[P(H)P(D/H) + P(\sim H)P(D/\sim H)]$$

$$P(H/D) = (.001)(1.0)/[(.001)(1.0) + (.999)(.05)] = .001/(.001 + .04995) = .0198$$

In both of these problems there is a tendency to overweight individual-case evidence and underweight statistical information. The case evidence (the witness's identification, the laboratory test result) seems "tangible" and "concrete" to most people—it is more vivid. In contrast, the probabilistic evidence seems, well—probabilistic! This reasoning is of course fallacious because case evidence itself is always probabilistic. A witness can make correct identifications with only a certain degree of accuracy, and a clinical test misidentifies the presence of a disease with a certain probability.

The problems presented thus far are often termed *noncausal base rates*—those involving base rates with no obvious causal relationship to the criterion behavior (Ajzen, 1977; Barbey & Sloman, 2007; Bar-Hillel, 1980, 1990; Koehler, 1996; Tversky & Kahneman, 1982). The cab problem discussed earlier is an example of a noncausal base rate. The *causal* variant of the same problem substitutes for the first fact the phrase "Although the two companies are roughly equal in size, 85% of cab accidents in the city involve Green cabs and 15% involve Blue cabs" (Tversky & Kahneman, 1982, p. 157). In this version, the base rates seem more relevant to the probability of the Green cab being involved in the accident. People are more prone to use causal base rates than noncausal ones.

In all versions of these problems, the situation is one in which two probabilities, the probable diagnosticity of the case evidence and the prior probability, must be combined if one is to arrive at a correct decision. There are right and wrong ways of combining these probabilities, and more often than not—particularly when the case evidence gives the illusion of concreteness—people combine the information in the wrong way. The right way is to use Bayes' rule, or, more specifically, the insight from Bayes' rule. As I mentioned previously, I emphasize here the *insight* from Bayes' rule: that the diagnosticity of evidence must be weighted by the base rate. I do not wish to imply in this discussion of Bayesian reasoning that we do, or should, always explicitly calculate using the Bayesian formula in our minds. It is enough that people learn to "think Bayesian" in a qualitative sense— that they have what might be called "Bayesian instincts," not that they have necessarily memorized the rule. It is enough, for example, simply to realize the importance of the base rate. That would allow a person to see the critical insight embedded in the XYZ virus problem—that when a test with a substantial false-alarm rate is applied to a disease with a very small base rate, then the majority of individuals with a positive test will not have the disease. This is all the knowledge of the Bayesian reasoning that is needed (of course, greater depth of understanding would be an additional plus). Such a qualitative understanding will allow a person to make a guesstimate that is close enough to prevent serious errors in action in daily life.

In short, the issue is whether people's natural judgments of probabilities follow—to an order of approximation—the dictates of the theorem. Theorists take for granted that people making probabilistic judgments are making spontaneous "guesstimates"; the experimental evidence concerns whether these spontaneous judgments capture some of the restrictions that Bayes' theorem puts on probabilities. When we fall to the ground, our body can be described as behaving according to a law of Newton's. We do not consciously *calculate* Newton's law as our falling behavior is taking place—but we can in fact be described *as if* we were adhering to that law.

Dawkins (1976/1989) emphasizes the point I am stressing here:

> Just as we may use a slide rule without appreciating that we are, in effect, using logarithms, so an animal may be pre-programmed in such a way that it behaves as if it had made a complicated calculation.... When a man throws a ball high in the air and catches it again, he behaves as if he had solved a set of differential equations in predicting the trajectory of the ball. He may neither know nor care what a differential equation is, but this does not affect his skill with the ball. At some subconscious level, something functionally equivalent to the mathematical calculations is going on. (p. 96)

The analogous question for our present discussion is whether people's judgments can be described as adhering to the model of rational reasoning provided by Bayes' rule. The probability judgments of people might be described as consistent with Bayes' rule without them having *any* knowledge of the formula or being aware of any conscious calculation. We will see in some of the following problems that much experimentation has examined whether subjects' probability judgments simply move *in the right direction* after being presented with evidence—and research has found that sometimes with regard to one particular reasoning error, ignoring P(D/~H), they do not!

Ignoring P(D/~H)

We have seen in the previous section how the failure to weight diagnostic evidence with the base rate probability is an error of Bayesian reasoning. In this section, we will see that sometimes it is not the base rate that is the problem but the processing of the data that should lead to belief updating.

In order to illustrate this thinking error, I will utilize a different form of Bayes' rule—one arrived at by simple mathematical transformation. The formula presented earlier was written in terms of the posterior probability of the focal hypothesis (H) given a new datum (D). It of course would be possible to write the formula in terms of the posterior probability of the nonfocal hypothesis (~H) given a new datum (D):

$$P\left(\sim H/D\right) = \frac{P(\sim H) * P\left(D/\sim H\right)}{P(\sim H) * P\left(D/\sim H\right) + P(H) * P\left(D/H\right)}$$

By dividing the two formulas we can arrive at the most theoretically transparent form of Bayes' formula (see Fischhoff & Beyth-Marom, 1983)—one which is written in so-called odds form:

$$\frac{P(H/D)}{P(\sim H/D)} = \frac{P(D/H)}{P(D/\sim H)} * \frac{P(H)}{P(\sim H)}$$

In this ratio, or odds form, from left to right, the three ratio terms represent: the posterior odds favoring the focal hypothesis (H) after receipt of the new data (D); the so-called likelihood ratio (LR) composed of the probability of the data given the focal hypothesis divided by the probability of the data given the alternative hypothesis; and the prior odds favoring the focal hypothesis. Specifically:

posterior odds = P(H/D)/P(~H/D)
likelihood ratio = P(H/D)/P(D/~H/)
prior odds = P(H)/P(~H)

The formula tells us that the odds favoring the focal hypothesis (H) after receipt of the data are arrived at by multiplying together the other two terms—the likelihood ratio and the prior odds favoring the focal hypothesis:

posterior odds favoring the focal hypothesis = LR × prior odds

There are several ways in which reasoning has been found to deviate from the prescriptions of Bayes' rule, but in this section I wish to concentrate on just one: Often, when evaluating the diagnosticity of evidence [that is, the likelihood ratio: P(D/H)/P(D/~H)], people fail to appreciate the relevance of the denominator term [P(D/~H)]. They fail to see the necessity of evaluating the probability of obtaining the data observed if the focal hypothesis were *false*.

This is the formal reason why failing to "think of the opposite" leads to serious reasoning errors. A large research literature has grown up demonstrating that the tendency to ignore the probability of the evidence given that the nonfocal hypothesis is true—P(D/~H)—is a ubiquitous psychological tendency. For example, Doherty and Mynatt (1990) used a simple paradigm in which subjects were asked to imagine that they were a doctor examining a patient with a red rash. They were shown four pieces of evidence and were asked to choose which pieces of information they would need in order to determine whether the patient had the disease "Digirosa." The four pieces of information were:

The percentage of people with Digirosa.
The percentage of people without Digirosa.
The percentage of people with Digirosa who have a red rash.
The percentage of people without Digirosa who have a red rash.

These pieces of information corresponded to the four terms in the Bayesian formula: P(H), P(~H), P(D/H), and P(D/~H). Because P(H) and P(~H) are complements, only three pieces of information are necessary to calculate the posterior probability. However, P(D/~H)—the percentage of people who have a red rash among those *without* Digirosa—clearly must be selected because it is a critical component of the likelihood ratio in Bayes' formula. Nevertheless, 48.8% of the individuals who participated in the Doherty and Mynatt (1990) study failed to select the P(D/~H) card. Thus, to many subjects presented with this problem, the people with a red rash but without Digirosa do not seem relevant—they seem (mistakenly) to be a nonevent.

The importance of P(D/~H) often seems counterintuitive. People have to be taught that it is important or else their default is to ignore it. Consider, for example, the following problem that has implications that might still seem strange even though you have been amply warned about the importance of P(D/~H):

Imagine yourself meeting David Maxwell. Your task is to assess the *probability that he is a university professor* based on some information that you will be given. This will be done in two steps. At each step you will get some information that you may or may not find useful in making your assessment. After each piece of information you will be asked to assess the probability that David Maxwell is a university professor. In doing so, consider all the information you have received to that point if you consider it to be relevant.

Step 1: You are told that David Maxwell attended a party in which 25 male university professors and 75 male business executives took part, 100 people all together. Question: What do you think the probability is that David Maxwell is a university professor? _____%

Step 2: You are told that David Maxwell is a member of the Bears Club. At the party mentioned in step 1, 70% of the male university professors were members of the Bears Club, and 90% of the male business executives were members of the Bears Club. Question: What do you think the probability is that David Maxwell is a university professor? _____%

This problem is used in studies to assess whether people can deal correctly (or at all) with the P(D/~H) information (Beyth-Marom & Fischhoff, 1983; Stanovich & West, 1998d). The first step is simple. The probability of the focal hypothesis is .25 because 25 of the 100 are university professors. It is step 2 that is the tricky one. It might seem that because 70% of the male university professors were members of the Bears Club and that this percentage is greater than 50%, that the probability that David Maxwell is a university professor should go up (that it should now be judged to be higher than the base rate of 25%). But that would be making the error of ignoring P(D/~H). In fact, it is *more* likely that a business executive is a member of the Bears Club. Being a member of the Bears Club is more diagnostic of being a business executive than a university professor, so it actually *lowers* the probability of the latter. The likelihood ratio here is less than 1 (.70/.90), so the odds against David Maxwell being a university professor, after the information about the Bears Club is received, get worse—from 1 to 3 against (.25/.75) to:

posterior odds = likelihood ratio × prior odds

posterior odds = (.70 / .90) × (.25 / .75)

posterior odds = .175 / .675 = 1 to 3.86

In terms of the probability version of Bayes' rule, the proper Bayesian adjustment is from .25 in step 1 to .206 in step 2 [(.70 × .25) / (.70 × .25 + .90 × .75)]. In a study that my research group ran using this problem (Stanovich & West, 1998d), we found, however, that only 42% of the sample moved their probability assessments in the right direction (lowered it from .25 after receiving the evidence). Many subjects raised their probabilities after receiving the evidence, indicating that their focus was on the relatively high value of P(D/H)—.70—and that they failed to contextualize this conditional probability with the even higher value of P(D/~H).

Here is a parallel problem that is tricky, but in a slightly different way, and it will again test whether you understand the implications of the likelihood ratio, and more specifically, the importance of P(D/~H):

Again, imagine yourself meeting Mark Smith. Your task is to assess the *probability that he is a university professor* based on some information that you will be given.

Step 1: You are told that Mark Smith attended a party in which 80 male university professors and 20 male business executives took part, 100 people all together. Question: What do you think the probability is that Mark Smith is a university professor? _____%

Step 2: You are told that Mark Smith is a member of the Bears Club. At the party mentioned in step 1, 40% of the male university professors were members of the Bears Club, and 5% of the male business executives were members of the Bears Club. Question: What do you think the probability is that Mark Smith is a university professor? _____%

In this problem, reliance on the base rate at step 1 would result in an estimate of .80. Step 2 is structured so that although the likelihood ratio is considerably greater than 1 (.40/.05), P(D/H) is less than .50. This might suggest to someone ignoring P(D/~H)—which is in fact lower than P(D/H)—that these data should *decrease* the probability that David is a university professor. In fact, the proper Bayesian adjustment is from .80 in step 1 to .97 in step 2 [(.40 × .80) / (.40 × .80 + .05 × .20)]). Any adjustment upward from step 1 to step 2 would suggest that the subject had been attentive to P(D/~H). Moving in the right direction is all that is necessary to show that one is a Bayesian thinker. However, in the study that my research group ran using this problem (Stanovich & West, 1998d), we found that only 30% of the sample moved their probability assessments in the right direction (raised it from .80 after receiving the evidence).

The failure to attend to the alternative hypothesis—to the denominator of the likelihood ratio when receiving evidence—is not a trivial reasoning error. Paying attention to the probability of the observation under the alternative hypothesis is a critical component of clinical judgment in medicine and many other applied sciences. It is the reason we use control groups. It is of course essential to know what would have happened if the variable of interest had not been changed. Both clinical and scientific inference is fatally compromised if we have information about only the treated group.

A further example of the difficulty people have in processing P(D/~H) is provided by another problem, used by Mynatt, Doherty, and Dragan (1993) to study whether people use rational search strategies when looking for evidence. The problem is phrased as follows:

Your sister has a car she bought a couple of years ago. It is either a car X or a car Y, but you cannot remember which. You do remember that her car gets over 25 miles to the gallon of gasoline and has not had any major mechanical problems in the 2 years she has owned it. You have the following piece of information:

65% of car Xs get over 25 miles per gallon

Three additional pieces of information are also available:

1. The percentage of car Ys that get over 25 miles per gallon.
2. The percentage of car Xs that have had no major mechanical problems for the first 2 years of ownership.
3. The percentage of car Ys that have had no major mechanical problems for the first 2 years of ownership.

The question asked of subjects is the following: Assuming you could find out only *one* of these three pieces of information (1, 2, or 3), which would you want in order to help you decide what car your sister owns?

The structure of the problem is as follows. There are two hypotheses—that the car is an instance of brand X (H1) and that the car is an instance of Y (H2), and these two hypotheses are mutually exclusive. There are two potentially diagnostic indicators—that a car gets over 25 miles per gallon (D1) and that a car has had no major mechanical problems for the first 2 years of ownership (D2). You have been given one piece of information, $P(D1/H1)$—concerning all brand X cars: what proportion gets over 25 miles per gallon. There are two likelihood ratios available:

$P(D1/H1)/P(D1/H2)$ and $P(D2/H1)/P(D2/H2)$

However, you cannot attain information on both, because you are allowed only one other piece of information—beyond $P(D1/H1)$, which you have. Obviously, the choice is $P(D1/H2)$ so that you can get at least one complete likelihood ratio—the percentage of X cars getting over 25 miles per gallon compared to the percentage of Y cars getting over 25 miles per gallon. If these percentages are different, they will help you determine which car your sister has, because you know that hers gets over 25 miles per gallon. The choice seems obvious, but it is not in fact the one that untrained subjects make. Mynatt et al. (1993) found that the majority of subjects (60.4%) chose to examine the percentage of car Xs having no major mechanical problems [$P(D2/H1)$]. This piece of information is totally useless because the subject cannot obtain $P(D2/H2)$. Without knowing whether Ys have a higher or lower incidence of mechanical problems than Xs, knowing that a certain percentage of Xs have problems is uninformative.

Disturbingly, Kern and Doherty (1982) found performance to be no better in a structurally analogous medical diagnosis task with the participants being senior medical students enrolled in clinical clerkships at Ohio State University. These medical students were trying to diagnose the existence of tropical disease type A or type B in a patient. Given the information on the incidence of one symptom, P(symptom 1/ disease A), they were given the choice of one of three pieces of information analogous to that in the Mynatt et al. (1993) experiment: P(symptom 1/ disease B), P(symptom 2/ disease A), and P(symptom 2/ disease B). Obviously, only the first gives a useful likelihood ratio. However, 69.3% of the medical students in this experiment failed to select a useful piece of information in either of the two problems like this. The medical students persistently picked diagnostically useless information.

Psychologists have done extensive research on the tendency for people to ignore essential comparative (control group) information. For example, in a much researched covariation detection paradigm (Levin, Wasserman, & Kao, 1993; Shanks, 1995; Wasserman, Dorner, & Kao, 1990), subjects are shown a 2 × 2 matrix summarizing the data from an experiment examining the relation between a treatment and patient response:

	Condition Improved	No Improvement
Treatment Given	200	75
No Treatment	50	15

The numbers in the matrix represent the number of people in each cell. Specifically, 200 people were given the treatment and the condition improved, 75 people were given the treatment and no improvement occurred, 50 people were not given the treatment and the condition improved, and 15 people were not given the treatment and the condition did not improve. In covariation detection experiments, subjects are asked to indicate whether the treatment was effective. Many think that the treatment in this example is effective. They focus on the large number of cases (200) in which improvement followed the treatment. Secondarily, they focus on the fact that more people who received treatment showed improvement (200) than showed no improvement (75). Because this probability (200/275 = .727) seems high, subjects are enticed into thinking that the treatment works. This is an error of rational thinking.

Such an approach ignores the probability of improvement given that treatment was *not* given. Since this probability is even higher (50/65 = .769), the particular treatment tested in this experiment can be judged to be completely *ineffective*. The tendency to ignore the outcomes in the no-treatment cells and focus on the large number in the treatment/improvement cell seduces many people into viewing the treatment as effective. Disturbingly, this nonoptimal way of treating evidence has been found even among those who specialize in clinical diagnosis (for example, among medical personnel; see Chapman & Elstein, 2000; Groopman, 2007; Wolf, Gruppen, & Billi, 1985).

The tendency to ignore the alternative hypothesis is exemplified in a well-known effect that has been studied by psychologists for over 50 years (Dickson & Kelly, 1985; Forer, 1949; King & Koehler, 2000; Marks, 2001)—the so-called P. T. Barnum effect. Barnum, the famous carnival and circus operator, coined the statement "There's a sucker born every minute." In a classroom demonstration that is commonly used in introductory psychology classes, the instructor takes handwriting samples from all of the students and returns the next week with their "personalized personality descriptions" based on his or her knowledge of graphology. After reading their "individualized" reports, the students invariably find their descriptions highly accurate—rating them from 7 to 9 on a 10-point scale of accuracy. They are embarrassed and, one hopes, learn something about pseudosciences such as graphology when they are told to look at their neighbor's report to see that everyone was given exactly the same personality description—for example, a whole paragraph of statements such as "At times you are extroverted, affable, and sociable, but at other times you are wary and reserved."

This particular demonstration of the P. T. Barnum effect depends on the fact that there are certain sets of statements and phrases that most people see as applicable to themselves. Many of these phrases have been studied by psychologists. The upshot however is that anyone can feed them to a "client" as individualized psychological "analysis." The client is usually very impressed by the individualized accuracy of the "personality reading," not knowing that the same reading is being given to everyone. Of course, the Barnum effect is the basis of belief in the accuracy of palm readers and astrologists.

If we look more carefully at what is going on here, we will see that it is our old friend—the failure to consider P(D/~H). Implicitly, the students fooled by the Barnum demonstration are evaluating the probability that "at times you are extroverted, affable, and sociable, but at other times you are wary and reserved" applies to them and finding it high. A bit more technically, students were thinking that the following probability was high:

P (extroverted, affable, wary . . ./this description applies specifically to me)

But of course this is not the likelihood ratio. It is merely P(D/H). To calculate the proper posterior probability, we need to take into account the denominator of the likelihood ratio—P(D/~H). What is that in this instance? It is simply the probability that "at times you are extroverted, affable, and sociable, but at other times you are wary and reserved" applies to a random person. Of course we can immediately detect that the probability of *that* quantity is also high. The phrase "at times extroverted, affable, and sociable, but at other times wary and reserved" is so slippery and open to interpretation that virtually anyone would find it highly likely that it applied to them. So in terms of the likelihood ratio, although the numerator might well be .90 (it *does* apply to me), the denominator is perhaps almost .90 as well (it applies to almost everyone else).

So the likelihood ratio (LR) in this case is the ratio of two high numbers. The likelihood ratio is

P (extroverted, affable, wary . . ./this description is applied to me) divided by P (extroverted, affable, wary . . ./this description is applied to a random person)

Because the denominator is a high number (perhaps .90?), then even if the numerator is judged to be higher, the LR cannot be that high a number (even if the numerator is judged to be 1.0, the LR could not be much higher than 1). Now, look at the entire equation again:

posterior odds = likelihood ratio × prior odds

Whatever the odds were before the "data" were collected, they cannot be much changed because the LR is close to 1.0. The so-called evidence of predictive accuracy given to the students was in fact pseudoevidence. It was not diagnostic at all—and is immediately recognized as worthless once attention is focused on P(D/~H).

Overconfidence in Knowledge Calibration

Let us begin this section with a little test of your knowledge calibration ability. For each of the following items, provide a low and high guess such that you are 90% sure the correct answer falls between the two. Write down your answers:

1. I am 90% confident that Martin Luther King's age at the time of his death was somewhere between _____ years and _____ years.

2. I am 90% confident that the number of books in the Old Testament is between _____ books and _____ books.

3. I am 90% confident that the year in which Wolfgang Amadeus Mozart was born was between the year _____ and the year _____.

4. I am 90% confident that the gestation period (in days) of an Asian elephant is between _____ days and _____ days.

5. I am 90% confident that the deepest known point in the oceans is between _____ feet and _____ feet.

6. I am 90% confident that the length of the Nile River is between _____ miles and _____ miles.

7. I am 90% confident that the number of countries that are members of Organization of Petroleum Exporting Countries is between _____ and _____.

8. I am 90% confident that the diameter of the moon is between _____ miles and _____ miles.

9. I am 90% confident that the weight of an empty Boeing 747 is between _____ pounds and _____ pounds.

10. I am 90% confident that the air distance from London to Tokyo is between _____ miles and _____ miles.

These questions relate to another important domain in which people have difficulty assessing probabilities. Psychologists have done numerous studies using the so-called knowledge calibration paradigm (Fischhoff, 1988; Fischhoff, Slovic, & Lichtenstein, 1977; Griffin & Tversky, 1992; Sieck & Arkes, 2005; Tetlock, 2005; Yates, Lee, & Bush, 1997). In this paradigm, a large set of probability judgments of knowledge confidence are made. Of course, a single probability judgment by itself is impossible to evaluate. How would I know if you were correct in saying there is a 95% chance that your nephew will be married in a year? However, a large set of such judgments can be evaluated because, collectively, the set must adhere to certain statistical criteria.

For example, if the weather forecaster says there is a 90% chance of rain tomorrow and it is sunny and hot, there may be nothing wrong with that particular judgment. The weather forecaster might have processed all the information that was available and processed it correctly. It just happened to be unexpectedly sunny on that particular day. However, if you found out that on half of the days the weatherperson said there was a 90% chance of rain it did not rain, then you would be justified in seriously questioning the accuracy of weather reports from this outlet. You expect it to rain on 90% of the days that the weatherperson says have a 90% chance of rain. You accept that the weatherperson does not know on which 10% of the days it will not rain (otherwise he or she would have claimed to be 100% certain), but overall you expect that if, over the years, the weatherperson has predicted "90% chance of rain" on 50 different days, that on about 45 of them it will have rained.

The assessment of how well people calibrate their knowledge proceeds in exactly the same way as we evaluate the weatherperson. People answer multiple choice or true/false questions and, for each item, provide a confidence judgment indicating their subjective probability that their answer is correct. Epistemic rationality is apparent only when one-to-one calibration is achieved—that the set of items assigned a subjective probability of .70 should be answered correctly 70% of the time, that the set of items assigned a subjective probability of .80 should be answered correctly 80% of the time, and so forth. This is what is meant by good knowledge calibration. It means, in a sense, that a person must know what he or she knows and what he or she does *not* know as well. If such close calibration is not achieved, then a person is not epistemically rational because his or her beliefs do not map on to the world in an important way. Such epistemic miscalibration will make it impossible to choose the best actions to take, because probabilistic guesses about future states of the world will be inaccurate.

The standard finding across a wide variety of knowledge calibration experiments has been one of overconfidence. Subjective probability estimates are consistently higher than the obtained percentage correct. So, for example, people tend to get 88% items correct when they say they are 100% sure that they were correct. When people say they are 90% sure they are correct, they actually get about 75% of the items correct, and so on. Often, people will say they are 70 to 80% certain when in fact their performance is at chance—50% in a true/false paradigm.

The overconfidence effect in knowledge calibration is thought to derive at least in part from our tendency to fix on the first answer that comes to mind, to then assume "ownership" of that answer, and to cut mental costs by then privileging that answer as "our own" in subsequent thinking. Subjects make the first-occurring answer a focal hypothesis and then concentrate attention on the focal hypothesis, thereby leading to inattention to alternative, or nonfocal, answers. In short, "One reason for inappropriately high confidence is failure to think of reasons why one might be wrong" (Baron, 2008, p. 144). The evidence retrieved for each of the alternatives forms the basis for the confidence judgments, but the subject remains unaware that the recruitment of evidence was biased— that evidence was recruited only for the favored alternative. As a result, subjects end up with too much confidence in their answers.

You can see if you were subject to the phenomenon of overconfidence by looking at the end of this chapter. There you will find the answers to the questions at the beginning of this section. See how you did. Note that you were forewarned about the phenomenon of overconfidence by the title of this section. Because you were forming 90% confidence intervals, 90% of the time your confidence interval should contain the true value. Only 1 time in 10 should your interval fail to contain the actual answer. So because you answered only 10 such questions, your intervals should have contained the correct answer 9 times. Chances are, based on past research with these items, that your confidence intervals missed the answer more than once, indicating that your probability judgments were characterized by overconfidence (despite the warning in the title), like those of most people.

Overconfidence effects have been found in perceptual and motor domains as well as in knowledge calibration paradigms (Baranski & Petrusic, 1994, 1995; Mamassian, 2008; West & Stanovich, 1997). They are not just laboratory phenomena, but have been found in a variety of real-life domains, such as the prediction of sports outcomes (Ronis & Yates, 1987), prediction of one's own behavior or life outcomes (Hoch, 1985; Vallone, Griffin, Lin, & Ross, 1990), and economic forecasts (Åstebro, Jeffrey, & Adomdza, 2007; Braun & Yaniv, 1992; Tetlock, 2005). Overconfidence is manifest in the so-called *planning fallacy* (see Buehler, Griffin, & Ross, 2002)—the fact that we often underestimate the time it will take to complete projects in the future (for example, to complete an honors thesis, to complete this year's tax forms, to finish a construction project).

Overconfidence in knowledge calibration has many real-world consequences. People who think they know more than they really do have less incentive to learn more or to correct errors in their knowledge base. People who think their motor or perceptual skills are excellent are critical of the performance of other people but do not subject their own behavior to criticism. For example, surveys consistently show that most people think that their driving skill is above average. Consider a survey by the Canada Safety Council in which 75% of drivers admitted to either talking on the phone, eating, shaving, or applying makeup while driving (Perreaux, 2001). Oddly, 75% of the same people said they were frustrated and appalled by other drivers they saw eating or talking on the phone! Similarly, thousands of people overconfidently think that their driving is unimpaired while talking on their cell phones. This failure of epistemic rationality (beliefs tracking reality) is proving increasingly costly as inattention-based accidents increase due to the addition of more technological distractions to the driver's environment. Cell phone use—even the use of hands-free phones—impairs driving ability to an extent that substantially increases the probability of an accident (McEvoy et al., 2005; Strayer & Drews, 2007; Strayer & Johnston, 2001). The failure to achieve good probabilistic calibration represents an epistemic irrationality in humans that appears to be widespread and that may have pervasive consequences. For example, overconfidence among physicians is a pervasive and dangerous problem (Groopman, 2007).

Additional Problems of Probabilistic Reasoning

Conjunction Fallacy

Consider another problem that is famous in the literature of cognitive psychology, the so-called Linda problem. The Linda problem was first investigated by Tversky and Kahneman (1983). The literature on it is voluminous (e.g., Dulany & Hilton, 1991; Girotto, 2004; Mellers, Hertwig, & Kahneman, 2001; Politzer & Macchi, 2000), as is the case with most of the tasks discussed in this book:

Linda is 31 years old, single, outspoken, and very bright. She majored in philosophy. As a student, she was deeply concerned with issues of discrimination and social justice, and also participated in antinuclear demonstrations. Please rank the following statements by their probability, using 1 for the most probable and 8 for the least probable.

a. Linda is a teacher in an elementary school _____
b. Linda works in a bookstore and takes yoga classes _____
c. Linda is active in the feminist movement _____
d. Linda is a psychiatric social worker _____
e. Linda is a member of the League of Women Voters _____
f. Linda is a bank teller _____
g. Linda is an insurance salesperson _____
h. Linda is a bank teller and is active in the feminist movement _____

Most people make what is called a "conjunction error" on this problem. Because alternative h (Linda is a bank teller and is active in the feminist movement) is the conjunction of alternative c and alternative f, the probability of alternative h cannot be higher than that of either alternative c (Linda is active in the feminist movement) or alternative f (Linda is a bank teller). All feminist bank tellers are also bank tellers, so alternative h cannot be more probable than alternative f—yet often over 80% of the subjects in studies rate alternative h as more probable than alternative f, thus displaying a conjunction error. When subjects answer incorrectly on this problem, it is often because they have engaged in attribute substitution (see Kahneman & Frederick, 2002, 2005). Attribute substitution occurs when a person needs to assess attribute A but finds that assessing attribute B (which is correlated with A) is easier cognitively and so uses B instead. In simpler terms, attribute substitution amounts to substituting an easier question for a harder one. In this case, rather than think carefully and see the Linda problem as a probabilistic scenario, subjects instead answer on the basis of a simpler similarity assessment (a feminist bank teller seems to overlap more with the description of Linda than does the alternative "bank teller"). Of course, logic dictates that the subset (feminist bank teller)–superset (bank teller) relationship should trump assessments of similarity when judgments of probability are at issue.

Inverting Conditional Probabilities

An error of probabilistic thinking with many implications for real-life decision making is the inverting of conditional probabilities (Gigerenzer, 2002). The inversion error in probabilistic reasoning is thinking that the probability of A, given B, is the same as the probability of B, given A. The two are not the same, yet they are frequently treated as if they are. Sometimes the difference between these two probabilities is easy to see because of the content of the problem. For example, it is obvious that the probability of pregnancy, given that intercourse has occurred, is different from the probability of intercourse, given that pregnancy has occurred. However, sometimes the content of the problem does not give away the difference so easily.

Recall from the earlier discussion that each of the conditional probabilities depends on the probability of the conditioning event in the following manner:

$$P(A/B) = P(A \text{ and } B) / P(B)$$
$$P(B/A) = P(A \text{ and } B) / P(A)$$

When conditioning event A is much more probable than conditioning event B, then P(A/B) will be much larger than P(B/A). For example, Dawes (1988) described an article in a California newspaper that ran a headline implying that a student survey indicated that use of marijuana led to the use of hard drugs. The headline implied that the survey was about the probability of using hard drugs, given previous smoking of marijuana. But, actually, the article was about the inverse probability: the probability of having smoked marijuana, given that the student was using hard drugs. The problem is that the two probabilities are vastly different. The probability that students use hard drugs, given that they have smoked marijuana, is much, much smaller than the probability of having smoked marijuana given that students are using hard drugs. The reason is that most people who smoke marijuana do not use hard drugs, but most people who use hard drugs have tried marijuana. The conditioning event "smoked marijuana" is much more probable than the conditioning event "used hard drugs," thus ensuring that P(smoked marijuana /used hard drugs) is much larger than P(used hard drugs /smoked marijuana). Consider the situation in the following table.

	Used Hard Drugs	No Use of Hard Drugs
Smoked Marijuana	50	950
Not Smoked Marijuana	10	2000

Very few people (60 out of 3010; less than 2%) have used hard drugs, but almost 33% have smoked marijuana. The probability of having smoked marijuana given that someone has used hard drugs is quite high:

$$P(\text{smoked marijuana/used hard drugs}) = 50/60 = .83$$

Nevertheless, the probability of having used hard drugs given that someone has smoked marijuana is still quite low:

P(used hard drugs/smoked marijuana) = 50/1000 = .05

An important domain in which the inversion of conditional probabilities happens quite often is medical diagnosis (Eddy, 1982; Groopman,
2007; Schwartz & Griffin, 1986). It has been found that both patients
and medical practitioners can sometimes invert probabilities, thinking,
mistakenly, that the probability of disease, given a particular symptom,
is the same as the probability of the symptom, given the disease (as a
patient, you are concerned with the former). For example, what if I told
you that you had been given a cancer test and that the results were positive? Furthermore, what if I told you that this particular test had a diagnostic accuracy of 90%—that is, that 90% of the time when cancer was
present this test gave a positive result? You might well be extremely upset.
However, you might be much less upset if I told you that the chances
that you had cancer were less than 20%. How can this be if the test has
a diagnostic accuracy of 90%? Imagine that a study of this test was done
in which 1,000 patients were tested, and that 100 of them actually had
cancer. Imagine that the results were as follows:

	Cancer present	Cancer absent
Test Positive	90	500
Test Negative	10	400

In this table, we can see the test's diagnostic accuracy of 90%. Of the
100 people with cancer, the test gave a positive result for 90. But you can
immediately see that this is not the probability that is relevant to you.
The 90% figure is the probability that the test result will be positive for
someone who has cancer, P(positive test/cancer). But what you are inter-
ested in is the inverse: the probability that you have cancer, given that the
test result is positive, P(cancer/positive test). That probability is only 15.3
percent (90 divided by 590).

Unfortunately, this example is not just imaginary. Dawes (1988) discussed a physician who was recommending a type of preventive treatment because he confused the probability of cancer, given the diagnostic
indicator, with the probability of the diagnostic indicator, given that the
patient had cancer (p. 73). Since the preventive treatment was a type of

mastectomy, we can readily understand how serious this error in probabilistic reasoning can be.

The Certainty Effect

In a famous paper introducing prospect theory, their descriptive theory of decision making, Kahneman and Tversky (1979) presented several examples of the so-called certainty effect—that people overweight outcomes that are considered certain compared to outcomes that are only probable. Here is one of their examples:

Imagine that you must choose one of the following two alternatives. Pick the alternative that you would prefer:

A. a .33 probability of $2,500; a .66 probability of $2,400 and a .01 probability of receiving nothing
B. $2,400 with certainty

Now again imagine that you must choose one of the following two alternatives. Pick the alternative that you would prefer:

C. a .33 probability of $2,500; and a .67 probability of receiving nothing
D. a .34 probability of $2,400; and a .66 probability of receiving nothing

Kahneman and Tversky found that 82% of their subjects preferred alternative B in the first choice. There is nothing wrong with this preference, in and of itself. The problem is that 83% of their subjects favored alternative C in the second choice. That, in fact, *is* problematic, because it is flatly inconsistent with the preference for B in the first choice. Here is why.

The preference for B in the first choice means that the utility of $2,400 is greater than the utility of a .33 probability of $2,500 plus the utility of a .66 probability of $2,400. Symbolically, we can write this:

$$u(\$2,400) > .33u(\$2,500) + .66u(\$2,400)$$

Subtracting $.66u(\$2,400)$ from both sides, we get:

$$.34u(\$2,400) > .33u(\$2,500)$$

But looking at the second choice, we can see that this is exactly what is offered in the choice between C and D, and most subjects chose C, thus indicating, in complete contradiction to the first choice, that:

$.33u(\$2,500) > .34u(\$2,400)$

Kahneman and Tversky (1979) argued that the reason for this inconsistency was that probabilities near certainty are overweighted. In the second choice (C vs. D) the extra .01 slice of probability for getting $2,400 simply moves a .33 probability to .34. In the first choice however, the same .01 slice moves the .99 probability of getting a payoff to the certainty of getting a payoff. What the inconsistency in preferences demonstrates is that probability differences that raise an alternative to certainty are weighted more than the same difference at some other point in the probability weighting function. Likewise, Kahneman and Tversky found that probabilities around zero were overweighted—moving from impossibility to possibility also has extra salience. Descriptively, we do not weight probabilities as we should (linearly with their actual values), but in terms of a weighting function shaped somewhat like that proposed in Kahneman and Tversky's prospect theory and illustrated in Figure 3.1. This example also provides us with a quantitative way of thinking about the causes of the Allais paradox discussed in chapter 2 (with which it is analogous) in terms of probability weightings.

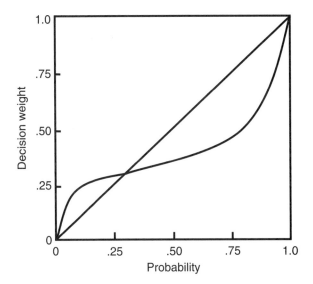

FIGURE 3.1 Probability weighting function according to prospect theory.

Problems "Unpacking" Disjunctions in Probability Judgments

Previously we saw problems that people have when dealing with conjunctions. In the Linda problem, of course, it is likely that the conjunction is never directly experienced—that is, that the problem is not thought of in probabilistic terms because attribute substitution is taking place (Kahneman & Frederick, 2002, 2005). Instead of viewing the Linda problem as a probabilistic scenario, subjects instead answer on the basis of a simpler similarity assessment (a feminist bank teller seems to overlap more with the description of Linda than does the alternative "bank teller"). But conjunctions are not the only difficulty. People have problems dealing with disjunctions too, especially when the disjunctive components are implicit.

Tversky and Koehler (1994) reported a study in which one group of subjects estimated that the percentage of deaths in the United States due to natural causes was 58%. Another group rated the probability of death by cancer, death by heart attack, and death by "other natural causes." The second group rated these probabilities at 18%, 22%, and 33%, respectively. Of course, the combination of death by cancer, death by heart attack, and death by "other natural causes" amounts to the same thing as deaths due to natural causes. But note that something is not adding up here. The total for the second group's estimates of death by all natural causes is 73% (18% + 22% + 33%), significantly higher than the group who estimated the category directly without explicitly unpacking it (58%).

The "deaths due to natural causes" example is typical of the evaluation of implicit disjunctions. When estimating the disjunction (death by all natural causes) the subjects are subadditive—the estimate for the category as a whole is often lower than the additive combination of the estimates of the components of the category. People minimize cognitive effort when making disjunctive judgments. They do not explicitly unpack the category components. Were they to do so and focus attention on each of the subcomponents in turn, each of the components would trigger the retrieval of evidence suggesting its likelihood. There are many more such cues retrieved when the components are thought about separately than when the category as a whole is used as a retrieval cue.

The Gambler's Fallacy

Please answer the following two problems:

Problem A: Imagine that we are tossing a fair coin (a coin that has a 50/50 chance of coming up heads or tails) and it has just come up heads five times in a row. For the sixth toss, do you think that:

_____ It is more likely that tails will come up than heads.
_____ It is more likely that heads will come up than tails.
_____ Heads and tails are equally probable on the sixth toss.

Problem B: When playing slot machines, people win something 1 out of every 10 times. Julie, however, has just won on her first three plays. What are her chances of winning the next time she plays? _____ out of _____

These two problems probe whether a person is prone to the so-called *gambler's fallacy*—the tendency for people to see links between events in the past and events in the future when the two are really independent (Ayton & Fischer, 2004; Burns & Corpus, 2004; Croson & Sundali, 2005). Two outcomes are independent when the occurrence of one does not affect the probability of the other. Most games of chance that use proper equipment have this property. For example, the number that comes up on a roulette wheel is independent of the outcome that preceded it. Half the numbers on a roulette wheel are red, and half are black (for purposes of simplification, we will ignore the green zero and double zero), so the odds are even (.50) that any given spin will come up red. Yet after five or six consecutive reds, many bettors switch to black, thinking that it is now more likely to come up. This is the gambler's fallacy: acting as if previous outcomes affect the probability of the next outcome when the events are independent. In this case, the bettors are wrong in their belief. The roulette wheel has no memory of what has happened previously. Even if 15 reds in a row come up, the probability of red coming up on the next spin is still .50. Of course, it should be stressed that this is the case only when the events are *truly* independent (no "crooked" roulette wheels, loaded dice, or fake coins, etc.).

In problem A above, some people think that it is more likely that either heads or tails will come up after five heads, and they are displaying the gambler's fallacy by thinking so. The correct answer is that heads and tails are equally probable on the sixth toss. Likewise, on problem B any answer other than 1 out of 10 indicates the gambler's fallacy.

The gambler's fallacy is not restricted to the inexperienced. Research has shown that even habitual gamblers, who play games of chance over 20 hours a week, still display belief in the gambler's fallacy (Petry, 2005; Wagenaar, 1988). In fact, research has shown that individuals in treatment for pathological gambling problems were more likely to believe in the gambler's fallacy compared to control subjects (Toplak, Liu, Macpherson, Toneatto, & Stanovich, 2007).

It is important to realize that the gambler's fallacy is not restricted to games of chance. It operates in any domain in which chance plays a substantial role, that is, in almost everything. The genetic makeup of babies is an example. Psychologists, physicians, and marriage counselors often see couples who, after having two female children, are planning a third child because "We want a boy, and it's bound to be a boy this time." This, of course, is the gambler's fallacy. The probability of having a boy (approximately 50%) is exactly the same after having two girls as it was in the beginning (roughly 50%). The two previous girls make it no more likely that the third baby will be a boy.

The gambler's fallacy is related to several mistakes that people make in thinking about the probability of chance events. One is the belief that if a process is truly random, no sequence—not even a small one (six coin flips, for instance)—should display runs or patterns. People routinely underestimate the likelihood of runs (HHHH) and patterns (HHT-THHTTHHTT) in a random sequence. For this reason, people cannot generate truly random sequences when they try to do so. The sequences that they generate tend to have too few runs and patterns. When generating such sequences, people alternate their choices too much in a mistaken effort to destroy any structure that might appear (Nickerson, 2002; Towse & Neil, 1998).

Those who claim to have psychic powers can easily exploit this tendency. Consider a demonstration sometimes conducted in psychology classes. A student is told to prepare a list of 200 numbers by randomly choosing from the numbers 1, 2, and 3 over and over again. After it is completed, the list of numbers is kept out of view of the instructor. The student is now told to concentrate on the first number on the list, and the instructor tries to guess what the number is. After the instructor guesses, the student tells the class and the instructor the correct choice. A record is kept of whether the instructor's guess matched, and the process continues until the complete record of 200 matches and nonmatches is recorded. Before the procedure begins, the instructor announces that he or she will demonstrate "psychic powers" by reading the subject's mind during the experiment. The class is asked what level of performance—that is, percentage of "hits"—would constitute empirically solid evidence of psychic powers. Usually a student who has taken a statistics course volunteers that, because a result of 33% hits could be expected purely on the basis of chance, the instructor would have to achieve a larger proportion than this, probably at least 40%, before one should believe that he or she has psychic powers. The class usually understands and agrees with this argument. The demonstration is then conducted, and a result of more than 40% hits is obtained, to the surprise of many.

The students then learn some lessons about randomness and about how easy it is to fake psychic powers. The instructor in this example merely takes advantage of the fact that people do not generate enough runs: They alternate too much when producing "random" numbers. In a truly random sequence of numbers, what should the probability of a 2 be after three consecutive 2s? One third, the same as the probability of a 1 or a 3. But this is not how most people generate such numbers. After even a small run, they tend to alternate numbers in order to produce a representative sequence. Thus, on each trial in our example, the instructor merely picks one of the two numbers that the student did not pick on the previous trial. Thus, if on the previous trial the student generated a 2, the instructor picks a 1 or a 3 for the next trial. If on the previous trial the subject generated a 3, the instructor picks a 1 or a 2 on the next trial. This simple procedure usually ensures a percentage of hits greater than 33%—greater than chance accuracy without a hint of psychic power.

The tendency for people to believe that if a sequence is random then it should display no runs or patterns was illustrated quite humorously in the controversy over the iPod's "shuffle" feature that broke out in 2005 (Levy, 2005). This feature plays the songs loaded into the iPod in a random sequence. Of course, knowing the research I have just discussed, many psychologists and statisticians chuckled to themselves when the inevitable happened—users complained that the shuffle feature could not be random because they often experienced sequences of songs from the same album or genre. Technical writer Steven Levy (2005) described how he had experienced the same thing. His player seemed always to have a fondness for Steely Dan in the first hour of play! But Levy was smart enough to accept what the experts told him: that truly random sequences will often not seem random to people because of our tendency to impose patterns on everything. After conducting his research into the issue, Levy concluded that "life may indeed be random, and the iPod probably is, too. But we humans will always provide our own narratives and patterns to bring chaos under control. The fault, if there is any, lies not in shuffle but in ourselves" (p. 10).

Probability Matching: Clinical Versus Actuarial Prediction

Understanding and avoiding the gambler's fallacy is one of the conceptual lessons of probability—one of the nonmathematical lessons of great generality. A related insight is a deep understanding of the fact that most events that we observe in the world are a complex mixture of chance and systematic factors. It is important to understand that part of the variability in events is random (determined by chance).

The reluctance to acknowledge the role of chance when trying to explain outcomes in the world can actually decrease our ability to predict real-world events. Acknowledging the role of chance in determining outcomes in a domain means that we must accept the fact that our predictions will never be 100% accurate, that we will always make some errors in our predictions. Interestingly, however, acknowledging that our predictions will be less than 100% accurate can actually help us to increase our overall predictive accuracy (Dawes, 1991; Einhorn, 1986). This is illustrated by a very simple experimental task that has been studied for decades in cognitive psychology laboratories (Fantino & Esfandiari, 2002; Gal & Baron, 1996). The subject sits in front of two lights (one red and one blue) and is told that he or she is to predict which of the lights will be flashed on each trial and that there will be several dozen such trials (subjects are often paid money for correct predictions). The experimenter has actually programmed the lights to flash randomly, with the provision that the red light will flash 70% of the time and the blue light 30% of the time. Subjects do quickly pick up the fact that the red light is flashing more, and they predict that it will flash on more trials than they predict that the blue light will flash. In fact, they predict that the red light will flash approximately 70% of the time. Subjects come to believe that there is a pattern in the light flashes and almost never think that the sequence is random. Instead, they attempt to get every prediction correct, switching back and forth from red to blue, predicting the red light roughly 70% of the time and the blue light roughly 30% of the time. This is not the optimal strategy.

Let us consider the logic of the situation. How many predictions will subjects get correct if they predict the red light roughly 70% of the time and the blue light roughly 30% of the time and the lights are really coming on randomly in a ratio of 70:30? We will do the calculation on 100 trials in the middle of the experiment—after the subject has noticed that the red light comes on more often and is, thus, predicting the red light roughly 70% of the time. In 70 of the 100 trials, the red light will come on and the subject will be correct on about 70% of those 70 trials (because the subject predicts the red light 70% of the time). That is, in 49 of the 70 trials (70 times .70), the subject will correctly predict that the red light will come on. In 30 of the 100 trials, the blue light will come on, and the subject will be correct in 30% of those 30 trials (because the subject predicts the blue light 30% of the time). That is, in 9 of the 30 trials (30 times .30), the subject will correctly predict that the blue light will come on. Thus, in 100 trials, the subject is correct 58% of the time (49 correct predictions in red light trials and 9 correct predictions in blue light trials). But notice that this is a poorer performance than could be achieved if the subject simply noticed which light was coming on more often and then predicted it in every trial—in this case, noticing that the red light came on more often and predicting it in every trial (let's call this the 100% red strategy). Of the 100 trials, 70 would be red flashes, and the subject would have predicted all 70 of these correctly. Of the 30 blue flashes, the subject would have predicted none correctly but still would have a prediction accuracy of 70%—12% better than the 58% correct that the subject achieved by switching back and forth, trying to get every trial correct!

The optimal strategy does have the implication though, that you will be wrong every time a blue occurs. Since blue-light stimuli are occurring on at least *some* of the trials, it just does not seem right *never* to predict them. But this is just what correct probabilistic thinking requires. It requires accepting the errors that will be made on blue trials in order to attain the higher overall hit rate that will be obtained when predicting red each time. In short, we must *accept* the blue errors in order to make *fewer* errors overall.

Accepting error in order to make fewer errors is a difficult thing to do, however, as evidenced by the 40-year history of research on clinical versus actuarial prediction in psychology. The term *actuarial prediction* refers to predictions based on group (i.e., aggregate) trends derived from statistical records. A simple actuarial prediction is one that predicts the same outcome for all individuals sharing a certain characteristic. So predicting a life span of 77.5 years for people who do not smoke and a life span of 64.3 years for individuals who smoke would be an example of an actuarial prediction. More accurate predictions can be made if we take more than one group characteristic into account (using statistical techniques such as multiple regression). For example, predicting a life span of 58.2 years for people who smoke, are overweight, and do not exercise would be an example of an actuarial prediction based on a set of variables (smoking behavior, weight, and amount of exercise), and such predictions are almost always more accurate than predictions made from a single variable. Such actuarial predictions are common in economics, human resources, criminology, business and marketing, the medical sciences, and most subareas of psychology, such as cognitive psychology, developmental psychology, organizational psychology, personality psychology, and social psychology. In contrast, some subgroups of clinical psychological practitioners claim to be able to go beyond group predictions and to make accurate predictions of the outcomes for particular individuals. This is called clinical, or case, prediction. When engaged in clinical prediction, as opposed to actuarial prediction

> Professional psychologists claim to be able to make predictions about individuals that transcend predictions about "people in general" or about various categories of people.... Where professional psychologists differ is in their claim to understand the single individual as unique rather than as part of a group about which statistical generalizations are possible. They claim to be able to analyze "what caused what" in an individual's life rather than to state what is "in general" true. (Dawes, 1994, pp. 79–80)

Clinical prediction would seem to be a very useful addition to actuarial prediction. There is just one problem, however. Clinical prediction does not work.

For clinical prediction to be useful, the clinician's experience with the client and his or her use of information about the client would have to result in better predictions than we can get from simply coding information about the client and submitting it to statistical procedures that optimize the process of combining quantitative data in order to derive predictions. In short, the claim is that the experience of psychological practitioners allows them to go beyond the aggregate relationships that have been uncovered by research. The claim that clinical prediction is efficacious is, thus, easily testable. Unfortunately, the claim has been tested, and it has been falsified.

Research on the issue of clinical versus actuarial prediction has been consistent. Since the publication in 1954 of Paul Meehl's classic book *Clinical Versus Statistical Prediction,* four decades of research consisting of over 100 research studies have shown that, in just about every clinical prediction domain that has ever been examined (psychotherapy outcome, parole behavior, college graduation rates, response to electro-shock therapy, criminal recidivism, length of psychiatric hospitalization, and many more), actuarial prediction has been found to be superior to clinical prediction (e.g., Dawes, Faust, & Meehl, 1989; Goldberg, 1959, 1968, 1991; Swets, Dawes, & Monahan, 2000; Tetlock, 2005).

In a variety of clinical domains, when a clinician is given informa-tion about a client and asked to predict the client's behavior, and when the same information is quantified and processed by a statistical equation that has been developed based on actuarial relationships that research has uncovered, invariably the equation wins. That is, the actuarial predic-tion is more accurate than the clinician's prediction. In fact, even when the clinician has more information available than is used in the actuarial method, the latter is superior. That is, when the clinician has information from personal contact and interviews with the client, in addition to the same information that goes into the actuarial equation, the clinical pre-dictions still do not achieve an accuracy as great as the actuarial method: "Even when given an information edge, the clinical judge still fails to surpass the actuarial method; in fact, access to additional information often does nothing to close the gap between the two methods" (Dawes et al., 1989, p. 1670). The reason is of course that the equation integrates information accurately and consistently. This factor—consistency—can overcome any informational advantage the clinician has from informa-tion gleaned informally.

A final type of test in the clinical-actuarial prediction literature involves actually giving the clinician the predictions from the actu-arial equation and asking the clinician to adjust the predictions based on his or her personal experience with the clients. When the clinician makes adjustments in the actuarial predictions, the adjustments actu-ally decrease the accuracy of the predictions (see Dawes, 1994). Here we have an example of failing to "accept error in order to reduce error" that is directly analogous to the light-prediction experiment previously described. Rather than relying on the actuarial information that the red light came on more often and predicting red each time (and getting 70% correct), the subjects tried to be correct on each trial by alternating red and blue predictions and ended up being 12% less accurate (they were correct on only 58% of the trials). Analogously, the clinicians in these studies believed that their experience gave them "clinical insight" and allowed them to make better predictions than those that can be made from quantified information in the client's file. In fact, their "insight" is nonexistent and leads them to make predictions that are worse than those they would make if they relied only on the public, actuarial information. It should be noted, though, that the superiority of actuarial prediction is not confined to psychology but extends to many other clinical sciences as well—for example, to the reading of electrocardiograms in medicine (Gawande, 1998).

Wagenaar and Keren (1986) illustrated how overconfidence in personal knowledge and the discounting of statistical information can undermine safety campaigns advocating seat belt use because people think, "I am different, I drive safely." The problem is that over 85% of the population thinks that they are "better than the average driver" (Svenson, 1981)—obviously a patent absurdity.

The same fallacy of believing that "statistics do apply to the single case" is an important factor in the thinking of individuals with chronic gambling problems. In his study of gambling behavior, Wagenaar (1988) concluded:

> From our discussions with gamblers it has become abundantly clear that gamblers are generally aware of the negative long-term result. They know that they have lost more than they have won, and that it will be the same in the future. But they fail to apply these statistical considerations to the next round, the next hour, or the next night. A rich repertoire of heuristics... gives them the suggestion that statistics do not apply in the next round, or the next hour. That they can predict the next outcome. (p. 117)

Wagenaar found that compulsive gamblers had a strong tendency not to "accept error in order to reduce error." For example, blackjack players had a tendency to reject a strategy called *basic* that is guaranteed to decrease the casino's advantage from 6% or 8% to less than 1%. Basic is a long-term statistical strategy, and the compulsive players tended to reject it because they believed that "an effective strategy ought to be effective in every single instance" (p. 110). The gamblers in Wagenaar's study "invariably said that the general prescriptions of such systems could not work, because they neglect the idiosyncrasies of each specific situation" (p. 110). Instead of using an actuarial strategy that was guaranteed to save them thousands of dollars, these gamblers were on a futile chase to find a way to make a clinical prediction based on the idiosyncrasies of each specific situation.

Other Aspects of Epistemic Rationality: Hypothesis Testing and Falsifiability

Just as people have difficulty learning to assess data in light of an alternative hypothesis, people have a hard time thinking about evidence and tests that could falsify their focal hypotheses. Instead, people (including scientists) tend to seek to confirm theories rather than falsify them. One of the most investigated problems in four decades of reasoning research illustrates this quite dramatically. The task was invented by Peter Wason (1966, 1968) and has been investigated in dozens, if not hundreds, of studies (Evans, 1972, 1996, 2007; Evans, Newstead, & Byrne, 1993; Johnson-Laird, 1999, 2006; Klauer, Stahl, & Erdfelder, 2007; Oaksford & Chater, 1994, 2007; Stenning & van Lambalgen, 2004). Try to answer it before reading ahead:

Each of the boxes in the following illustration represents a card lying on a table. Each one of the cards has a letter on one side and a number on the other side. Here is a rule: If a card has a vowel on its letter side, then it has an even number on its number side. As you can see, two of the cards are letter-side up, and two of the cards are number-side up. Your task is to decide which card or cards must be turned over in order to find out whether the rule is true or false. Indicate which cards must be turned over.

This task is called the four-card selection task and has been intensively investigated for two reasons—most people get the problem wrong and it has been devilishly hard to figure out why. The answer seems obvious. The hypothesized rule is as follows: If a card has a vowel on its letter side, then it has an even number on its number side. So the answer would seem to be to pick the A and the 8—the A, the vowel, to see if there is an even number on its back, and the 8 (the even number) to see if there is a vowel on the back. The problem is that this answer—given by about 50% of the people completing the problem—is wrong! The second most common answer, to turn over the A card only (to see if there is an even number on the back)—given by about 20% of the responders—is also wrong! Another 20% of the responders turn over other combinations (e.g., K and 8) that are also not correct.

If you were like 90% of the people who have completed this problem in dozens of studies during the past several decades, you answered it incorrectly too. Let us see how most people go wrong. First, where they do not go wrong is on the K and A cards. Most people do not choose the K and they do choose the A. Because the rule says nothing about what should be on the backs of consonants, the K is irrelevant to the rule. The A is not. It could have an even or odd number on the back, and although the former would be consistent with the rule, the latter is the critical potential outcome—it could prove that the rule is false. In short, in order to show that the rule is not false, the A must be turned. That is the part that most people get right.

However, it is the 8 and 5 that are the hard cards. Many people get these two cards wrong. They mistakenly think that the 8 card must be chosen. This card is mistakenly turned because people think that they must check to see if there is a vowel rather than a nonvowel on the back. But, for example, if there were a K on the back of the 8 it would not show that the rule is false because although the rule says that a vowel must have even numbers on the back, it does not say that even numbers must have vowels on the back. So finding a nonvowel on the back says nothing about whether the rule is true or false. In contrast, the 5 card, which most people do not choose, is absolutely essential. The 5 card might have a vowel on the back and, if it did, the rule would be shown to be false because all vowels would not have even numbers on the back. In short, in order to show that the rule is not false, the 5 card must be turned.

In summary, the rule is in the form of an "if P, then Q" conditional, and it can only be shown to be false by showing an instance of P and not-Q, so the P and not-Q cards (A and 5 in our example) are the only two that need to be turned to determine whether the rule is true or false. If the P and not-Q combination is there, the rule is false. If it is not there, then the rule is true.

Why do most people answer incorrectly when this problem, after explanation, is so easy? Many theories exist (see Cosmides, 1989; Evans, 2007; Johnson-Laird, 1999, 2006; Klauer et al., 2007; Margolis, 1987; Oaksford & Chater, 1994, 2007; Sperber, Cara, & Girotto, 1995), but one of the oldest theories that certainly plays at least a partial role in the poor performance is that people focus on confirming the rule. This is what sets them about turning the 8 card (in hopes of confirming the rule by observing a vowel on the other side) and turning the A card (in search of the confirming even number). What they do not set about doing is looking at what would falsify the rule—a thought pattern that would immediately suggest the relevance of the 5 card (which might contain a disconfirming vowel on the back). As I have noted, there are many other theories of the poor performance on the task, but regardless of which of these descriptive theories explains the error, there is no question that a concern for falsifiability would rectify the error.

As useful as the falsifiability principle is in general reasoning, there is a large amount of evidence indicating that it is not a natural strategy. Another paradigm which illustrates the problems that people have in dealing with falsification is the so-called 2–4–6 task, another famous reasoning problem invented by Peter Wason (1960). As with the four-card selection task, there are several alternative theories about why subjects perform poorly in the 2–4–6 task (Evans, 1989, 2007; Evans & Over, 1996; Gale & Ball, 2006; Klayman & Ha, 1987; Poletiek, 2001). Again like the four-card selection task, regardless of which of these descriptive theories explains the poor performance on the task, it is clear from research that a concern for falsifiability would facilitate performance.

Subjects are told that the experimenter has a rule in mind that classifies sets of three integers (triplets) and that the triplet 2–4–6 conforms to the rule. Subject are then to propose triplets and, when they do, the experimenter tells them whether their triplet conforms to the rule. Subjects are to continue proposing triplets and receiving feedback until they think they have figured out what the experimenter's rule is, at which time they should announce what they think the rule is.

The experimenter's rule in the 2–4–6 task is actually "any set of three increasing numbers." Typically, subjects have a very difficult time discovering this rule because they initially adopt an overly restrictive hypothesis about what the rule is. They develop rules like "even numbers increasing" or "numbers increasing in equal intervals" and proceed to generate triplets that are consistent with their overly restrictive hypothesis. Subjects thus receive much feedback from the experimenter that their triplets are correct, and when they announce their hypothesis they are often surprised when told it is not correct. For example, a typical sequence (see Evans, 1989) is for the subject to generate triplets like 8–10–12; 14–16–18; 40–42–44. Receiving three confirmations, they announce the rule "numbers increasing by two." Told this is incorrect, they then might proceed to generate 2–6–10; 0–3–6; and 1–50–99 and again receive confirmatory feedback. They then proceed to announce a rule like "the rule is that the difference between numbers next to each other is the same"— which again is incorrect. What they fail to do with any frequency is to generate sequences seriously at odds with their hypothesis so that they might falsify it—sequences like 100–90–80 or 1–15–2.

That subjects are not seriously attempting to refute their focal hypothesis is suggested by one manipulation that has been found to strongly facilitate performance. Tweney, Doherty, Warner, and Pliske (1980) ran an experiment in which the subject was told that the experimenter was thinking of two rules—one rule would apply to a group of triples called DAX and the other to a set of triples called MED. Each time the subject announced a triple, he or she was told whether it was DAX or MED. The subject was then told that 2–4–6 was a DAX, and the experiment proceeded as before. DAX was defined, as before, as "any set of three increasing numbers" and MED was defined as "anything else." Under these conditions, the subjects solved the problem much more easily, often alternating between positive tests of DAX and MED. Of course—now—a positive test of MED is an attempt to falsify DAX. The subject is drawn into falsifying tests of DAX because there is another positive, salient, and vivid hypothesis to focus upon (MED). Because the alternative exhausts the universe of hypotheses and it is mutually exclusive of the old focal hypothesis, each time the subjects try to get a confirmation of one they are simultaneously attempting a falsification of the other. In this way, the subjects were drawn to do something they did not normally do—focus on the alternative hypothesis and falsify the focal hypothesis. Of course, the fact that they had to be lured into it in this contrived way only serves to reinforce how difficult it is to focus on the focal hypothesis not being true.

Thus, the bad news is that people have a difficult time thinking about the evidence that would falsify their focal hypothesis. The good news is that this thinking skill is teachable. All scientists go through training that includes much practice at trying to falsify their focal hypothesis, and they automatize the verbal query "What alternative hypotheses should I consider?"

Summary and Implications

Determining the best action involves estimating the probabilities of various outcomes. If these probabilistic estimates are wrong, then utility will not be maximized. In short, instrumental rationality depends on epistemic rationality.

Most generally, epistemic rationality means having our beliefs properly calibrated to evidence. We weight the confidence in our beliefs in terms of subjective probability judgments. In this chapter we have seen various ways in which the probabilistic judgments of people are sometimes less than optimal. The normative model for subjective probability assessment involves following the rules of the probability calculus. We have seen a variety of ways in which people fail to follow these rules. For example, people display the conjunction fallacy and they fail to unpack implicit disjunctions.

People violate several strictures embodied in Bayes' rule. Sometime they fail to weight diagnostic evidence with the base rate. They are particularly prone to do this when the base rate is presented as pallid and abstract statistical information with no apparent causal connection to the hypothesis of interest. A ubiquitous tendency is to underweight, or ignore entirely, $P(D/\sim H)$, the probability of the datum given the alternative hypothesis. Finally, when asked to actively test their hypotheses about the world, they do not go about this task correctly—usually because they are insufficiently sensitive to the necessity of finding evidence that falsifies their prior belief.

The heuristics and biases research program seems to have as its conclusion that people make a plethora of reasoning errors related to epistemic rationality, just as they make various reasoning errors related to instrumental rationality. The list of thinking errors in all domains of rational thought seems surprisingly long. Can human reasoning really be this bad? Some researchers have indeed found this list so surprisingly long that they have questioned whether we are interpreting responses correctly in these experiments. In the next chapter, we will discuss the alternative interpretations of several research groups that question the conclusion that irrational human thinking is so widespread.

Suggestions for Further Readings

Gigerenzer, G. (2002). *Calculated risks: How to know when numbers deceive you.* New York: Simon & Schuster.

Gilovich, T., Griffin, D., & Kahneman, D. (Eds.). (2002). *Heuristics and biases: The psychology of intuitive judgment.* New York: Cambridge University Press.

Answers to Knowledge Calibration Questions

These questions were taken from Plous (1993) and Russo and Schoemaker (1989), and the answers are the following:

1. 39 years 2. 39 books 3. the year 1756 4. 645 days 5. 36,198 feet 6. 4,187 miles 7. 13 countries 8. 2,160 miles 9. 390,000 pounds 10. 5,949 miles

Hacking, I. (2001). *An introduction to probability and inductive logic*. New York: Cambridge University Press.

Kahneman, D. (2003). A perspective on judgment and choice: Mapping bounded rationality. *American Psychologist, 58,* 697–720.

Koehler, D. J., & Harvey, N. (Eds.). (2004). *Blackwell handbook of judgment and decision making*. Oxford: Blackwell.

Mlodinow, L. (2008). *The drunkard's walk: How randomness rules our lives*. New York: Pantheon.

Nickerson, R. S. (2004). *Cognition and chance: The psychology of probabilistic reasoning*. Mahwah, NJ: Erlbaum.

Pohl, R. (Ed.). (2004). *Cognitive illusions: A handbook on fallacies and biases in thinking, judgment and memory*. Hove, UK: Psychology Press.

Tversky, A. (2003). *Preference, belief, and similarity: Selected writings of Amos Tversky* (E. Shafir, Ed.). Cambridge, MA: MIT Press.

CHAPTER 4

How Bad Is Our Decision Making?
The Great Rationality Debate

In the previous two chapters we have seen that a substantial research literature—one comprising literally hundreds of empirical studies conducted over nearly three decades—has firmly established that people's responses sometimes deviate from the performance considered normative on many reasoning tasks. They have thinking habits that lead to suboptimal actions (instrumental rationality) and beliefs (epistemic rationality). For example, people assess probabilities incorrectly; they test hypotheses inefficiently; they violate the axioms of utility theory; they do not properly calibrate degrees of belief; their choices are affected by irrelevant context; they ignore the alternative hypothesis when evaluating data; and they display numerous other information-processing biases (Baron, 2008; Evans, 2007; Kahneman & Tversky, 2000). We have seen that demonstrating that descriptive accounts of human behavior diverge from normative models is a main theme of the heuristics and biases research program.

Researchers working in the heuristics and biases tradition tend to be so-called *Meliorists* (Stanovich, 1999, 2004). They assume that human reasoning is not as good as it could be and that thinking could be improved. The Dictionary.com definition of meliorism is "the doctrine that the world tends to become better or may be made better by human effort." Thus, a Meliorist is one who feels that education and the provision of information could help make people more rational—that is, help them to further their goals more efficiently and to bring their beliefs more in line with the actual state of the world[1]. Expressed this way, Meliorism seems to be an optimistic doctrine, and in one sense it is. But this optimistic part of the Meliorist message derives from the fact that Meliorists see a large gap between normative models of rational responding and descriptive models of what people actually do. Emphasizing the gap, of course, entails that Meliorists will be attributing a good deal of irrationality to human cognition.

Some readers might feel that it is insulting to people to make widespread ascriptions of human irrationality, as Meliorists do. In this concern lies a well-motivated anti-elitist tendency as well, no doubt, as some kind of inchoate concern for human self-esteem. For these reasons, but more importantly for empirical and theoretical reasons, we need to consider another perspective on the research we have reviewed in chapters 2 and 3.

Over the last two decades, an alternative interpretation of the findings from the heuristics and biases research program has been championed. Contributing to this alternative interpretation have been evolutionary psychologists, adaptationist modelers, and ecological theorists (Anderson, 1990, 1991; Cosmides & Tooby, 1992, 1994, 1996; Gigerenzer, 1996a, 1996b, 2007; Oaksford & Chater, 2001, 2007; Todd & Gigerenzer, 2000). They have reinterpreted the modal response in most of the classic heuristics and biases experiments as indicating an optimal information-processing adaptation on the part of the subjects. These investigators argue that the research in the heuristics and biases tradition has not demonstrated human irrationality at all. This group of theorists—who assert that an assumption of perfect human rationality is the proper default

---

1. It is important to note that the Meliorist recognizes two different ways in which human decision-making performance might be improved. These might be termed *cognitive change* and *environmental change*. First, it might be possible to teach people better reasoning strategies and to have them learn rules of decision making that are helpful (see Stanovich, 2009). These would represent instances of cognitive change. In chapters 2 and 3 I am attempting to teach just such reasoning strategies and rules of decision making. Additionally, however, research has shown that it is possible to change the environment so that natural human reasoning strategies will not lead to error (Gigerenzer, 2002; Thaler & Sunstein, 2008). For example, choosing the right default values for a decision (discussed in chapter 2) would be an example of an environmental change. In short, environmental alterations (as well as cognitive changes) can prevent rational thinking problems. Thus, in cases where teaching people the correct reasoning strategies might be difficult, it may well be easier to change the environment so that decision-making errors are less likely to occur.

position to take—have been termed the Panglossians. The Panglossian position is named after the character in Voltaire's *Candide* who argued, after every apparently bad event, that actually we live in the best of all possible worlds. This position posits no difference between descriptive and normative models of performance because human performance is actually normative.

But how could a Panglossian position be maintained in light of the findings discussed in the previous two chapters—in particular, the many demonstrations that human performance deviates from normative models of rationality? The Panglossian theorists have several responses to this question, but two predominate. The first is that the normative model being applied is not the appropriate one because the subject's interpretation of the task is different from what the researcher assumes it is. The second is that the modal response in the task makes perfect sense from an evolutionary perspective. We will see in this chapter how various Panglossian theorists reinterpret the performance patterns that were introduced in chapters 2 and 3.

The Great Rationality Debate

The contrasting positions of the Panglossians and Meliorists define the differing poles in what has been termed the *Great Rationality Debate* in cognitive science (Cohen, 1981; W. Edwards & von Winterfeldt, 1986; Gigerenzer, 1996a; Jungermann, 1986; Kahneman & Tversky, 1996; Stanovich, 1999; Stein, 1996)—the debate about how much irrationality to attribute to human cognition. As mentioned in the preface, Tetlock and Mellers (2002) have noted that "the debate over human rationality is a high-stakes controversy that mixes primordial political and psychological prejudices in combustible combinations" (p. 97).

The Great Debate about human rationality is a "high-stakes controversy" because it involves nothing less than the models of human nature that underlie economics, moral philosophy, and the personal theories (folk theories) we use to understand the behavior of other humans. For example, a very influential part of the Panglossian camp is represented by the mainstream of the discipline of economics, which is notable for using strong rationality assumptions as fundamental tools and pressing them quite far: "Economic agents, either firms, households, or individuals, are presumed to behave in a rational, self-interested manner....a manner that is consistent with solutions of rather complicated calculations under conditions of even imperfect information" (Davis & Holt, 1993,

p. 435). These strong rationality assumptions are essential to much work in modern economics, and they account for some of the hostility that economists have displayed toward psychological findings that suggest nontrivial human irrationality.

The work of cognitive psychologists engenders hostility among economists because the former expose the implausibly Panglossian assumptions that lie behind economic pronouncements about human behavior. For example, *The New York Times,* citing evidence that most people do not save enough for the retirement life that they desire, notes that this evidence is directly contrary to mainstream economics, which assumes that people rationally save the optimal amount: "Confronted with the reality that people do not save enough, the mainstream has no solution, except to reiterate that people are rational, so whatever they save must be enough" (Uchitelle, 2002, p. 4). Increasingly though, there are dissenters from the Panglossian view even within economics itself. In response to other examples like the one in *The New York Times,* University of Chicago economist Richard Thaler (1992) exasperatedly pleads, "Surely another possibility is that people simply get it wrong" (p. 2).

Whether or not people "simply get it wrong" is an important background dispute in many public policy discussions about the advisability of government intervention. For example, the difference between the Panglossian and the Meliorist was captured colloquially in an article in *The Economist* magazine (Author, February 14, 1998) where a subheading asked, "Economists Make Sense of the World by Assuming That People Know What They Want. Advertisers Assume That They Do Not. Who Is Right?" The Meliorist thinks that the advertisers are right—people often do not know what they want, and can be influenced so as to maximize the advertiser's profits rather than their own utility. In contrast, a Panglossian view of perfect rationality in the marketplace would need to defend the view that people take only from advertising what optimizes their consumption utility. Such a view is a very effective tool for advertisers to use when trying to repel government strictures prohibiting certain types of ads. In contrast, the Meliorist does not assume that consumers will process the advertiser's information in a way that optimizes things for the consumer (as opposed to the advertiser). Thus, Meliorists are much more sympathetic to government attempts to regulate advertising because, in the Meliorist view, such regulation can act to increase the utility of the total population. This is just one example of how the Great Rationality Debate has profound political implications.

That people "simply get it wrong" was the tacit assumption in much of the early work by the heuristics and biases researchers in cognitive psychology discussed in the previous two chapters. We shall now proceed to illustrate how Panglossian theorists question this assumption by reinterpreting the responses commonly given on some of the most well-known tasks in the heuristics and biases literature.

Alternative Interpretations of Performance on the Four-Card Selection Task

Consider Wason's (1966) four-card selection task discussed in the previous chapter. Subjects are shown four cards lying on a table showing two letters and two numbers (K, A, 8, 5). They are told that each card has a number on one side and a letter on the other and that the experimenter has the following rule (of the "if P, then Q" type) in mind with respect to the four cards: "If there is a vowel on one side of the card, then there is an even number on the other side." Typically, less than 10% of participants make the correct selections of the A card (P) and 5 card (not-Q)—the only two cards that could falsify the rule. The most common incorrect choices made by participants are the A card and the 8 card (P and Q) or the selection of the A card only (P).

The oldest explanation of the poor performance on the task was formulated in terms of a widespread failure to adopt a disconfirmatory stance toward hypothesis testing. However, Oaksford and Chater (1994) have an alternative interpretation of task performance which posits that a typical subject is testing hypotheses in a much more rational fashion once one critical assumption is allowed—that he or she is reading more into the instructions than is actually there. Oaksford and Chater's analysis of the selection task assumes that subjects approach the task as an inductive problem in data selection with assumptions about the relative rarity of the various classes (vowels, odd numbers) of cards. That is, despite the fact the instructions refer to four cards only, it is proposed that the participant is thinking that they are sampling from four classes (a bunch of vowels, a bunch of consonants, etc.). Now imagine that you are verifying the statement "If you eat tripe you will get sick" in the real world. Of course you would sample from the class "people who eat tripe" to verify or falsify it. However, would you sample from the class of "people who are not sick?" Probably not, because this class is too big. But you might well sample from the class "people who are sick" to see if any of them have eaten tripe.

Such an approach is not warranted by the task instructions. Nothing at all has been said in the instructions about classes—the instructions refer to four cards only. But the alternative explanation of Oaksford and Chater (1994) assumes that the subjects are thinking in terms of sampling from classes of cards. They even have implicit hypotheses about the relative rarity of these classes, according to the particular model of performance championed by Oaksford and Chater. Subjects assume that the classes mentioned in the rule are rare. Also, despite the fact that the instructions speak in terms of determining truth and falsity, most subjects ignore this and instead think in terms of inductive probabilities, in Oaksford and Chater's view. Whether or not this alternative reading of the instructions is warranted, Oaksford and Chater show that once this alternative reading is allowed, then the subsequent choices of P and Q seem much more rational.

There are continuing disputes about whether the Oaksford and Chater (1994) explanation of performance on the task is the right one (Evans, 2007; Johnson-Laird, 1999, 2006; Klauer et al., 2007; Stenning & van Lambalgen, 2004). The key point is that if we allow this alternative interpretation of the task instructions, then performance seems more rational.

Evolutionary psychologists have shown that many of the problems that are difficult for people in their abstract forms can be made easier to solve if they are contextualized—particularly if they are contextualized in ways that are compatible with the representations used by specific evolutionarily adapted modules. Some of their work has involved the four-card selection task. For example, in the early history of work on this task, it was first thought that the abstract content of the vowel/number rule made the problem hard for people and that more real-life or "thematic," nonabstract problems would raise performance markedly. Investigators tried examples like the following Destination Rule: "If 'Baltimore' is on one side of the ticket, then 'plane' is on the other side of the ticket." The fours cards facing the participant read, respectively:

Destination: Baltimore
Destination: Washington
Mode of Travel: Plane
Mode of Travel: Train

These four cards corresponded, respectively, to the P, not-P, Q, and not-Q alternatives for the "if P, then Q" rule. Surprisingly, this type of content did not improve performance at all (Cummins, 1996; Manktelow & Evans, 1979; Newstead & Evans, 1995). Most people still picked either P and Q or the P card only. The correct P (Baltimore), not-Q (Train) solution escaped the vast majority.

Griggs and Cox (1982) were the first to use a thematic version of the task that did markedly improve performance in their experiment and in many subsequent experiments by other investigators (Cummins, 1996; Dominowski, 1995; Newstead & Evans, 1995; Pollard & Evans, 1987). Here is a particularly easy version of the Griggs and Cox (1982) rule used by my research group (Stanovich & West, 1998a). Do the problem and experience for yourself how easy it is:

Imagine that you are a police officer on duty, walking through a local bar. It is your job to ensure that the drinking laws are in effect in this bar. When you see a person engaging in certain activities, the laws specify that certain conditions must first be met. One such law is "If a person is drinking beer, then the person must be over 21 years of age." There are four cards lying on a table. There are two pieces of information about a person on each card. Whether or not the person is drinking beer is on one side of the card and the person's age is on the other side. For two of the people, you can see their age, but you cannot see what they are drinking. For the other two people, you can see what they are drinking, but you cannot see their age. Your task is to decide whether or not this law is being broken in the bar. Choose the card or cards you would definitely need to turn over to decide whether or not the law is being broken. You may select any or all of the cards.

The fours cards facing the subject read, respectively:

Age: 22
Age: 18
Drink: Beer
Drink: Coke

Most people answer the Drinking Age problem correctly, including many people who answer the abstract version incorrectly. This is true even though the underlying logical structure of the two problems is seemingly the same. The answer to both is to pick P and not-Q—in this problem, Beer and Age 18.

With the invention of the Drinking Age problem, researchers had finally found a way after 15 years of research (at the time of the Griggs & Cox, 1982, report) to get participants to give the right answer to the

Wason four-card selection task. Joy was short-lived however, because researchers immediately began to doubt whether the reasoning process leading to correct responses on the abstract version was anything like the reasoning process leading to correct responding on the Drinking Age version. That is, despite the surface similarity of the two rules, investigators began to think that they were actually tapping fundamentally different reasoning mechanisms. The Destination rule, for example, is what is called an *indicative rule*—a rule concerning the truth status of a statement about the world. In contrast, the Drinking Age rule is a so-called *deontic rule*. Deontic reasoning concerns thinking about the rules used to guide human behavior—about what "ought to" or "must" be done. Cummins (1996) terms a deontic rule a rule about "what one may, ought, or must not do in a given set of circumstances" (p. 161; see also Manktelow, 1999; Manktelow & Over, 1991). A number of theorists have argued that deontic rules and indicative rules engage different types of mental mechanisms.

The most famous of these proposals was in a highly influential paper by Cosmides (1989), one of the leading figures in the move to ground psychology in evolutionary theory that swept through psychology in the 1990s (Cosmides & Tooby, 1992, 1994). She proposed that evolution has built processing systems (what she termed Darwinian algorithms) exclusively concerned with social exchange in human interactions. These algorithms embody the basic rule "if you take a benefit, then you must pay a cost" and are extremely sensitive "cheater detectors"—they react strongly to instances where an individual takes a benefit without paying the cost. In the Drinking Age problem, an individual underage and drinking beer is just that—a cheater. Thus, with this rule, the possibility of an 18-year-old drinking beer (the P and not-Q case) becomes very salient because the rule automatically triggers an evolutionary algorithm specifically concerned with detecting card selections that happen to be correct. The indicative rule of course does not trigger such a Darwinian algorithm. Evolution has provided no special module in the brain for solving indicative problems. The tools for solving such problems are largely cultural inventions, and the brain processes supporting them are fragile because they demand much computational capacity (Dennett, 1991; Evans, 2007; Stanovich, 2004, 2009).

Cosmides' (1989) hypothesis is not the only explanation for the superior performance in the Drinking Age problem (see Evans & Over, 1996; Manktelow, 1999; Manktelow & Over, 1991). Other theorists have taken issue with her emphasis on domain-specific and informationally encapsulated modules for regulating social exchange. However, the alternative explanations do share some family resemblances with Cosmides' (1989) account. They tend to view the Drinking Age task as a problem of instrumental rationality rather than epistemic rationality. Indicative selection tasks tap epistemic rationality: They probe how people test hypotheses about the nature of the world. In contrast, deontic tasks tap instrumental rationality: They concern how actions should be regulated and what people should do in certain situations.

Alternative Interpretations of Conjunction Errors

Our second example of theorists defending as rational the response that heuristics and biases researchers have long considered incorrect is provided by the much-investigated Linda problem ("Linda is 31 years old, single, outspoken, and very bright…") discussed in the previous chapter. People rated the probability of Linda being a feminist bank teller as higher than the probability that she was a bank teller, thus committing a conjunction error. Tversky and Kahneman (1983) argued that logical reasoning on the problem (all feminist bank tellers are also bank tellers) was trumped by a heuristic based on so-called representativeness that primes answers to problems based on an assessment of similarity (a feminist bank teller seems to overlap more with the description of Linda than does the alternative "bank teller"). Of course, logic dictates that the subset (feminist bank teller)–superset (bank teller) relationship should trump assessments of representativeness when judgments of probability are at issue.

However, several investigators have suggested that rather than illogical cognition, it is rational pragmatic inferences that lead to the violation of the logic of probability theory in the Linda problem. Hilton (1995) summarizes the view articulated in these critiques by arguing that "the inductive nature of conversational inference suggests that many of the experimental results that have been attributed to faulty reasoning may be reinterpreted as being due to rational interpretations of experimenter-given information" (p. 264). In short, these critiques imply that displaying the conjunction fallacy is a rational response triggered by the adaptive use of social cues, linguistic cues, and background knowledge.

Here is an example of the type of alternative interpretation of performance on the Linda problem that Hilton is positing. Under the assumption that the detailed information given about the target means that the experimenter knows a considerable amount about Linda, then it is reasonable to think that the phrase "Linda is a bank teller" does not contain the phrase "and is not active in the feminist movement" because the experimenter already knows this to be the case. If "Linda is a bank teller" is interpreted in this way, then rating the conjunction (Linda is a bank teller and is active in the feminist movement) as more probable than Linda is a bank teller no longer represents a conjunction fallacy.

Several investigators have suggested that pragmatic inferences lead to seeming violations of the logic of probability theory in the Linda problem (see Adler, 1984, 1991; Hertwig & Gigerenzer, 1999; Politzer & Noveck, 1991). Most of these can be analyzed in terms of Grice's (1975) norms of rational communication (see Sperber & Wilson, 1995), which require that the speaker be cooperative with the listener—and one of the primary ways that speakers attempt to be cooperative is by not being redundant. The key to understanding the so-called Gricean maxims of communication is to realize that to understand a speaker's meaning, the listener must comprehend not only the meaning of what is spoken but also what is implicated in a given context, assuming that the speaker intends to be cooperative. Hilton (1995) is at pains to remind us that these are rational aspects of communicative cognition. They are rational heuristics as opposed to the suboptimal shortcuts emphasized in the heuristics and biases literature.

Many theorists have linked their explanation of Linda problem performance to evolutionary adaptations in the domain of social intelligence (Cummins, 1996; Dunbar, 1998; Humphrey, 1976; Mithen, 1996). That such social intelligence forms the basic substrate upon which all higher forms of intelligence must build leads to the important assumption that a social orientation toward problems is always available as a default processing mode when computational demands become onerous. The cognitive illusions demonstrated by three decades of work in problem solving, reasoning, and decision making seem to bear this out. As in the Linda problem and the four-card selection task discussed earlier, the literature is full of problems where it is necessary to use an abstract, decontextualized—but computationally expensive—approach in order to arrive at the correct answer. However, alongside such a solution often resides a tempting social approach ("Oh, yeah, the author of this knows a lot about Linda") that with little computational effort will prime an alternative response.

Alternative Interpretations of Base Rate Neglect

Recall from the previous chapter the phenomenon of base rate neglect illustrated with the cab problem (85% of the cabs in the city are Green and...) and the XYZ virus problem (Imagine that the XYZ virus causes a serious disease...). People ignore the prior probability of an event, especially when it is seemingly noncausal and when it is presented as pallid statistical evidence. Cosmides and Tooby (1996) as well as Gigerenzer (1991, 1996a, 2007; see also, Koehler, 1996) have argued that we have evolved mental mechanisms for dealing with frequencies but not single-event probabilities. These investigators have argued that the problems in the heuristics and biases literature are difficult because they are presented in terms of single-event probabilities rather than frequencies. Let us analyze an example of a problem in each of the two formats.

Here is a problem that people find difficult: For symptom-free women ages 40–50 who participate in screening using mammography, the following information is available for this region. The probability that one of these women has breast cancer is 1%. If a woman has breast cancer, the probability is 80% that she will have a positive mammography test. If a woman does not have breast cancer, the probability is 10% that she will still have a positive mammography test. Imagine a woman (ages 40–50, no symptoms) who has a positive mammography test in your breast cancer screening. What is the probability that she actually has breast cancer? _____ %

Here is a different version of the same problem (from Gigerenzer, 1996b) that makes it much easier: For symptom-free women ages 40–50 who participate in screening using mammography, the following information is available for this region. Ten out of every 1,000 women have breast cancer. Of these 10 women with breast cancer, 8 will have a positive mammography test. Of the remaining 990 women without breast cancer, 99 will still have a positive mammography test. Imagine a sample of women (ages 40–50, no symptoms) who have positive mammography tests in your breast cancer screening. How many of these women actually have breast cancer? _____ out of _____

The second version of the problem makes it much easier to see that probabilities refer to instances of a class. It is easier to see in the second example that there will be a total of 107 women (8 plus 99) with positive mammographies and that 8 of these will have cancer. Thus, only 8 of 107 (7.5%) of women with a positive test will actually have cancer. Gigerenzer and other investigators have shown that presenting problems in frequency formats facilitates the processing of probabilistic information by not only laboratory subjects but also by practicing physicians (Cosmides & Tooby, 1996; Gigerenzer, 2002, 2007).

What seems to be critical, though, is that frequency formats clarify the point that probabilistic information refers to instances of a class. Frequency formats are not necessary for improved performance. There are also ways of clarifying the presentation of single-event probabilities so that they are more understandable. Several studies have demonstrated a variety of means of presenting probabilistic information so that the relationship between instance and class is clarified in ways that make processing the information easier and that result in much better performance (Barbey & Sloman, 2007; Evans, Simon, Perham, Over, & Thompson, 2000; Sloman & Over, 2003; Sloman et al., 2003).

Alternative Interpretations of Overconfidence in Knowledge Calibration

In Chapter 3 we discussed the overconfidence effect in knowledge calibration experiments. In one popular laboratory paradigm, people answer multiple choice or true/false questions and, for each item, provide a judgment indicating their subjective probability that their answer is correct. The standard finding of overconfidence on this task (that subjective probability estimates are consistently higher than the obtained percentage correct) has been considered normatively inappropriate.

However, Gigerenzer, Hoffrage, and Kleinbolting (1991; see also Juslin, 1994; Juslin, Winman, & Persson, 1994) have argued that if the subject construes the task situation in a certain way, then some degree of overconfidence might well be considered normative. For example, it is common to posit that people base confidence judgments on probabilistic cues that they retrieve from memory that are related to the target judgment. That is, when asked whether Philadelphia or Columbus, Ohio, has more people, an individual might retrieve the cue that Philadelphia has a major league baseball team and Columbus does not. This cue has a certain validity in the natural environment of U.S. cities (in a random selection of pairs of cities in which one has baseball team and another does not, the former has a greater than 50% probability of being the larger).

Gigerenzer et al. (1991) hypothesize that people use such probabilistic cues not only to derive the answer to the question but to determine their level of confidence. The use of cues with high validity will lead to high degrees of confidence. Gigerenzer et al. (1991) assume that the cue validities stored in memory are well adapted to the actual environment: "Cue validities correspond well to ecological validities" (p. 510). However, overconfidence results when people employ cue validities stored in memory that are well adapted to the information in the actual environment to derive degrees of confidence about questions that have been nonrandomly sampled. For example, the baseball team cue, although highly valid for a random selection of U.S. cities, would not be as diagnostic for the types of pairs that are usually employed in knowledge calibration experiments. Such experiments most often select items that would be analogous to the comparison between Columbus and Cincinnati (here, the generally valid baseball team cue leads the assessor astray).

When in the unrepresentative environment of the typical knowledge calibration experiment, reliance on cue validities that are generally well adapted to a representative environment to derive confidence judgments will result in overconfident estimates of knowledge. In a series of elegant experiments, Gigerenzer et al. (1991) demonstrated that perhaps some of the overconfidence effect in knowledge calibration studies is due to the unrepresentative stimuli used in such experiments—stimuli that do not match the participants' stored cue validities, which are optimally tuned to the environment (however, see Brenner, Koehler, Liberman, & Tversky, 1996). But the Meliorist would surely reply to such an argument that there are many instances in real-life when we are suddenly placed in environments where the cue validities have changed. Metacognitive awareness of such situations and strategies for suppressing incorrect confidence judgments generated by automatic responses to cues will be crucial here (such suppression will be discussed in the next chapter, when we take up dual-process models). High school musicians who aspire to a career in music have to recalibrate when they arrive at a university and see large numbers of other talented musicians for the first time. If they persist in their old confidence judgments they may not change majors when they should. Many real-life situations where accomplishment yields a new environment with even more stringent performance requirements share this logic. Each time we "ratchet up" in the competitive environment of a capitalist economy we are in a situation just like the overconfidence knowledge calibration experiments with their unrepresentative materials. The Meliorist would argue that it is important to have learned strategies that will temper one's overconfidence in such situations. Therefore, overconfidence—even when displayed in paradigms with unrepresentative materials—is still a concern.

Alternative Interpretations of Probability Matching

The probabilistic contingency experiment has many versions in psychology (Gal & Baron, 1996; Tversky & Edwards, 1966), and it yields the phenomenon of probability matching. Described in the last chapter, this was the paradigm where, when faced with lights that flash red or blue in a 70:30 ratio, people match the ratio rather than engage in the optimally predictive behavior of choosing the most probable color each time.

Probability matching behavior has been observed in many different choice situations for both animals and humans (e.g., Estes, 1964; Gallistel, 1990). The research exploring probability matching in humans has often studied probability learning in choice situations, where reinforcement frequencies must be inferred across a large number of trials. Estes (1964) reviewed over 80 studies that were predominately of this type and reported that probability matching was a common finding. In most of these studies, a subject was asked to make a choice between two alternatives that each had a fixed probability of being correct, and then, following their choice, received immediate feedback as to which alternative was correct. An alternative procedure, in the tradition of research exploring human probability judgments (Kahneman & Tversky, 1972), involves presenting verbal problems where the frequencies of hypothetical outcomes are either directly given or easily inferable from the outset (e.g., Gal & Baron, 1996).

Does probability matching in choice situations reflect optimal or rational behavior? Gallistel (1990) comes down on the side of conceptualizing probability matching as an optimizing behavior by suggesting that matching makes perfect sense from the perspective of a foraging organism. In natural foraging environments, many animals normally will gather wherever food is plentiful, with the result that the plentiful state is unlikely to persist for long. Similarly, Gigerenzer (1996a) suggests that probability matching may be adaptive under some conditions: "If all choose to forage in the spot where previous experience suggests food is to be found in greatest abundance, then each may get only a small share.... Maximization is not always an evolutionarily stable strategy in situations of competition among individuals" (p. 325). In short he argues that probability matching could, under some conditions, actually be an evolutionarily stable strategy (see Skyrms, 1996, for many such examples). Gigerenzer (1996a) borrows the concept of adaptive coin-flipping from theoretical biology (Cooper, 1989; Cooper & Kaplan, 1982) to make his point. Adaptive coin-flipping is an "intra-genotypic strategy mixing...in which it can be to the selective advantage of the genotype for its individual phenotypic expressions to make their choices randomly" (Cooper, 1989, p. 460). It functions much like hedging a bet by providing a safety net against the catastrophic loss that might occur when less probable events eventually happen. Likewise, the instability in preference orderings that signal the failure of individual utility maximization is defended by Cooper (1989) because "perhaps some of the observed instability is due to adaptive strategy mixing. If so, instability would have to be reevaluated; when one is acting as an agent of one's genotype, it could sometimes be a sound strategy" (p. 473).

Both Gigerenzer (1996a) and Cooper (1989) argue that the genes are served in the long run by the existence of a random mechanism that ensures that all individuals do not respond to choice in the same fashion and that a given person does not respond the same all the time to an identical situation—even though one particular choice is maximizing for the individual. In short, there are several arguments in the literature indicating that, while not utility maximizing, a strategy of probability matching might make sense from an evolutionary point of view.

Alternative Interpretations of Belief Bias in Syllogistic Reasoning

An aspect of epistemic rationality that was not discussed in the last chapter relates to the consistency of beliefs in a knowledge network. From a set of beliefs currently held, a person needs to be able to infer further beliefs that follow logically. When inferences lead to an inconsistency, it is usually a sign that some belief in the network is not accurately tracking reality. Thus, logical reasoning is a facilitator of epistemic rationality. A full discussion of logical reasoning is beyond the scope of this book (see Evans et al., 1993; Johnson-Laird, 1999, 2006), but one particular bias in logical reasoning does deserve discussion because it has been extensively examined in the heuristics and biases literature. It is *belief bias*—the tendency for conclusions to be accepted on the basis of believability rather than logical necessity.

Consider the following syllogism. Ask yourself if it is valid—whether the conclusion follows logically from the two premises:

Premise 1: All living things need water.
Premise 2: Roses need water.

Therefore, roses are living things.

What do you think? Judge the conclusion either logically valid or invalid before reading on.

If you are like about 70% of the university students who have been given this problem, you will think that the conclusion is valid. And if you did think that it was valid, like 70% of university students who have been given this problem, you would be wrong (Markovits & Nantel, 1989; Sá, West, & Stanovich, 1999; Stanovich & West, 1998c). Premise 1 says that all living things need water, not that all things that need water are living things. So just because roses need water, it does not follow from premise 1 that they are living things. If that is still not clear, it probably will be after you consider the following syllogism with exactly the same structure:

Premise 1: All insects need oxygen.
Premise 2: Mice need oxygen.

Therefore, mice are insects.

Now it seems pretty clear that the conclusion does not follow from the premises.

If the logically equivalent "mice" syllogism is solved so easily, why is the "rose" problem so hard? Well for one thing, the conclusion (roses are living things) seems so reasonable, and you know it to be true in the real world. That is the rub. Logical validity is not about the believability of the conclusion—it is about whether the conclusion necessarily follows from the premises. The same thing that made the rose problem so hard made the mice problem easy. The fact that "mice are insects" is not definitionally true in the world we live in might have made it easier to see that the conclusion did not follow logically from the two premises.

In both of these problems, prior knowledge about the nature of the world (that roses are living things and that mice are not insects) was becoming implicated in a type of judgment (of logical validity) that is supposed to be independent of content. In the rose problem prior knowledge was interfering, and in the mice problem prior knowledge was facilitative. These differences prove that factual knowledge is implicated in both the rose and mice problems—even though the *content* of syllogisms should have no impact on their logical validity. This effect is termed the *belief bias effect* in syllogistic reasoning. The effect on the rose problem is large. Only about 32% of university students solve it (Sá et al., 1999), whereas the same participants respond correctly 78% of the time on logically equivalent versions with unfamiliar material (versions where prior knowledge does not get in the way).

The rose problem illustrates one of the fundamental computational biases of human cognition—the tendency to automatically bring prior knowledge to bear when solving problems (Evans, 2002; Stanovich, 1999, 2004). That prior knowledge is implicated in performance on this problem even when the person is explicitly told to ignore the real-world believability of the conclusion illustrates that this tendency toward contextualizing problems with prior knowledge is so ubiquitous that it cannot easily be turned off—hence its characterization here as a fundamental computational bias (one that pervades virtually all thinking, whether we like it or not). Of course, the tendency to use prior knowledge to supplement problem solving is more often a help than a hindrance. Nevertheless, there are certain improbable but important situations in modern life in which the fundamental computational biases must be overridden, and wherein failure to do so can have negative real-life consequences.

The property of cognition illustrated in the rose syllogism problem is sometimes termed *belief projection*. Automatic belief projection is not limited to syllogistic reasoning problems. Experiments have shown it to operate in several different problem-solving domains and in several different paradigms.

One belief projection paradigm has been extensively studied in the reasoning literature: the evaluation of information in 2 × 2 contingency tables discussed in the last chapter. For example, in one such paradigm subjects are asked to evaluate the efficacy of a drug based on a hypothetical well-designed scientific experiment. They are told that

150 people received the drug and were not cured
150 people received the drug and were cured

75 people did not receive the drug and were not cured
300 people did not receive the drug and were cured

They are asked to evaluate the effectiveness of the drug based on this information. In this case, they have to detect that the drug is ineffective. In fact, not only is it ineffective, it is positively harmful. Only 50% of the people who received the drug were cured (150 out of 300), but 80% of those who did not receive the drug were cured (300 out of 375).

The drug context of this problem is fairly neutral to most participants. However, it is easy to trigger prior knowledge and belief by using problems that have more content. For example, in one study, we (see Stanovich & West, 1998d) asked subjects to evaluate the outcome of an experiment to test whether having siblings is associated with sociability. The association presented was the same as in the drug experiment:

150 children had siblings and were not sociable
150 children had siblings and were sociable
75 children did not have siblings and were not sociable
300 children did not have siblings and were sociable

Now, however, it was more difficult for our subjects (who, as a group, did think that sociability was positively associated with having siblings) to see that, in these data, having siblings was negatively associated with sociability. As in the rose syllogism problem, prior knowledge/belief automatically colored the evaluation of the data. The fact that the numerical paradigm here was quite different from the verbal reasoning domain of syllogistic reasoning indicates the generality of the phenomenon.

Controlled studies (e.g., Broniarczyk & Alba, 1994; King & Koehler, 2000; Levin et al., 1993; Nisbett & Ross, 1980) have demonstrated that when people have a prior belief that two variables are connected, they tend to see that connection even in data in which the two variables are totally unconnected. Unfortunately, this finding generalizes to some real-world situations that adversely affect people's lives. For example, many psychological practitioners continue to believe in the efficacy of the Rorschach Test. This is the famous inkblot test in which the client responds to blotches on a white card. Because the inkblots lack structure, the theory is that people will respond to them in the same style that they typically respond to ambiguity and thus reveal "hidden" psychological traits. The problem with all of this is that there is no evidence that the Rorschach

Test provides any additional diagnostic utility (Dawes, 1994; Lilienfeld, 1999; Wood, Nezworski, Lilienfeld, & Garb, 2003). Belief in the Rorschach Test arises from the phenomenon of illusory correlation. Clinicians see relationships in response patterns because they believe they are there, not because they are actually present in the pattern of responses being observed.

There are certainly situations in modern society where processing the evidence as is and not projecting prior beliefs is useful (jury trials, for example). However, numerous theorists have argued that the emphasis on treating knowledge projection as a dysfunctional bias sometimes obscures the basic fact that, overall, it is a useful aspect of cognition. Philosopher Hilary Kornblith (1993) reminds us that

> mistaken beliefs will, as a result of belief perseverance, taint our perception of new data. By the same token, however, belief perseverance will serve to color our perception of new data when our preexisting beliefs are accurate.... If, overall, our belief-generating mechanisms give us a fairly accurate picture of the world, then the phenomenon of belief perseverance may do more to inform our understanding than it does to distort it. (p. 105)

This argument—that in a natural ecology where most of our prior beliefs are true, projecting our beliefs onto new data will lead to faster accumulation of knowledge—recurs throughout the literature on numerous reasoning tasks. For example, Alloy and Tabachnik (1984) echo it in their review of the covariation detection literature on humans and other animals: "When individuals' expectations accurately reflect the contingencies encountered in their natural environments... it is not irrational for them to assimilate incoming information about covariation between events to these expectations" (p. 140). Of course, Alloy and Tabachnik emphasize that we must project from a largely accurate set of beliefs in order to obtain the benefit of knowledge projection. In a sea of inaccurate beliefs, the situation is quite different.

Evans, Over, and Manktelow (1993) rely on a variant of this argument when considering the normative status of belief bias in syllogistic reasoning. They consider the status of selective scrutiny explanations of the belief bias phenomenon. Such theories posit that subjects accept conclusions that are believable without engaging in logical reasoning at all. Only when faced with unbelievable conclusions do subjects engage in logical reasoning about the premises. Evans et al. (1993) consider whether such a processing strategy could be rational in the sense of serving to achieve the person's goals, and they conclude that it could. They argue that any adult is likely to hold a large number of true beliefs that are interconnected in complex ways. Because single-belief revision has interactive effects on the rest of the belief network, it may be computationally costly. Evans et al. (1993) argue that under such conditions it is quite right that conclusions that contradict one's beliefs "should be subjected to the closest possible scrutiny and refuted if at all possible" (p. 174). Again, the argument works when the selective scrutiny mechanism is applied using a subset of beliefs that are largely true in the domain to which the scrutiny strategy is being applied.

Finally, Edwards and Smith (1996) found a disconfirmation bias in the evaluation of arguments. Arguments that were incompatible with prior beliefs were subjected to a more intense analysis than those compatible with prior belief. Edwards and Smith (1996) developed a selective scrutiny account of this effect similar to that developed for the syllogistic reasoning task by Evans et al. (1993). But Edwards and Smith (1996) also emphasize the caveat mentioned previously—selective scrutiny will only work when the prior beliefs upon which we are conditioning our selectivity are true:

> The preceding considerations indicate that a disconfirmation bias can be normatively justified. Still, we do not want to leave the reader with the impression that all aspects of the behavior of the participants in our experiments were rational. The case for total rationality hinges on the assumption that the prior beliefs involved (which determine whether an argument is compatible or not) were themselves arrived at by a normative process. It seems unlikely that this would always be the case.... Thus, when one looks at the details of the search for disconfirming evidence, irrationalities begin to surface. (p. 22)

Again, the pitfall here is the same as that mentioned previously—when the subset of beliefs that the individual is projecting contains substantial false information, selective scrutiny will delay the assimilation of the correct information. In summary, though, the point of this section was to emphasize that the tendency to treat all belief bias effects as non-normative should be avoided. Sometimes it is perfectly rational for people to project their prior beliefs.

Alternative Interpretations of Framing Effects

Framing effects provide another example of an area of research where alternative interpretations of the results obtained have been proposed. Recall the disease framing effect discussed in chapter 2. People preferred the sure-thing option (saving 200 for sure) in decision 1:

Decision 1. Imagine that the United States is preparing for the outbreak of an unusual disease, which is expected to kill 600 people. Two alternative programs to combat the disease have been proposed. Assume that the exact scientific estimates of the consequences of the programs are as follows: If program A is adopted, 200 people will be saved. If program B is adopted, there is a one-third probability that 600 people will be saved and a two-thirds probability that no people will be saved.

Most people when given this problem prefer program A—the one that saves 200 lives for sure. They are risk averse in this "gain" framing. However, inconsistent responses to another problem define a framing effect:

Decision 2. Imagine that the United States is preparing for the outbreak of an unusual disease, which is expected to kill 600 people. Two alternative programs to combat the disease have been proposed. Assume that the exact scientific estimates of the consequences of the programs are as follows: If program C is adopted, 400 people will die. If program D is adopted, there is a one-third probability that nobody will die and a two-thirds probability that 600 people will die.

The program outcomes are identical in decision 2, but now in this "loss" framing people are risk seeking. They prefer program D—the one-third probability that nobody will die. This framing effect—subjects preferences flipping based on simply a rephrasing of the alternatives as gains or losses—violates the principle of descriptive invariance that underlies most basic frameworks of instrumental rationality. Nevertheless, McKenzie and Nelson (2003) present an analysis in defense of subjects who display framing effects that violate descriptive invariance. Their argument is that frames provide additional *implicit* information, in addition to what is explicitly stated. As an example, they make reference to a previous study in which people rated beef described as 75% lean as leaner than beef described as having 25% fat. This could be viewed as an irrational framing effect. In contrast though, McKenzie and Nelson (2003) argue that it would be reasonable to describe beef as 25% fat if *most* beef had less than that. Thus, describing the beef in that way might be thought to convey information.

In an experiment, they demonstrate a similar effect by showing that most people interpreted a glass described as "half empty" as previously full—as opposed to a glass described as "half full" which was interpreted as previously being empty. McKenzie and Nelson's point is that although the "half empty" and "half full" framings could be viewed, on the surface, as formally equivalent, this would be a narrow view of the situation. "Half empty" implies a previous state of full, whereas "half full" implies a previous state of empty, and in some situations the previous state might be relevant. For example, when people are sensitive to signs of improvement or deterioration, what the frame implies about the previous states might have some relevance.

McKenzie and Nelson (2003) argue that the famous disease problem might be subject to interpretation in terms of implicit information. Specifically the idea is that alternative A—200 will be saved—could contain an implicit suggestion of a previous state in which no one was saved, whereas alternative C—400 will die—could contain an implicit suggestion of a previous state in which no one died. If this is the case, then, based on the implied previous state, the developmental trajectory of alternative A seems to be better than alternative C. Such an implication would lead to choices consistent with the previous finding of risk aversion for problem 1 (the gain frame) and risk seeking for problem 2 (the loss frame). The key point though is that if McKenzie and Nelson (2003) are correct that frames carry implicit information that could vary from condition to condition, then failures of descriptive invariance are not necessarily a sign of irrationality.

Some investigators have argued that demonstrations of the sunk-cost fallacy are examples of framing effects (Frisch, 1993; Sieck & Yates, 1997). Standard economic theory dictates that all decisions should be future oriented, that is, our decisions should be oriented toward consequences in the future rather than what has happened in the past. Giving weight to past economic history (what has already been invested) when deciding about the future is known as the sunk-cost fallacy. Here is a example of sunk-cost problem commonly used in the research literature:

Decision 1. You are staying in a hotel room on vacation. You turn on the TV and there is a movie on. After 5 minutes you are bored and the movie seems pretty bad. Would you continue to watch the movie or not?

a. Continue to watch   b. Turn it off

In a study in my lab (Stanovich & West, 1998b), only 7.2% of a sample of subjects would watch the movie after hearing this description. Now consider another version used in the same study:

Decision 2. You are staying in a hotel room on vacation. You paid $6.95 to see a movie on pay TV. After 5 minutes you are bored and the movie seems pretty bad. Would you continue to watch the movie or not?

a. Continue to watch   b. Turn it off

Here the situation is exactly the same except that you have paid for the movie. The cost is in the past—it is water under the bridge. You cannot get it back. The only rational thing to do, says conventional economic theory, is to look to the future to see what action has the best consequences. The answer to decision 1 (only 7.2% would watch) tells us what subjects see as the best action in the future. Nonetheless, in response to decision 2, most subjects display a sunk-cost effect. Specifically, in our study, 62.5% of the sample said that they would continue watching if they had already paid for the movie. They continued to do something that in the future would make them *less* happy. They did so for the irrelevant reason that they had spent the money in the past. Viewed in this way, the sunk-cost fallacy seems to be an irrational framing effect.

Keys and Schwartz (2007) point out, however, that in one critical respect sunk-cost problems such as this one violate one of the prerequisites for a framing effect. As was discussed in Chapter 2, the most straightforward examples of framing effects are those where the *subjects themselves* view as irrelevant the contextual feature that causes their choices to reverse. But this is not the case in many sunk-cost problems. Both Frisch (1993) and Stanovich and West (1998b) found that when both problems are presented to the subjects side by side, the majority do not agree that they represent the same choice. In our study, only 35.4% of the sample responded that the two choice situations defined by decision 1 and decision 2 are the same. Not surprisingly, these subjects overwhelmingly avoided the sunk-cost fallacy. However, 33.9% of our subjects thought that the two decisions were subjectively different, and 30.7% of the subjects thought that the two decisions were *objectively* different. Two thirds of these two groups of subjects displayed a sunk-cost effect.

Keys and Schwartz (2007) point out that it makes sense to think that if you failed to watch the movie in decision 2 that you would remember that you had paid the money and that this memory would negatively impact whatever you decided to do instead. From this standpoint, it is understandable that subjects do not see the consequences of the action "turn it off" in decision 2 as the same as the consequences of the action "turn it off" in decision 1. People view the contextual difference in the two decisions (whether they have already paid for the movie or not) as relevant even though economic theory does not. The Meliorist might still argue that regret is overly influential on our future decisions—unnecessarily dampening our the enjoyment of our future choices (infecting our enjoyment after turning off the movie in decision 2). As a long-term strategy, we might want to learn how to alter our feelings of regret in situations where it would lead us to commit the sunk-cost fallacy, the Meliorist would argue. Nevertheless, the Panglossian position is that, with respect to evaluating a single choice such as that in this example, it is difficult to sanction someone who commits the sunk-cost fallacy with the charge of irrationality.

Balancing the Meliorist and Panglossian Perspectives

In this chapter, we have balanced the perspective that dominated Chapters 2 and 3. In those chapters we saw numerous ways in which heuristics and biases researchers have demonstrated gaps between descriptive and normative models of both instrumental and epistemic rationality. These researchers interpret the gaps as real and indicative of irrational response patterns that are characteristic of human cognition. As Meliorists, however, they view the gaps as remediable. They think that with training in the appropriate rational thinking strategies and the necessary knowledge in the domains of probabilistic thinking and scientific inference, people can think and respond better. Meliorists think that people are not, in general, perfectly rational but that they can be made more so.

In this chapter, however, we have seen that performance on many of the same tasks can be interpreted so as to make the performance of the average subject seem more rational. This is the approach taken by Panglossian theorists. If we accept the alternative task interpretations discussed in this chapter, then the response patterns of many of the subjects on these tasks seems much more rational. Meliorism and the Panglossian view are sometimes called metatheoretical approaches in that they are not theories tied to *particular* tasks, but instead are broad frameworks that bias our overall conclusions in one direction or another.

There are unique and complementary advantages and disadvantages to both approaches.

In a balanced and nuanced essay, Adler (1991) argues that it is best to view an individual facing a reasoning task as balancing different sets of goals and trading one type of real cost for another. He points out that many classic problems ask people to trade off predictive accuracy and explanatory coherence. In the Linda problem for example, predictive accuracy is lost if the subject displays the conjunction fallacy—it is a bad bet to favor the probability of Linda being a feminist bank teller over the probability of her being a bank teller. To avoid this bad bet, one must ignore Linda's personality description. If, on the other hand, an individual is focused on developing an overall coherent view of Linda—one that might help in developing expectations for her behavior in the future—then paying close attention to the personality description and weighing it heavily would seem to serve this end. Thus, a focus on explanatory coherence will lead one into a bad bet, whereas a focus on predictive accuracy will sacrifice explanatory coherence.

Adler (1991) warns the Meliorists that a myopic focus on the static one-shot goals of the problem as set by the experimenter potentially ignores legitimate long-run goals that individuals may bring to the task. Similarly, he warns Panglossians that "the fact that favoring one set of goals over others is reasonable does not eliminate the fact that sacrifice of legitimate objectives has taken place" (p. 274). So, for example, the finding that a frequentist representation of a problem often leads to better performance than the single-event probability version, as was discussed previously in this chapter, does not negate the fact that inaccuracies will result when single-event probabilities must be dealt with. Adler's (1991) balanced view contains a warning for both camps:

> Even if subjects' answers are wrong, that does not exclude those answers being appropriate on other relevant evaluative dimensions. Correlatively, if there is a legitimate framework that subjects apply, within which their answers are justified, that doesn't exempt them from criticism. The studies of judgment and reasoning are best understood along a number of evaluative dimensions. (p. 274)

Adler argues that it is the basic weakness of the Meliorist–Panglossian opposition to attempt to reduce these to only one evaluative dimension.

Thus, a more nuanced debate would recognize that each of the camps in the rationality debate has its own strengths and its own blind spots.

Each has advanced the theoretical and practical debate about human rationality: The Panglossians have demonstrated the power of evolutionary explanations and the necessity of matching stimulus representations to those to which evolution has shaped cognition (e.g., Cosmides & Tooby, 1996); the Meliorists have championed the possibility of cognitive change and warned against the dire consequences of mismatches between human cognitive tendencies and the thinking requirements of a technological society.

Correspondingly, however, the Meliorists are often to quick to claim flaws in human reasoning and they may miss real strengths in human cognition that could be exploited for behavioral betterment, whereas the Panglossians sometimes fail to acknowledge that a real cognitive disability results when a technological society confronts the human cognitive apparatus with a representation for which it is not evolutionarily adapted—and they sometimes fail to stress that representational flexibility is something that can increase with instruction. The Panglossians also often ignore opportunities to remediate correctable cognitive mistakes.

All camps in the debate acknowledge the same facts about behavior, but they choose to foreground and background different things. Meliorists see a world seemingly full of shockingly awful events—pyramid sales schemes going "bust" and causing financial distress, Holocaust deniers generating media attention, $10 billion spent annually on medical quackery, respected physical scientists announcing that they believe in creationism, financial institutions seemingly self-destructing and costing taxpayers billions of dollars—and think that there must be something fundamentally wrong in human cognition to be accounting for all this mayhem. Of course, in the background for the Meliorist are the very things that represent the foreground for the Panglossians—all of the cognitive feats that humans perform amazingly well. For the latter camp, it is a marvel that humans are exquisite frequency detectors, that they infer the intention of others with almost supernatural ease, that they acquire a complex language code from impoverished input, and that they perceive three dimensions with incredible accuracy (see Levinson, 1995; Pinker, 1994, 1997).

Obviously, both camps recognize that there are costs and benefits to their positions, but they calculate the probabilities of incurring those costs and reaping the benefits differently. For example, the camps are in strong disagreement about the probability that evolutionarily adapted mechanisms will match the representations called for in many real-world situations that occur in a technological society. The Meliorists think that there will be many such situations and that it is no consolation to be told that the ill-suited mechanisms that we do possess work marvelously efficiently on some other representation. The Panglossians think that the number of such situations is small and that our ability to prepare for them is reduced by Meliorist fixation on attributions of irrationality. In short, the camps make different assumptions about the extent of the ecological match with the cognitive representations that are stored in the brain.

It is also likely that preexisting biases related to cognitive remediation have partially motivated the positions of the Meliorist reformers in the heuristics and biases literature as well as their critics in the Panglossian camp. Pretheoretical biases also arise because of different weightings of the relative costs and benefits of varying assumptions about the nature of human rationality. For example, if Panglossians happen to be wrong in their assumptions, then we might miss opportunities to remediate reasoning. Conversely, unjustified Meliorism has its associated costs as well. Effort might well be wasted at cognitive remediation efforts. We might fail to appreciate and celebrate the astonishing efficiency of unaided human cognition. Excessive Meliorism might lead to a tendency to ignore the possibility that environmental change might be an easier route to performance enhancement than cognitive change.

Some commentators in these disputes feel that it is insulting to people to make widespread ascriptions of human irrationality, as Meliorists do. Such sentiments show a commendable concern for the folk psychological and social implications of the interpretation of research findings. But other commentators wonder whether our immediate reaction—to think that ascriptions of human irrationality are a bad thing—might not be a bit hasty itself. The world is full of catastrophes caused by human action. Meliorists think that some of these might be avoided by teaching people to be less prone to irrational judgments and actions.

What are the alternatives to the Meliorist position? Assume that the Meliorist is wrong. Is it not disturbing that none of our wars, economic busts, technological accidents, pyramid sales schemes, telemarketing fraud, religious fanaticism, psychic scams, environmental degradation, broken marriages, and mortgage lending scandals are due to remediable irrational thought? If these are not due to irrationality, what else is at fault? In fact, there are alternative explanations. One alternative is that the causes of these disasters must reside in much more intractable social dilemmas, such as the famous Prisoner's Dilemma (Colman,

1995; Hardin, 1968; Komorita & Parks, 1994) which we will discuss in chapter 6.

If not intractable social dilemmas as the cause, then there is in fact another alternative explanation, but it is even less palatable. Recall that instrumental rationality means attaining our goals via the most efficient means—regardless of what those goals are. If the world seems to be full of disastrous events despite the fact that everyone is assumed (by the Panglossians) to be rationally pursuing their goals and there is no social dilemma involved, then it seems we are left with a most distressing alternative. Large numbers of people must be pursuing truly evil human desires. The problems of a thin theory of rationality were discussed in chapter 1, where it was noted that such thin theories might well deem Hitler rational. Positing that there are many "rational Hitlers" in the world is a way to square a Panglossian assumption of human rationality with the observation that myriad human-caused catastrophes occur daily. In the face of this type of conclusion it appears that ascribing some irrationality to human beings is not quite the bogey we once thought it was and, ironically, a Panglossian assumption of perfect human rationality is not the warm fuzzy that it initially seems. If we feel queasy about insulting people, it seems less insulting to say they are irrational than that they are evil or despicably selfish.

These then, are some of the metatheoretical concerns that have fueled the great debate about human rationality. It seems reasonable to ask though, whether there are more empirical means for adjudicating these disputes. Or, beyond the issue of resolving the dispute, might there be way of integrating the two perspectives—the frameworks of the Meliorist and the Panglossian? In fact, in the next chapter, I present a theory that attempts to do exactly that. Before we take up that theory, we need to discuss a major class of evidence that has fueled interest in the theory presented in chapter 5.

Individual Differences in Rational Thought

In chapters 2 and 3 we saw how three decades of research in the heuristics and biases tradition have demonstrated numerous instances wherein people's responses deviate from the response considered normative on many reasoning tasks. In this chapter, we saw that the reason for this discrepancy between the normative and descriptive is still the subject of intense controversy. Until quite recently, however, one aspect of performance had been largely neglected by all parties in these disputes.

What has largely been ignored is that—although the average person in the classic heuristics and biases experiments might well display an overconfidence effect, underutilize base rates, ignore P(D/~H), violate the axioms of utility theory, choose P and Q in the selection task, commit the conjunction fallacy, and so forth—on each of these tasks some people give the standard normative response. What has been ignored is individual differences. For example, in knowledge calibration studies, although the mean performance level of the entire sample may be represented by a calibration curve that indicates overconfidence, almost always some people do display near perfect calibration. Likewise, in probabilistic assessment, the majority of subjects might well ignore the noncausal base rate evidence but a minority of subjects often makes use of this information in exactly the way prescribed by Bayes' theorem. A few people even respond correctly on the notoriously difficult abstract selection task (Evans et al., 1993; Stanovich & West, 1998a, 2008). It is similar with respect to all of the other tasks discussed in chapters 2 and 3. While the modal subject might well give a response that deviates from what has traditionally been interpreted as the normatively appropriate response, a minority of subjects does in fact respond exactly according to the strictures of instrumental and epistemic rationality.

In short, some people give the response traditionally considered normative, and others do not. There is variability in responding on all of these tasks, so it is incorrect to say that a specific experiment shows that people, in general, display a particular irrational thought pattern or response pattern. The experiment might instead be said to show that the average person, or perhaps the modal person, displays suboptimal thinking. Other people, often a minority to be sure, do not. Might anything be learned from this variability? It depends on whether or not the variability is in any way systematic. In theory, the variability might just be error variance. By chance, some people might answer a particular problem of rational thought correctly, and on the next problem a different set of people might guess, get lucky, and land on the normatively correct answer. If this were the case, the variability in responding would not correlate with any other variable. Is this the case, or is something more interesting determining these individual differences?

One aspect of this variability that researchers have examined is whether it is correlated at all with cognitive sophistication. The question has been as follows: Do people who display more complex cognition tend to give the response traditionally considered normative? Or, alternatively and quite interestingly: Do people who display more complex cognition tend to give the modal response—the response that is justified by the alternative interpretations of these tasks favored by the Panglossians? In fact, there is some suggestive data on what correlates with these individual differences.

Individual differences in cognitive sophistication have been indexed in three different ways in the research literature. The first is developmentally. It is straightforward to assume that adolescents are more cognitively sophisticated than young children and that, in turn, adults are more cognitively advanced than adolescents. The question then becomes whether cognitive developmental level, as indexed by age, is correlated with performance on rational thinking tasks. For a group of subjects of the same age, the natural index of cognitive ability is intelligence test performance. The question then becomes whether cognitive developmental level, as indexed by intelligence, is correlated with performance on rational thinking tasks.

Intelligence, however, is not an exhaustive measure of cognitive functioning. For one thing, intelligence tests fail to tap important metacognitive strategies and cognitive styles that are critical components of what has been termed the reflective mind (Stanovich, 2009; Sternberg, 2003). These components of cognition travel under a variety of names in psychology, with "thinking dispositions" or "cognitive styles" being the two most popular, and I will use the former here. Many thinking dispositions concern beliefs, belief structure, and, importantly, attitudes toward forming and changing beliefs—in short, they tap aspects of epistemic rationality. Other thinking dispositions concern a person's goals and goal hierarchy—in short, they tap aspects of instrumental rationality. Examples of some thinking dispositions that have been investigated by psychologists are actively open-minded thinking, need for cognition (the tendency to think a lot), consideration of future consequences, need for closure, superstitious thinking, and dogmatism. With regard to these aspects of cognition, the question then becomes whether cognitive developmental level, as indexed by various thinking dispositions, is correlated with performance on rational thinking tasks.

What does the data say about these relationships, that is, about the correlations between performance on rational thinking tasks and age, intelligence, and thinking dispositions? The data on intelligence is most extensive. Intelligence displays positive correlations with rational thinking on a variety of heuristics and biases tasks, but not all (Stanovich & West, 2008). On some tasks, there is no correlation. However, there is never a negative correlation—that is, it is never the case that subjects giving the non-normative response that is defended by the Panglossians (the responses defended in this chapter, for example) are higher in intelligence than those giving the normative response.

Briefly, some examples of the relationships that have been found are as follows: Intelligence correlates roughly (in absolute magnitude) .35.–45 with belief bias in syllogistic reasoning, in the range of .25–.35 with the use of causal base rates, in the range of .20–.25 with various covariation detection and hypothesis-testing tasks, .15–.20 with outcome bias measured within-subjects, .20–.40 with performance in the four-card selection task, and 05–.15 with various indices of overconfidence (Bruine de Bruin, Parker, & Fischhoff, 2007; Handley, Capon, Beveridge, Dennis, & Evans, 2004; Klaczynski & Lavallee, 2005; Kokis, Macpherson, Toplak, West, & Stanovich, 2002; Newstead, Handley, Harley, Wright, & Farrelly, 2004; Parker & Fischhoff, 2005; Stanovich & West, 1998c, 1998d, 1999, 2000, 2008; Toplak & Stanovich, 2002). These correlations are all modest to low, but they are all in the direction of more intelligent individuals giving more normative responses. Other cognitive errors revealed in the heuristics and biases literature show almost no correlation with intelligence, such as noncausal base rate usage, the sunk-cost effect, and the certainty effect (Stanovich & West, 2008).

The data on thinking dispositions largely parallels that on intelligence. A variety of the thinking dispositions mentioned earlier display positive correlations with rational thinking on a variety of heuristics and biases tasks, but not all. On some tasks, there is no correlation. However, there is never a negative correlation—that is, it is never the case that subjects giving the non-normative response that is defended by the Panglossians are higher on efficacious thinking dispositions (e.g., need for cognition) than those giving the normative response (Bruine de Bruin et al., 2007; Klaczynski & Lavellee, 2005; Kokis et al., 2002; LeBoeuf & Shafir, 2003; Parker & Fischhoff, 2005; Smith & Levin, 1996; Stanovich & West, 1999; Toplak & Stanovich, 2002; West, Toplak, & Stanovich, 2008).

The data on developmental trends are not quite so consistent, however (see Stanovich, Toplak, & West, 2008), in part because there are many fewer developmental comparisons than there are studies of intelligence or thinking dispositions. Age is correlated with the use of causal base rates (Jacobs & Potenza, 1991; Kokis et al., 2002). However, the developmental research on framing effects is quite confusing. Some studies have failed to find a developmental trend (Levin & Hart, 2003; Levin, Hart, Weller, & Harshman, 2007) and others have actually found that sometimes framing effects increase with age (Reyna & Ellis, 1994). In contrast, belief bias does attenuate with age (Kokis et al., 2002), as does the gambler's fallacy (Klaczynski, 2000, 2001; Klaczynski & Narasimham, 1998). Performance on the four-card selection task improves with age (Overton, Byrnes, & O'Brien, 1985).

The data on intelligence, thinking dispositions, and development are not monolithic in their trends, and on many tasks the data are still sparse, yet they seem to be trending in one direction. Overall, rational thinking, as defined by the standard task interpretations described in chapters 2 and 3, tends to increase with cognitive sophistication. In short, there is variability in responses to heuristics and biases tasks, and this variability is systematic and not error variance. We will see in the next chapter that if this variability in human behavior is fully acknowledged by all sides, then it is possible to reconcile the basic insights that motivate both camps in the Great Rationality Debate.

Suggestions for Further Readings

Cohen, L. J. (1981). Can human irrationality be experimentally demonstrated? *Behavioral and Brain Sciences, 4,* 317–370.

Cosmides, L., & Tooby, J. (1992). Cognitive adaptations for social exchange. In J. Barkow, L. Cosmides & J. Tooby (Eds.), *The adapted mind* (pp. 163–228). New York: Oxford University Press.

Cosmides, L., & Tooby, J. (1996). Are humans good intuitive statisticians after all? Rethinking some conclusions from the literature on judgment under uncertainty. *Cognition, 58,* 1–73.

Gigerenzer, G. (2007). *Gut feelings: The intelligence of the unconscious.* New York: Viking Penguin.

Keys, D. J., & Schwartz, B. (2007). "Leaky" rationality: How research on behavioral decision making challenges normative standards of rationality. *Perspectives on Psychological Science, 2,* 162–180.

McKenzie, C. R. M. (2003). Rational models as theories—not standards—of behavior. *Trends in Cognitive Sciences, 7,* 403–406.

Oaksford, M., & Chater, N. (2007). *Bayesian rationality: The probabilistic approach to human reasoning.* Oxford: Oxford University Press.

Samuels, R., & Stich, S. P. (2004). Rationality and psychology. In A. R. Mele & P. Rawling (Eds.), *The Oxford handbook of rationality* (pp. 279–300). Oxford: Oxford University Press.

Stein, E. (1996). *Without good reason: The rationality debate in philosophy and cognitive science*. Oxford: Oxford University Press.

Todd, P. M., & Gigerenzer, G. (2007). Environments that make us smart: Ecological rationality. *Current Directions in Psychological Science, 16,* 167–171.

....

CHAPTER 5

Resolving the Debate About the Rationality of Judgment and Decision Making

A Dual-Process Account

In chapters 2 and 3, we saw that there is a normative-descriptive gap on a variety of tasks from the heuristics and biases literature. A descriptive model of how people actually perform deviates from a normative model that prescribes what an ideally rational response would be. We have also seen that there are two different ways to describe this normative-descriptive gap. In the early days of the heuristics and biases research program, the gap was taken—in the manner of the discussion in chapters 2 and 3—as an indication that there were systematic irrationalities present in human cognition.

In chapter 4, we introduced several alternative interpretations of the gap—many in terms of alternative task interpretations held by subjects. Several of the arguments in that chapter amounted to a defense of the subject's non-normative response by viewing it as a rational response to a different task: that is, subjects were said to be giving rational responses to tasks different from those intended by the experimenters. Because this alternative response is often the modal one—the most common response given by subjects—it might be argued that the alternative interpretations discussed in chapter 4 should be considered the rational ones. However, such an argument would ignore the data patterns discussed at the end of chapter 4—those involving individual differences. Although on many of these tasks most subjects give the non-normative response, some give the normative response, and this variability is systematic.

Not uniformly, but somewhat consistently, the magnitude of the normative-descriptive gap correlates inversely with cognitive sophistication.

Another way to say this is that giving the normative response, as opposed to the non-normative response, is correlated with cognitive sophistication, as indicated by intelligence, thinking dispositions, or developmental level. In this chapter, I try to reconcile these two dominant data patterns—the modal response pattern and the correlations with individual differences. The evolutionary psychologists and optimal data selection theorists correctly predict the modal response in a host of heuristics and biases tasks. Yet in all of these cases—despite the fact that the adaptationist models predict the modal response quite well—individual differences analyses demonstrate associations that also must be accounted for. The conceptualization that I develop here accounts for both of these patterns, and it also provides a reasonable way to reconcile the differing metatheoretical positions of the Meliorist and the Panglossian. This framework is known as dual-process theory.

Dual-Process Theory

Evidence from cognitive neuroscience and cognitive psychology is converging on the conclusion that the functioning of the brain can be characterized by two different types of cognition having somewhat different functions and different strengths and weaknesses (Evans, 1984, 2003, 2006, 2007; Evans & Over, 1996, 2004; Sloman, 1996, 2002; Stanovich, 1999, 2004). That there is a wide variety of evidence converging on this conclusion is indicated by the fact that theorists in a diverse set of specialty areas (including cognitive psychology, social psychology, cognitive neuroscience, and decision theory) have proposed that there are both Type 1 and Type 2 processes in the brain (e.g., Brainerd & Reyna, 2001; Feldman Barrett, Tugade, & Engle, 2004; Haidt, 2001; Metcalfe & Mischel, 1999; Smith & DeCoster, 2000). Type 1 processing is fast and automatic heuristic processing. Type 2 is, slow, analytic, and computationally expensive.

In fact, a dual-process view was implicit within the early writings in the groundbreaking heuristics and biases research program (Kahneman, 2000, 2003; Kahneman & Frederick, 2002, 2005; Kahneman & Tversky, 1996; Tversky & Kahneman, 1974, 1983). Such models are now ubiquitous in cognitive science. A list of over 23 dual-process models is presented in table 2.1 in Stanovich (2004). The details and terminology of the various dual-process theories differ, but they all share a family resemblance. Neurophysiological work supporting a dual-process conception continues to grow (Bechara, 2005; Goel & Dolan, 2003;

Lieberman, 2003; McClure, Laibson, Loewenstein, & Cohen, 2004; Prado & Noveck, 2007).

The defining feature of Type 1 processing is its autonomy. Type 1 processes are termed autonomous because (a) their execution is rapid, (b) their execution is mandatory when the triggering stimuli are encountered, (c) they do not put a heavy load on central processing capacity (i.e., they do not require conscious attention), (d) they are not dependent on input from high-level control systems, and (e) they can operate in parallel without interfering with themselves or with Type 2 processing. Type 1 processing would include behavioral regulation by the emotions, the encapsulated modules for solving specific adaptive problems that have been posited by evolutionary psychologists, processes of implicit learning, and the automatic firing of overlearned associations.

There has been much research on each of the different kinds of Type 1 processing (e.g., Buss, 2005; Fodor, 1983; Lieberman, 2000, 2003; Ohman & Mineka, 2001; Pinker, 1997; Willingham, 1998, 1999). Type 1 processes conjoin the properties of automaticity, modularity, and heuristic processing, as these constructs have been variously discussed in cognitive science (e.g., Bargh & Chartrand, 1999; Barrett & Kurzban, 2006; Carruthers, 2006; Coltheart, 1999; Samuels, 2005, 2008; Shiffrin & Schneider, 1977; Sperber, 1994).

Type 1 processing, because of its computational ease, is a common processing default. Type 1 processes are sometimes termed the adaptive unconscious (Wilson, 2002) in order to emphasize that Type 1 processes accomplish a host of useful things—face recognition, proprioception, language ambiguity resolution, depth perception, and so on—all of which are beyond our awareness. *Heuristic processing* is a term often used for Type 1 processing—processing that is fast, automatic, computationally inexpensive, and that does not engage in extensive analysis of all the possibilities. The term *heuristics* in the original phrase *heuristics and biases* was referring to the different kinds of Type 1 processing that lead to the biases that cause the deviations from the normative response in many rational thinking tasks. Type 1 processing (i.e., heuristic processing) is what makes possible what Kahneman and Frederick (2002, 2005) term *attribute substitution*—the generic trick used by people to lighten their cognitive load. Attribute substitution occurs when a person needs to assess attribute A but finds that assessing attribute B (which is correlated with A) is easier cognitively and so uses B instead. In simpler terms, attribute substitution amounts to substituting an easier question for a harder one.

Type 2 processing contrasts with Type 1 processing on each of the critical properties that define the latter. Type 2 processing is relatively slow and computationally expensive—it is the focus of our awareness. And what we can attend to—be aware of—is limited. We call it *"paying attention"* for a reason—attention is a limited resource and it has costs in terms of available computational power. Many Type 1 processes can operate at once in parallel, but only one (or a very few) Type 2 thoughts can be executing at once. Type 2 processing is thus serial processing. Type 2 processing is often language based and rule based. It is what psychologists call *controlled processing*, and it is the type of processing going on when we talk of things like "conscious problem solving."

One of the most critical functions of Type 2 processing is to override Type 1 processing. This is sometimes necessary because Type 1 processing is "quick and dirty." This so-called heuristic processing is designed to get you into the right ballpark when solving a problem or making a decision, but it is not designed for the type of fine-grained analysis called for in situations of unusual importance (financial decisions, fairness judgments, employment decisions, legal judgments, etc.). Heuristic processing depends on benign environments. In hostile environments, it can be costly.

All of the different kinds of Type 1 processing (processes of emotional regulation, Darwinian modules, associative and implicit learning processes) can produce responses that are irrational in a particular context if not overridden. People will engage in attribute substitution—the substitution of an easy-to-evaluate characteristic for a harder one —even if the easier attribute is less accurate. For example, people will substitute the less effortful attributes of vividness or salience for the more effortful retrieval of relevant facts. But when we are evaluating important risks— such as the risk of certain activities and environments for our children— we do not want to substitute vividness for careful thought about the situation. In such situations, we want to employ Type 2 override processing to block the attribute substitution.

Misleading risk judgments based on the vividness of media-presented images are widespread. For example, risks that we face such as the possibility of developing diabetes cause less worry than risks such as developing staph infections in hospitals, even though the former will affect 45 million Americans and the latter only 1,500 in a year. This is despite the fact that, personally, we can do something about the former (by changing our diet and exercising) but not the latter. Reports of the staph infections are vivid, however, and Type 1 reactions to their salience must be overridden if we are to respond rationality to these different health risks.

In order to override Type 1 processing, Type 2 processing must display at least two related capabilities. One is the capability of interrupting Type 1 processing and suppressing its response tendencies while a better response is computed. Type 2 processing thus involves inhibitory mechanisms of the type that have been the focus of recent work on executive functioning (e.g., Hasher, Lustig, & Zacks, 2007; Kane & Engle, 2003; Miyake, Friedman, Emerson, & Witzki, 2000; Salthouse, Atkinson, & Berish, 2003; Zelazo, 2004).

But the ability to suppress Type 1 processing gets the job only half done. Suppressing one response is not helpful unless there is a better response available to substitute for it. Where do these better responses come from? One answer is that they come from processes of hypothetical reasoning and cognitive simulation (Byrne, 2005; Evans, 2007; Evans & Over, 2004; Oatley, 1999; Suddendorf & Corballis, 2007) that are another aspect of Type 2 processing. When we reason hypothetically, we create temporary models of the world and test out actions (or alternative causes) in that simulated world.

A dual-process framework like that outlined in this chapter can encompass both the impressive record of descriptive accuracy enjoyed by a variety of evolutionary/adaptationist models as well as the fact that cognitive ability sometimes dissociates from the response deemed optimal by an adaptationist analysis. These data patterns make sense if the following is assumed:

1. That there are two systems of processing with the properties just outlined
2. That the two systems of processing are optimized for different situations and different goals
3. That in individuals of higher cognitive ability there is a greater probability that Type 2 processing will override the response primed by Type 1 processing

The argument is that the natural processing tendency on many of these problems yields a Type 1 response—an automatic heuristic, as Tversky and Kahneman (1974) originally argued—that primes the wrong response. The evolutionary psychologists are probably correct that this Type 1 response is evolutionarily adaptive. Nevertheless, their evolutionary interpretations do not impeach the position of the heuristics and biases researchers that the alternative response given by the minority of subjects is rational at the level of the individual. Subjects of higher analytic intelligence are simply more prone to override their automatically primed Type 1 response in order to produce responses that are epistemically and instrumentally rational.

Evolutionary Optimization Versus Instrumental Rationality

To completely understand what is being posited by dual-process theorists, it necessary to invoke the distinction between evolutionary adaptation (optimization at the genetic level) and instrumental rationality (optimization of goals at the level of the whole person). In this distinction lies a possible rapprochement between the Meliorists, who have emphasized the flaws in human cognition, and the Panglossians, who have emphasized the optimality of human cognition. For example, a leading group of Panglossian theorists—the evolutionary psychologists—are fond of pointing to the optimality of cognitive functioning: for example, by showing that certain reasoning errors that cognitive psychologists have described as a characteristic and problematic aspect of human reasoning have in fact a logical evolutionary explanation. They have made a substantial contribution by providing empirical support for such explanations. However, such a finding does not necessarily imply that the concern with cognitive reform is misplaced. The possibility of a dissociation between genetic and human goals means that evolutionary adaptation does not guarantee instrumental rationality.

In short, it is critical to recognize the distinction between evolutionary adaptation and instrumental rationality. The key point is that for the latter, maximization is at the level of the individual person. Adaptive optimization in the former case is at the level of the genes. J. R. Anderson (1990, 1991) emphasizes this distinction in his treatment of adaptationist models in psychology by stressing that instrumental rationality is different than evolutionary optimization (i.e., evolution as a local genetic fitness maximizer). Anderson (1990) accepts Stich's (1990; see also Skyrms, 1996) argument that evolutionary adaptation (genetic fitness) does not guarantee perfect human rationality in the instrumental sense, which is focused on goals of the whole organism. As a result, a descriptive model of processing that is adaptively optimal could well deviate substantially from a normative model of instrumental rationality (Skyrms, 1996, devotes an entire book to demonstrating just this).

A key feature of this framework is that goals served by Type 1 and Type 2 processing are somewhat different. The goal structures that are primarily keyed to the genes' interests and the goal structures primarily keyed to the organism's interests are differentially represented by Type 1 and Type 2 processing (see Reber, 1992, 1993, for a theoretical and empirical basis for this claim). Theorists hypothesize that Type 1 processing is more keyed toward genetic optimization, whereas Type 2 processing serves a flexible goal hierarchy that is oriented toward maximizing goal satisfaction at the level of the whole organism. Because Type 2 processing is more attuned to instrumental rationality than is Type 1 processing, Type 2 processing will seek to fulfill the individual's goals in the minority of cases where those goals conflict with the responses triggered by Type 1 processing.

Psychometric intelligence and thinking dispositions are measures of the computational capacities of Type 2 processing (Stanovich, 1999, 2009). On tasks where Type 1 and Type 2 processing are triggering different responses, this viewpoint predicts that the instrumentally optimal response will be made by individuals with higher intelligence or higher rational thinking dispositions. It is precisely this situation that accounts for the pattern of results we have previously reviewed. In short, higher analytic intelligence may lead to task construals that track instrumental rationality, whereas the alternative construals of subjects low in analytic intelligence (and hence more dominated by Type 1 processing) might be more likely to track evolutionary adaptation in situations that put these goals in conflict (De Neys, 2006; Stanovich, 2004).

Reconciling the Positions of the Meliorists and the Panglossians

In chapter 2 the difference between descriptive and normative models was introduced. Descriptive models are accurate specifications of the actual response patterns of human beings. This type of model is the goal of most work in empirical psychology. In contrast, normative models embody standards for action and belief that serve to optimize the accuracy of beliefs and the efficacy of actions. Following Bayes' rule is a normative model of belief revision, for example.

It is important to realize, however, that not all divergences between normative and descriptive models represent instances of human irrationality. This conclusion is a point on which Meliorists and Panglossians agree because, as recognized long ago by Herb Simon (1956, 1957), human rationality is bounded by the limitations of the human brain and the information available in the environment. Simon coined the term *bounded rationality* to capture the fact that judgments about the rationality of actions and beliefs must take into account the resource-limited nature of the human cognitive apparatus and the constraints of the environment. As Harman (1995) explains, "Reasoning uses resources and there are limits to the available resources. Reasoners have limited attention spans, limited memories, and limited time. Ideal rationality is not always possible for limited beings" (p. 178). More humorously, Stich (1990) notes that "it seems simply perverse to judge that subjects are doing a bad job of reasoning because they are not using a strategy that requires a brain the size of a blimp" (p. 27).

Acknowledging cognitive resource limitations leads to the idea of replacing normative models with *prescriptive* models as the standard to be achieved (Baron, 2008; Bell, Raiffa, & Tversky, 1988; Simon, 1956, 1957). Prescriptive models are usually viewed as specifying how processes of belief formation and decision making should be carried out, given the limitations of the human cognitive apparatus and the situational constraints (e.g., time pressure) with which the decision maker must deal. Thus, in cases where the normative model is computable by the human brain, it is also prescriptive. In a case where the normative model is not computable, then the standard for human performance becomes the computable strategy closest to the normative model. Meliorists and Panglossians can often agree on this point. However, many of the tasks on which people display reasoning errors are not ones that have heavy computational demands (framing tasks, base rate tasks, etc.). Other arguments will thus have to be brought to bear to completely close the gap between the Meliorists and Panglossians.

Further rapprochement between the Meliorist camp and the Panglossian camp lies in the distinction between evolutionary adaptation (optimization for the genes in the environment of evolutionary adaptation) and instrumental rationality (optimization of the current goals of the individual). For example, evolutionary psychologists are fond of pointing to the optimality of cognitive functioning—showing that certain reasoning errors that cognitive psychologists have proposed are a characteristic and problematic aspect of human reasoning have in fact a logical evolutionary explanation (see chapter 4; Brase, Cosmides, & Tooby,

1998; Cosmides & Tooby, 1996; Rode, Cosmides, Hell, & Tooby, 1999). The problem is that evolutionary psychologists are prone to emphasize situations where the ancient evolutionary goals of the genes and personal goals coincide. They are not wrong to do so, because this is often the case. Accurately navigating around objects in the natural world was adaptive during the environment of evolutionary adaptation, and it similarly serves our personal goals as we carry out our lives in the modern world. It is likewise, with other evolutionary adaptations—most serve personal goal fulfillment in the modern world. But none of this means that the overlap is necessarily 100%.

Mechanisms designed for survival in preindustrial times are clearly sometimes maladaptive in a technological culture. Our mechanisms for storing and utilizing energy evolved in times when fat preservation was efficacious. These mechanisms no longer serve the goals of people in a technological society where a fast-food outlet is on every corner. Many other Type1 processes play a similar role.

Modern society creates many situations that require radical decontextualization—that require our natural Type 1 processing tendencies to be overridden. For example, many aspects of the contemporary legal system put a premium on detaching prior belief and world knowledge from the process of evidence evaluation. There has been understandable vexation at odd jury verdicts rendered because of jury theories and narratives concocted during deliberations that had nothing to do with the evidence but instead were based on jurors' background knowledge and personal experience. The point is that in a particular cultural situation where detachment and decoupling is required, the people who must carry out these demands for decontextualization are often unable to do so, even under legal compulsion.

The need to override Type 1 processing tendencies characterizes many work settings in contemporary society. Consider the common admonition in the retail service sector that "the customer is always right." This admonition is often interpreted to include even instances where customers unleash unwarranted verbal assaults that are astonishingly vitriolic. The service worker is supposed to remain polite and helpful under this onslaught, despite the fact that such emotional social stimuli are no doubt triggering evolutionarily instantiated modules of self-defense and emotional reaction. All of this emotion, all of these personalized attributions—all fundamental computational biases of Type 1 processing—must be set aside by the service worker, and instead an abstract rule that "the customer is always right" must be invoked in this special, socially constructed domain of the market-based transaction. The worker must realize that he or she is not in an actual social interaction with this person, but in a special, indeed unnatural, realm where different rules apply.

Hostile and Benign Environments for Heuristics

In short, the Panglossians have shown us that many reasoning errors might have an evolutionary or adaptive basis. But the Meliorist perspective on this is that the modern world is increasingly changing so as to render those responses less than instrumentally rational for an individual. In short, the requirements for rationality are becoming more stringent as modern technological societies develop. Decision scientists Hillel Einhorn and Robin Hogarth long ago cautioned that "in a rapidly changing world it is unclear what the relevant natural ecology will be. Thus, although the laboratory may be an unfamiliar environment, lack of ability to perform well in unfamiliar situations takes on added importance" (Einhorn & Hogarth, 1981, p. 82).

Critics of the abstract content of most laboratory tasks and standardized tests have been misguided on this very point. Evolutionary psychologists have singularly failed to understand the implications of Einhorn and Hogarth's warning. They regularly bemoan the "abstract" problems and tasks in the heuristics and biases literature and imply that since these tasks are not like "real life" we need not worry that people do poorly on them. The issue is that, ironically, the argument that the laboratory tasks and tests are not like "real life" is becoming less and less true. "Life," in fact, is becoming more like the tests! Try using an international ATM machine with which you are unfamiliar, or try arguing with your HMO about a disallowed medical procedure. In such circumstances, we invariably find out that our personal experience, our emotional responses, our Type 1 intuitions about social fairness—all are worthless. All are for naught when talking over the phone to the representative looking at a computer screen displaying a spreadsheet with a hierarchy of branching choices and conditions to be fulfilled. The social context, the idiosyncrasies of individual experience, the personal narrative—the "natural" aspects of Type 1 processing—all are abstracted away as the representatives of modernist technological-based services attempt to "apply the rules."

Unfortunately, the modern world tends to create situations where some of the default values of evolutionarily adapted cognitive systems are not optimal. Modern technological societies continually spawn situations where humans must decontextualize information—where they must deal abstractly and in a depersonalized manner with information, rather than in the context-specific way of the Type 1 processing modules discussed by evolutionary psychologists. The abstract tasks studied by the heuristics and biases researchers often accurately capture this real-life conflict. In short, the *requirements* for rationality are often more stringent in the modern world than they were in the environment of evolutionary adaptation. This puts a premium on the use of Type 2 processing capacity to override Type 1 responses. Likewise, market economies contain agents who will exploit automatic Type 1 responding for profit (better buy that "extended warranty" on a $150 electronic device!). This again puts a premium on overriding Type 1 responses that will be exploited by others in a market economy.

Of course, it should not be inferred that the use of heuristics always leads us astray. As previously discussed, they often give us a useful first approximation to the optimal response in a given situation, and they do so without stressing cognitive capacity. In fact, they are so useful that there are influential psychologists who extol their advantages even to the extent of minimizing the usefulness of the formal rules of rationality (Brandstatter, Gigerenzer, & Hertwig, 2006; Gigerenzer, 2002, 2007; Todd & Gigerenzer, 2000, 2007). Most psychologists, however, while still acknowledging the usefulness of heuristics, think that this view carries things too far. The reason is that the usefulness of the heuristics that we rely upon to lighten the cognitive load are dependent on a benign environment. A benign environment is an environment that contains useful cues that can be exploited by various heuristics (for example, affect-triggering cues, or vivid and salient stimulus components). Additionally, for an environment to be classified as benign, it also must contain no other individuals who will adjust their behavior to exploit those relying only on heuristics.

In contrast, a hostile environment for heuristics is one in which there are no cues that are usable by heuristic processes. Even when cues are present, another way that an environment can turn hostile is if other agents discern the simple cues that are triggering a person's heuristics and start to arrange the cues for their own advantage (for example, advertisements, or the deliberate design of supermarket floor space to maximize revenue).

Take as an example one chapter in an edited book that explains the usefulness of the so-called *recognition heuristic* (Gigerenzer & Todd,

1999). The chapter subheading is titled "How Ignorance Makes Us Smart." The idea behind such "ignorance-based decision making," as it is called, is that the fact that some items of a subset are unknown can be exploited to aid decisions. In short, the yes/no recognition response can be used as a estimation cue (Goldstein & Gigerenzer, 1999, 2002; Todd & Gigerenzer, 2007). For example, novice tennis fans correctly predicted the winner of 72% of all the men's matches at the 2003 Wimbledon by using the following simple recognition heuristic: If you recognize one player's name and not the other's, predict that the one you recognize will win. This heuristic does just as well as Wimbledon experts' rankings.

With ingenious simulations, Gigerenzer and colleagues have demonstrated how certain information environments can lead to such things as less-is-more effects: where those who know less about an environment can display more inferential accuracy in it. One is certainly convinced after reading material like this that the recognition heuristic is certainly efficacious in some situations, but then one immediately begins to worry when one ponders how it relates to a market environment specifically designed to exploit it. If I were to rely solely on the recognition heuristic as I went about my day tomorrow, I could easily be led to:

1. buy a $3 coffee when in fact a $1.25 one would satisfy me perfectly well
2. eat in a single snack the number of fat grams I should have in an entire day
3. pay the highest bank fees
4. incur credit card debt rather than pay cash
5. buy a mutual fund with a 6% sales charge rather than a no-load fund

None of these behaviors serves my long-term goals at all. Yet the recognition heuristic triggers these and dozens more that will trip me up while trying to make my way through the maze of modern society. The commercial environment of my city is not a benign environment for a cognitive miser.

The danger of such miserly tendencies and the necessity of relying on Type 2 processing in the domain of personal finance is suggested by the well-known finding (see Bazerman, 2001) that consumers of financial services overwhelmingly purchase high-cost products that underperform in terms of investment return when compared to the low-cost strategies recommended by true experts (e.g., dollar-cost averaging into no-load index mutual funds). The reason is, of course, that the high-cost fee-based products and services are the ones with high immediate recognizability in the marketplace, whereas the low-cost strategies must be sought out in financial and consumer publications. An article in a British publication (MacErlean, 2002) illustrates the situation by asking "Can 70 per cent of people be wrong?" and answers "yes, it seems." In the article we learn that, at that time, 7 out of 10 people in Britain had money in checking accounts earning 0.10% with one of the big four banks (Barclays, HSBC, Lloyds TSB, and Royal Bank of Scotland) when interest rates more than 30 times that amount were available from checking accounts recommended in the Best Buy columns of leading consumer publications. The reason millions of people were losing billions of dollars in interest is clear—the "big four" were the most recognizable banks and the cognitive miser defaulted to them. The marketplace of personal finance is not benign.

Experimental studies of choice indicate that errors due to insuffi-cient monitoring of Type 1 responses are probably made all the time. Neumann and Politser (1992) describe a study in which people were asked to choose between two insurance policies. Policy A had a $400 yearly deductible and a cost of $40 per month. Policy B had no deduct-ible and a cost of $80 a month. A number of subjects preferred policy B because of the certainty of never having to pay a deductible if an acci-dent occurs. However, it takes nothing more than simple arithmetic to see that people choosing policy B have fallen prey to a Type 1 tendency to avoid risk and seek certainty (see the discussion in chapter 3 on the certainty effect). Even if an accident occurs, policy B can never cost less than policy A. This is because paying the full deductible ($400) plus the monthly fee for 12 months ($480) would translate into a total cost of $880 for policy A, whereas the monthly fee of policy B for 12 months amounts to $960. Thus, even if accidents cause the maximum deduct-ible to be paid, policy A costs less. An automatic reaction triggered by a logic of "avoid the risk of large losses" biases responses against the more economical policy A.

Modern mass communication technicians have become quite skilled at exploiting Type 1 processing defaults. These defaults are exploited by advertisers, in election campaigns, and even by governments—for exam-ple in promoting their lottery systems. "You could be the one!" blares an ad from the Ontario Lottery Commission—thereby increasing the avail-ability of an outcome which, in the game called 6/49, has an objective probability of 1 in 14 million.

Just how easy it is to exploit Type 1 tendencies to rely on easily processed stimuli is illustrated in a study by Sinaceur, Heath, and Cole (2005). They presented subjects with the following hypothetical situation: "Imagine that you have just finished eating your dinner. You have eaten a packaged food product made with beef that was bought at the supermarket. While listening to the evening news on the television, you find out that eating this packaged food may have exposed you to the human variant of bovine spongiform encephalopathy (BSE)." After reading this, the subjects were asked to respond on a 7-point scale to the following questions: "After hearing this, to what extent would you decrease your consumption of this type of packaged beef?" and "To what extent would you alter your dietary habits to de-emphasize red meats and increase the consumption of other foods?" Not surprisingly, after hearing this hypothetical situation, subjects felt that they would decrease their consumption of beef. However, another group of subjects was even more likely to say they would decrease their consumption of beef when they heard the same story identically except for the very last words. Instead of "human variant of bovine spongiform encephalopathy (BSE)" the second group read "human variant of Mad Cow Disease." It is clear what is going on here. Mad Cow Disease automatically conjures creepy imagines of an animal-borne disease in a way that "bovine spongiform encephalopathy" does not. In short, when we rely on Type 1 processing, our actions and thoughts are too readily influenced by small changes in wording that alter the affective valence of our reactions. It is a pretty sure bet that Social Security taxes would be less if Social Security was called instead Welfare for the Elderly.

In short, if we rely solely on Type 1 processing, we literally do not have "a mind of our own." The response of the Type 1 processor is determined by the most vivid stimulus at hand, the most readily assimilated fact or the most salient cue available. This tendency can be easily exploited by those who control the labeling, who control what is vivid, and who control the framing. We saw some examples of how overreliance on shallow Type 1 processing threatens our autonomy as independent thinkers in chapter 2 where framing effects that flipped people's preferences were described. To the extent that modern society increasingly requires the Type 1 computational biases to be overridden, then Type 2 overrides will be more essential to personal well-being.

Thus, the long-standing debate between the Panglossians and the Meliorists can be viewed as an issue of figure and ground reversal. It is possible to accept most of the conclusions of the work of Panglossian theorists but to draw completely different morals from them. For example, evolutionary psychologists want to celebrate the astonishing job that evolution did in adapting the human cognitive apparatus to the Pleistocene environment. Certainly they are right to do so. The more we understand about evolutionary mechanisms, the more awed appreciation we have for them. But at the same time, it is not inconsistent for a person to be horrified that a multimillion dollar advertising industry is in part predicated on creating stimuli that will trigger Type 1 processing heuristics that many of us will not have the cognitive energy or cognitive disposition to override. To Meliorists, it is no great consolation that the heuristics so triggered were evolutionarily adaptive in their day.

As mentioned earlier in this chapter, evolutionary psychologists have shown that some problems can be more efficiently solved if represented in a way that coincides with how various brain modules represent information ("when people are given information in a format that meshes with the way they naturally think about probability, they can be remarkably accurate"; Pinker, 1997, p. 351). The Meliorist cautions, however, that the world will not always let us deal with representations that are optimally suited to our evolutionarily designed cognitive mechanisms. We are living in a technological society where we must decide which health maintenance organization to join based on abstract statistics rather than experienced frequencies, decide what type of mortgage to purchase, figure out what type of deductible to get on our auto insurance, decide whether to trade in a car or sell it ourselves, decide whether to lease or to buy a car, think about how to apportion our retirement funds, and decide whether we would save money by joining a book club—to simply list a random set of the plethora of modern-day decisions and choices. Furthermore, we must make all of these decisions based on information represented in a manner for which our brains are not adapted. In none of these cases have we coded individual frequency information from our own personal experience. In order to reason rationally in all of these domains (in order to maximize our personal utility) we are going to have to deal with probabilistic information represented in nonfrequentistic terms—in representations that the evolutionary psychologists have shown are different from our adapted algorithms for dealing with frequency information.

In choosing to emphasize the importance of the few situations where evolutionarily adapted processes might not achieve instrumental rationality, we are not disputing that evolutionary psychologists are right to point out that in a majority of cases evolutionary goals and personal goals coincide. On a purely quantitative basis, in terms of the micro-events in day-to-day life, this is no doubt true. Throughout the day we are detecting frequencies hundreds of times, detecting faces dozens of times, using our language modules repeatedly, inferring the thoughts of others constantly, and so on—all of which are adaptive and serve personal goal satisfaction. Nevertheless, the few instances involving the override of Type 1 tendencies may be of unusual importance. As several examples discussed previously illustrated, a market economy can very efficiently translate suboptimal behavioral tendencies into utility for those discovering a way to exploit the suboptimal Type 1 response. A consumer who buys $10,000 worth of shares in a mutual fund with a load (a 5% sales charge) because of the glossy brochure rather than buying the equivalently performing but unadvertised no-load (no sales charge) index fund has—in the most direct way imaginable—chosen to simply give away $500 to a salesperson and to the equity owners of the loaded mutual fund company. Modern market economies are simply littered with such Type 1 traps and, often, the more potentially costly the situation, the more such traps there are (automobile purchases, mutual fund investments, mortgage closing costs, and insurance come to mind). Increasingly, the modern world is a hostile environment for an uncritical reliance on heuristics.

Summary and Conclusions

In this chapter, the dual-process framework for understanding human cognition was introduced. Although there is much ongoing dispute about the details of these models (Carruthers, 2006; Evans & Frankish, 2009), the important function they serve is to provide a framework for integrating the insights of the Panglossian and Meliorist theorists. In fact, in terms of the Great Rationality Debate, these theorists are making important points that are less in conflict than is often apparent.

What has particular importance for the Great Rationality Debate is that the goal structures of Type 1 and Type 2 processing are different. This is because the goals of Type 1 processing are genetically short-leashed (online, stimulus-response), more tightly tied to the environment of evolutionary adaptation. In contrast, Type 2 processing is keyed to longer-term goals more attuned to the person's global situation than to the immediate environment. Thus, in the minority of cases where the outputs of the two types of processing conflict, people will generally be better off if they can accomplish an override of the response primed by Type 1 processing.

The evolutionary psychologists are certainly correct that most Type 1 processing is evolutionarily adaptive. Nevertheless, their evolutionary interpretations do not impeach the position of the heuristics and biases researchers that the alternative response given by the minority of subjects is rational at the level of the individual. Subjects of greater cognitive sophistication are simply more prone to override their automatically primed response in order to produce responses that are epistemically and instrumentally rational.

Suggestions for Further Readings

Barbey, A. K., & Sloman, S. A. (2007). Base-rate respect: From ecological rationality to dual processes. *Behavioral and Brain Sciences, 30,* 241–297.

deSousa, R. (2008). Logic and biology: Emotional inference and emotions in reasoning. In J. E. Adler & L. J. Rips (Eds.), *Reasoning: Studies of human inference and its foundations* (pp. 1002–1015). New York: Cambridge University Press.

Evans, J. St. B. T. (2007). *Hypothetical thinking: Dual processes in reasoning and judgment.* New York: Psychology Press.

Evans, J. St. B. T. (2008). Dual-processing accounts of reasoning, judgment and social cognition. *Annual Review of Psychology, 59,* 255–278.

Evans, J. St. B. T., & Frankish, K. (Eds.). (2009). *In two minds: Dual processes and beyond.* Oxford: Oxford University Press.

Kahneman, D., & Frederick, S. (2002). Representativeness revisited: Attribute substitution in intuitive judgment. In T. Gilovich, D. Griffin, & D. Kahneman (Eds.), *Heuristics and biases: The psychology of intuitive judgment* (pp. 49–81). New York: Cambridge University Press.

Samuels, R., & Stich, S. P. (2004). Rationality and psychology. In A. R. Mele & P. Rawling (Eds.), *The Oxford handbook of rationality* (pp. 279–300). Oxford: Oxford University Press.

Shafir, E., & LeBoeuf, R. A. (2002). Rationality. *Annual Review of Psychology, 53,* 491–517.

Stanovich, K. E. (2009). *What intelligence tests miss: The psychology of rational thought.* New Haven, CT: Yale University Press.

....

CHAPTER 6

Metarationality

Good Decision-Making Strategies
Are Self-Correcting

Rationality is a cultural achievement. Rational beliefs and actions are supported by strategies and knowledge that were not part of our biological endowment but that were cultural discoveries. The development of probability theory, concepts of empiricism, mathematics, scientific inference, and logic throughout the centuries have provided humans with conceptual tools to aid in the formation and revision of belief and in their reasoning about action. As a culture, we have been engaging in a progressive cultural critique of the cognitive tools we use to act and think more rationally. Chapter 4 was an example of such a critique. There we saw that certain applications of rational models were the subject of dispute. This is a good thing. Principles of rational thought are not set in stone, never to be changed. In fact, the best decision-making strategies will be those that are self-correcting. This we might call the insight of metarationality—that all reasoning principles, even those concerned with rationality itself, must be subject to critique.

In this chapter, we will consider some further critiques of the general framework of rational thought outlined in previous chapters. Recall from chapter 1 that the models discussed in the bulk of this book have been what Elster (1983) calls thin theories of rationality. They are means-ends models: They assess whether people are using efficient means to reach their previously existing desires and goals. Thin theories take beliefs and desires as given and simply ask whether people choose the right action *given* their beliefs and desires. Specifically, the content of desires is not evaluated. The strengths of such a thin theory of rationality are well known. For example, if the conception of rationality is restricted to a thin theory, many powerful formalisms (such as the axioms of decision theory discussed in chapter 2) are available to serve as standards of optimal behavior. However, in chapter 1 we mentioned the well-known weaknesses of the thin theory. For example, a thin theory of rationality might determine that Hitler was a rational person. Most people find this an unacceptable consequence of the thin theory. Metarationality rises above the thin theory in assessing the content of the desires that are being pursued by instrumentally rational means. So-called *broad theories of rationality* attempt to evaluate goals and desires, and we will discuss what it means to have such a metarational perspective in this chapter.

Another well-known area in which good decision making entails being critical of narrow views of rationality are situations of coordinate action such as the Prisoner's Dilemma and commons-dilemma situations (Colman, 1995, 2003; Hardin, 1968; Komorita & Parks, 1994). The logic of these situations will be explained later in this chapter, but what the Prisoner's Dilemma and other commons dilemmas show is that rationality must police itself.

Finally, the ability of narrow rationality to fulfill our needs may be context dependent. Metarationality demands that we ask the question of when it is rational to be (narrowly) rational and when not. I discuss this aspect of metarationality last. First, I discuss broad theories that critique the desires pursued in addition to evaluating means. This is followed by a discussion of the problems of collective action. I end with a discussion of when metarationality dictates that an irrelevant contextual factor is really not so irrelevant.

Evaluating Decisions: The Role of Values and Meaning

Philosopher John Searle (2001) began a book on rationality by referring to the famous chimpanzees on the island of Tenerife studied by the psychologist Wolfgang Kohler (1927) and the many feats of problem solving that the chimps displayed that have entered the lore of textbooks. In one situation, a chimp was presented with a box, a stick, and a bunch of bananas high out of reach. The chimp figured out that he should position the box under the bananas, climb up on it and use the stick to bring down the bananas. Searle (2001) pointed out how the chimp's behavior fulfilled all of the criteria of instrumental rationality—the chimp used efficient means to achieve its ends. The primary desire of obtaining the bananas was satisfied by taking the appropriate action (see Jensen, Call, & Tomasello, 2007).

Searle uses the instrumental rationality of Kohler's chimp to pose the provocative question of whether human rationality is just an extension of chimpanzee rationality. The answer can be given in terms of Elster's (1983) distinction between thin and broad theories of rationality. If all we aspire to as humans is a thin theory of instrumental rationality, then human rationality is indeed just like chimpanzee rationality in that rational choice would be evaluated in the same way in both cases. We would ask, in both cases, whether the sets of actions adhered to the axioms of choice. But there is every reason to believe that most people do not want to stop with a thin theory. Most people take a stance toward the choices they make and the goals that they pursue. Both the choices and the goals are often evaluated by external criteria. The choices are evaluated in terms of the meaning they convey to the person making the choice and the goals are evaluated in terms of whether they are consistent with the values the person holds.

In a series of papers on the meaning inherent in a decision, Medin and colleagues (Medin & Bazerman, 1999; Medin, Schwartz, Blok, & Birnbaum, 1999) have emphasized how decisions do more than convey utility to the agent but also send meaningful signals to other actors and symbolically reinforce the self-concept of the agent. Decision makers are often engaged in the symbolic act of signaling (either to themselves or to others) what kind of person they are. Medin and Bazerman discuss a number of experiments in which subjects are shown to be reluctant to trade and/or compare items when so-called protected values are at stake (see also, Baron & Leshner, 2000; Baron & Spranca, 1997). For example, people do not expect to be offered market transactions for their pet dog, for land that has been in the family for decades, or for their wedding rings. Among Medin and Bazerman's subjects, a typical justification for viewing such offers as insults was that "It's a meaning issue, not a money issue."

Philosopher Robert Nozick (1993) provides an especially good discussion of how symbolic actions that help maintain a valued concept of personhood are not irrational despite their lack of a causal connection to experienced utility. People may be fully aware that performing a particular act is characteristic of a certain type of person but does not contribute causally to their becoming that type of person. But in symbolizing the model of such a person, performing the act might enable the individual to maintain an image of him- or herself. For many of us, the act of voting serves just this symbolic function. Many of us are aware that the direct utility we derive from the influence of our vote on the political system (a weight of one-millionth or one-hundred-thousandth, depending on the election) is less than the effort that it takes to vote (Baron, 1998; Quattrone & Tversky, 1984), yet all the same we would never miss an election! Voting has symbolic utility for us. It represents who we are. We are "the type of person" who takes voting seriously. We use a value to evaluate the action of voting; we do not assess it in terms of its experienced utility.

Another example is provided by book buying—which has symbolic value for many intellectually inclined people. But often the symbolic utility of book buying has become totally disconnected from consumption utility or use value. I am like many people in that I buy many books that I will never read (I am fully aware that my "I'll have time for that in retirement" is a pipe dream). Nevertheless, I derive symbolic utility from buying many of these books despite the fact that they will never produce utility as a consumption good.

Sen (1977) points out that we have a tendency to critique our own choices based on their consistency with our values. However, such a critique is a threat to the traditional thin rationality assumptions of economics because it drives a wedge between choice and personal welfare. Choices based on values may actually lower the personal welfare (as economists measure it) of the individual, as when we vote for a political candidate who will act against our material interests but who will express other societal values that we treasure. The concept of ethical preferences (Anderson, 1993; Hirschman, 1986; Hollis, 1992) has the same function of severing the link between observed choice and the assumption of instrumental maximization in the economic literature. The boycott of nonunion grapes in the 1970s, the boycott of South African products in the 1980s, and the interest in fair-trade products that emerged in the 1990s are examples of ethical preferences affecting people's choices and severing the link between choice and the maximization of personal welfare that is so critical to standard economic analyses.

Metarationality: Evaluating Our First-Order Desires

Most people are accustomed to conflicts between their first-order desires ("If I buy that jacket I want, I won't be able to buy that CD that I also desire"). However, a person who forms ethical preferences creates new possibilities for conflict. So, for example, I watch a television documentary on the small Pakistani children who are unschooled because they work sewing soccer balls, and vow that someone should do something about this. I find myself at the sporting goods store 2 weeks later instinctively avoiding the more expensive union-made ball. A new conflict has been created for me. I can either attempt the difficult task of restructuring my first-order desires (e.g., learn to not automatically prefer the cheaper product) or I must ignore a newly formed ethical preference. Actions out of kilter with a political, moral, or social commitment likewise create inconsistency. Values and commitments create new attention-drawing inconsistencies that are not there when one is only aware of the necessity of scheduling action to efficiently fulfill first-order desires.

In short, our values are the main mechanism we use to initiate an evaluation of desires. Action/value inconsistency can signal the need to initiate normative criticism and evaluation of both the first-order desires and the values themselves. Values thus provide an impetus for the possible restructuring of the architecture of desires. They are what allow human rationality to be a broad rationality—one where the content of desires makes a difference—in contrast to the thin instrumental rationality characteristic of chimpanzees and other animals.

What I have been calling a critique of one's own desire structure can be a bit more formally explicated in terms of what philosopher Harry Frankfurt (1971), in a much-cited article, terms second-order desires—desires to have a certain desire. In the language more commonly used by economists and decision theorists (see Jeffrey, 1974), this higher-level state would be called a second-order preference: a preference for a particular set of first-order preferences. Frankfurt speculates that only humans have second-order desires, and he evocatively terms creatures without second-order desires (other animals, human babies) "wantons." To say that a wanton does not form second-order desires does not mean that they are heedless or careless about their first-order desires. Wantons can be rational in the thin, purely instrumental, sense. Wantons may well act in their environments to fulfill their goals with optimal efficiency. A wanton simply does not reflect upon his or her goals. Wantons want, but they do not care what they want.

To illustrate his concept, Frankfurt (1971) uses as an example three kinds of addict. The wanton addict simply wants to get his or her drug. That is the end of the story. The rest of the cognitive apparatus of the wanton is simply given over to finding the best way to satisfy the desire (i.e., the wanton addict could well be termed instrumentally rational). The wanton addict does not reflect on this desire—does not consider one way or another whether it is a good thing. The desire just is. The unwilling addict, in contrast, has the same first-order desire as the wanton addict, but has the second-order desire not to have it. The unwilling addict wants to want not to take the drug. But the desire to desire not to take it is not as strong as the desire to take it. So the unwilling addict ends up taking the drug just like the wanton. But the relation of the unwilling addict to his or her behavior is different than that of the wanton. The unwilling addict is alienated from the act of taking the drug in a way that the wanton is not. The unwilling addict may even feel a violation of self-concept when taking the drug. Such a feeling would never occur in the wanton's act of drug taking.

Finally, there is the interesting case of the willing addict (a possibility for humans). The willing addict has thought about his or her desire for drug taking and has decided that it is a good thing. This addict actually wants to want to take the drug. Frankfurt (1971) helps us understand this type by noting that the willing addict would, if the craving for the drug began to wane, try to take measures to reinstate the addiction. The willing addict has reflected on the addiction, just as the unwilling addict, but in this case has decided to endorse the first-order desire.

All three of Frankfurt's (1971) addicts are exhibiting the same behavior, but the cognitive structure of their desire hierarchies is quite different. This difference, although not manifest in current behavior, could well have implications for the likelihood of the addiction continuing. The unwilling addict is (statistically speaking, of course) the best candidate for behavioral change. This addict is the only one of the three to be characterized by an internal cognitive struggle. One would posit that this struggle at least has the possibility of destabilizing the first-order desire or perhaps weakening it. The wanton is characterized by no such internal struggle and thus has less of a chance of the first-order desire being disrupted. However, note that the wanton is actually more likely to lose the addiction than the willing addict. The latter has an internal governor keeping the addiction in place, namely, the second-order desire to have it. The willing addict would take steps to stop the natural waning of the addiction. A natural waning of the addiction would be unimpeded in the wanton addict, who would simply take up some other activity that is higher in his or her first-order goal hierarchy. The wanton would not be sad to be rid of the addiction, yet would not be happy either—for the logic of his or her condition is that the addict does not reflect on the coming and going of his or her desires.

What I have been calling a critique of one's own desire structure can be more formally explicated in terminology more commonly used by economists, decision theorists, and cognitive psychologists (see Jeffrey, 1974; Kahneman & Tversky, 2000; Slovic, 1995; Tversky, Slovic, & Kahneman, 1990)—that is, in terms of second-order preferences (a preference for a particular set of first-order preferences). For example, imagine that: John prefers to smoke (he prefers smoking to not smoking). Then using the preference relationship that is the basis for the formal axiomatization of utility theory, we have the following:

$$S \text{ pref } \sim S$$

However, humans alone appear to be able to represent a model of an idealized preference structure—perhaps, for example, a model based on a superordinate judgment of long-term life span considerations (or what Gauthier, 1986, calls *considered preferences*). Thus, a human can say, I would prefer to prefer not to smoke. Only humans can decouple from a first-order desire and represent, in preference notation:

$$(\sim S \text{ pref } S) \text{ pref } (S \text{ pref } \sim S)$$

This second-order preference then becomes a motivational competitor to the first-order preference. At the level of second-order preferences, John prefers to prefer to not smoke; nevertheless, as a first-order preference, he prefers to smoke. The resulting conflict signals that John lacks what Nozick (1993) terms rational integration in his preference structure. Such a mismatched first-order/second-order preference structure is one reason why humans are often less rational than other animals in an axiomatic sense (see Stanovich, 2004, pp. 243–247). This is because the struggle to achieve rational integration can destabilize first-order preferences in ways that make them more prone to the context effects that lead to the violation of the basic axioms of utility theory.

The struggle for rational integration is also what contributes to the feeling of alienation that people in the modern world often feel when contemplating the choices that they have made. People easily detect when their high-order preferences conflict with the choices actually made.

There of course is no limit to the hierarchy of higher-order desires that might be constructed. But the representational abilities of humans may set some limits—certainly three levels seems a realistic limit for most people in the nonsocial domain (Dworkin, 1988). However, third-order judgments can be called upon to help achieve rational integration at lower levels. So, for example, John, the smoker, might realize when he probes his feelings that:

> He prefers his preference to prefer not to smoke over his preference for smoking.

Symbolically, this could be represented as follows:

$$[(\sim S \text{ pref } S) \text{ pref } (S \text{ pref } \sim S)] \text{ pref } [S \text{ pref } \sim S]$$

We might in this case say that John's third-order judgment has ratified his second-order evaluation. Presumably this ratification of his second-order judgment would add to the cognitive pressure to change the first-order preference by taking behavioral measures that will make change more likely (entering a smoking secession program, consulting his physician, staying out of smoky bars, etc.). On the other hand, a third-order judgment might undermine the second-order preference by failing to ratify it:

> John might prefer to smoke more than he prefers his preference to prefer not to smoke.

$$[S \text{ pref } \sim S] \text{ pref } [(\sim S \text{ pref } S) \text{ pref } (S \text{ pref } \sim S)]$$

In this case, although John wishes he did not want to smoke, the preference for this preference is not as strong as his preference for smoking itself. We might suspect that this third-order judgment might not only prevent John from taking strong behavioral steps to rid himself of his addiction, but that over time it might erode his conviction in his second-order preference itself, thus bringing rational integration to all three levels.

Typically, philosophers have tended to bias their analyses toward the highest level desire that is constructed—privileging the highest point in the regress of higher-order evaluations, using that as the foundation, and defining it as the true self. Modern cognitive science would suggest instead a Neurathian project in which no level of analysis is uniquely privileged. Philosopher Otto Neurath (1932/1933; see Quine, 1960, pp. 3–4) employed the metaphor of a boat having some rotten planks. The best way to repair the planks would be to bring the boat ashore, stand on firm ground, and replace the planks. But what if the boat could not be brought ashore? Actually, the boat could still be repaired, but at some risk. We could repair the planks at sea by standing on some of the planks while repairing others. The project could work—we could repair the boat without being on the firm foundation of ground. The Neurathian project is not guaranteed, however, because we might choose to stand on a rotten plank. Nothing in Frankfurt's (1971) notion of higher-order desires guarantees against higher-order judgments being infected by ideas that are personally damaging (see Blackmore, 1999, 2005; Dawkins, 1993; Dennett, 1991, 2006; Distin, 2005; Laland & Brown, 2002; Mesoudi, Whiten, & Laland, 2006).

Rational integration is not always achieved by simply flipping preferences that are in the minority across the levels of analysis, nor can it always best be achieved by the simple rule of giving priority to the highest level. There is a philosophical literature (e.g., Bennett, 1974; McIntyre, 1990) on cases like that of the Mark Twain character, Huckleberry Finn. Huck helped his slave friend Jim run away because of very basic feelings of friendship and sympathy. However, Huck begins to have doubts about his action once he starts explicitly reasoning about how it is morally wrong for slaves to run away and for whites to help them. In this case, we want Huck to identify with his Type 1 emotional processing and to reject the explicit morality that he has been taught.

Philosophers have thought that unless we had a level of cognitive analysis (preferably the highest one) that was foundational, something that we value about ourselves (various candidates in the philosophical literature have been personhood, autonomy, identity, and free will) would be put in jeopardy. Hurley (1989), in contrast, endorses a Neurathian view in which there does not exist either a "highest platform" or a so-called true-self, outside of the interlocking nexus of desires. She argues that "the exercise of autonomy involves depending on certain of our values as a basis for criticizing and revising others, but not detachment from all of them, and that autonomy does not depend on a regress into higher and higher order attitudes, but on the first step" (p. 364). In short, the uniquely human project of self-definition begins at the first step, when an individual begins to climb the ladder of hierarchical values—when a person has, for the first time, a problem of rational integration. But how do we know that a person is engaging deeply in such a process of self-definition and rational integration? Interestingly, perhaps the best indicator is when we detect a mismatch between a person's first-order and second-order desires, with which the person is struggling: The person avows a certain set of values that implies that he or she should prefer to do something other than he or she is doing.

In short, people aspire to rationality broadly conceived, not just instrumental rationality. People want their desires satisfied, but they are concerned about having the right desires. Because humans aspire to rationality broadly rather than narrowly defined, a two-tiered evaluation of their rationality is necessary. The instrumental rationality we achieve must be evaluated by taking into account the complexity of the goals being pursued and by analyzing the dynamics of the cognitive critique. To put it another way, both thin and broad rationality need evaluation. The rules for examining instrumental rationality are well articulated. The criteria that should be applied when evaluating broad rationality are much more complex and contentious (see Nozick's [1993] discussion of 23 criteria for the evaluation of preferences) but would certainly include the following: the degree of strong evaluation undertaken, the degree to which a person finds lack of rational integration aversive and is willing to take steps to rectify it, whether the individual can state a reason for all second-order desires, whether it is the case that a person's desires are not such that acting on them leads to irrational beliefs, whether a person avoids forming desires that are impossible to fulfill, and others (see Nozick, 1993).

Metarationality: Collective Action

Decision theorists and cognitive psychologists have studied extensively the so-called *Prisoner's Dilemma* and *commons-dilemma* situations (Colman, 1995, 2003; Hargreaves Heap & Varoufakis, 1995; Komorita & Parks, 1994). The generic situation is one in which a narrowly rational response (NR) dominates a cooperative response (C), but if every player makes the NR response, the payoff for all is low. In the classic situation that gave the Prisoner's Dilemma its name (Sen, 1982), two criminals commit a crime together and are segregated in separate cells. The prosecutor has proof of a joint minor crime but does not have enough evidence to prove a joint major crime. Each prisoner is asked separately to confess to the major crime. If either confesses and the other does not, the confessor goes free and the other gets the full penalty of 20 years for the major crime. If both confess, both are convicted and get 10-year sentences. If neither confesses, they are both convicted of the minor crime and are both sentenced to 2 years. Each sees the dominance logic that dictates that no matter what the other person does, he is better off confessing. Thus, each does the narrowly rational thing and confesses (NR) and are both convicted of the major crime and given 10-year sentences—a much worse outcome than if they had not confessed (C, the cooperative response) and both received 2-year sentences.

The logic of the situation is displayed in the following table, where the two prisoners are displayed as players in a game and they are designated player 1 and player 2. We can more easily see in the table why NR is a dominating response for player 1. If player 2 chooses the C response, then by choosing NR, player 1 goes free rather than serves 2 years. Similarly, if player 2 chooses the NR response, player 1 is better off choosing NR. In such a scenario, player 1 will serve 10 years rather than 20. Thus, the NR response is the dominating response for player 1. But the NR response is also the dominant response for player 2. Thus, if they are both narrowly rational, both will choose NR and serve 10 years. This result may be narrowly rational, but it is hard to shake the feeling that there is something wrong here, since the CC outcome is so much better for them both.

		Player 2	
		NR	C
Player 1	NR	10 years, 10 years	Go free, 20 years
	C	20 years, go free	2 years, 2 years

Littering is a so-called multiple-player situation known as a commons dilemma (Hardin, 1968) that has an analogous logic. I gain a lot by driving through a faraway city and throwing an inconveniently full paper cup of beverage out the window of my car. Since I will never see the cup again, it will have no negative utility for me because it will never litter my landscape. In a very narrow sense it is rational for me to throw it out—it is an NR response. The problem is that it is narrowly rational for each driver to reason the same way. However, the result of everyone making the NR response is a totally trashed landscape that we all hate to view. Had we all sacrificed the small convenience of not throwing our cups (made the C response), we would all enjoy the immense benefit of an unlittered landscape. The C response is better in the collective sense, but notice the pernicious dominance of the NR response. If you all cooperated and did not throw your cups, then if I throw mine, I get the benefit of an unlittered landscape but I also get the convenience of throwing my cup (I do better than had I responded C). If the rest of you all threw your cups, then I am better off throwing (NR) because had I not thrown, the landscape would have still been littered but I would have forgone the convenience of throwing my cup. The problem is that everyone sees the same dominance logic and hence everyone throws their cups, and we are all less happy than we would have been if everyone had responded C.

What the Prisoner's Dilemma and commons dilemmas show is that rationality must police itself. With issues such as global warming looming, it is possible that world history has entered a stage where it is especially crucial that we exercise metarationality—using rational judgment to examine rationality itself. This is because the influence of markets in our lives may have already begun to become a threat to our broad rationality. Rational models drive some of our society's most successful institutions, such as corporations and financial markets, but the models tend to be narrow ones and thus may be having negative effects.

Numerous social commentators have described the paradoxical malaise that has descended upon the affluent, successful majority in Western societies (e.g., Myers, 2000). We seem to have a surfeit of goods that we certainly show no signs of wanting to give up, but we detect that the other aspects of our environment are deteriorating and we do not know what to do about it. Commuting times have doubled in many North American municipalities in just the last 10 years; childhood has been transformed into one long consumption binge; small communities die out as young adults see that in order to have a good job one must live in a large urban conurbation; music and movies become coarser and coarser, and children are exposed to this at earlier ages; food and water poisoning incidents increase in frequency and scope; we wait in lines of automobiles as we attempt to visit sites of natural beauty; obesity among young children is at an all time high; our rural areas and small towns are defaced by proliferating "big box" stores and their ugly architecture; libraries that were open full-time 30 years ago, when we were less rich, now cut back their hours; smog alerts during the summer increase yearly in most North American cities—all while we enjoy a cornucopia of goods and services that is unprecedented in scope. Several authors have written eloquently about the Prisoner's Dilemma logic that causes many of these problems and is the cause of the seeming paradox (e.g., Baron et al., 2006; Frank, 1999; Myers, 2000). We seem to be in need of a critical stance toward narrow rationality and its consequences. The empirical literature on interactive games does contain some optimistic findings (see Colman, 1995). For example, the more people are aware that they are immersed in a Prisoner's Dilemma logic and the more that they are able to communicate with each other, the greater is their tendency to mutually cooperate and obtain a better outcome than that available from the joint NR response.

Metarationality: Questioning the Applicability of Rational Principles

Engaging in a metarational critique can also be viewed as one way of reconciling the positions of the Panglossians and the Meliorists. Meliorists stress the importance of normative rules—the necessity of following them and of correcting ourselves when we deviate from them. Panglossians stress that deviations might be only apparent and that sometimes they are the result of normative rules that are inappropriately applied. An emphasis on metarationality recognizes the importance of normative rules while at the same time stressing that such rules are very much open to critique.

Consider the example of sunk costs that was discussed in chapter 4. The traditional rational stricture is that sunk costs should be ignored. Decisions should concern only future consequences, and sunk costs are in the past. So, to recall the movie example of Chapter 4, if one would turn off the movie if it were free, then one should also turn off the movie and do something else if one had already paid $7 for it. You should not continue to do something that in the future would make you less happy because you have spent the money in the past. But Keys and Schwartz (2007) point out that there seems nothing wrong with feeling that the memory that you had paid the $7 might depress the enjoyment of whatever else you decided to do. You might feel bad because you had "thrown money down the drain" by not watching. Whatever the normative status of the principle of ignoring sunk costs, it seems right for people to think that "not watching the movie and regretting that you spent the $7" is a worse outcome than that of "not watching the movie." Why shouldn't people take into account the regret that they will feel if they fail to honor sunk costs? Keys and Schwartz (2007) introduce the concept of "leakage" to help us understand this situation. Traditionally, we differentiate the decision itself from the experience of the consequences of that decision. At the time of the decision, the $7 already spent should not be a factor—so says the principle of ignoring sunk costs. But what if that $7 already spent will in fact affect your experience of one of the alternatives (here, specifically, the experience of the alternative of turning off the movie)? If so, then the effect of the $7 (the regret at having "wasted" it) has functionally leaked into the experience of the consequences—and if it is in fact part of the consequence of that option, then why should it be ignored?

Keys and Schwartz (2007) cite studies where (seemingly) irrelevant factors that are used to frame the choice actually leak into the experience of the alternative chosen. They cite studies in which beef labeled as "75% lean" was experienced as tasting better than beef labeled "25% fat," and ones in which people performed better after drinking an energy drink that cost $1.89 than after consuming the same drink when it cost only $0.89. Again, the way the alternatives were framed leaked into the *experience* of the alternatives. Therefore, one argument is that framing effects in such situations are not irrational because the frame leaks into the experience of the consequence. In fact, Keys and Schwartz (2007) point out that if leakage is a fact of life, then the wise decision maker might actually want to take it into account when making decisions.

Consider an example of regret as a leakage factor. Keys and Schwartz (2007) discuss the example of standing in the grocery store line and suspecting that the neighboring line would move faster. What should we do, stay or switch? On the one hand, our visual inspection of the neighboring line and the people in it leads us to suspect that it would move faster. Why would we ever hesitate if this were our judgment? Often, the reason we do in fact hesitate is because we can recall instances in the past where we have switched lines and then observed that our original line actually ended up moving faster. We want to kick ourselves when this happens—we regret our decision to switch. Furthermore, we tend to regret it more than when we fail to switch and the neighboring line does indeed move faster. If we take this anticipatory regret into account, we might well decide to stay in the line we are in even when the neighboring line looks like it will move faster.

In the grocery line and the movie examples, anticipated regret leads us to take actions that would otherwise not be best for us (in the absence of such anticipation). One response to these choices is to defend them as rational cases of taking into account aspects of decision framing that actually do leak into the experienced utility of the action once taken. Another response is to argue that if regret is leading us away from actions that would otherwise be better for us, then perhaps what should be questioned is whether the regret we feel in various situations is appropriate.

This response—that maybe we should *not* let aspects of how the choices are framed leak into our experience—Keys and Schwartz call "leak plugging." That leak plugging may sometimes be called for is suggested by another example that they discuss—that students think that if they change their responses on a multiple-choice test that they are more likely to change a correct response into an incorrect one than vice versa. Keys and Schwartz point out that this belief is false, but that it may be a superstition that arose to help prevent regret. That there is another response to regret other than avoidance is suggested by a question that we might ask about the situation surrounding the multiple-choice superstition: Are people better off with lower grades and reduced regret, or are they better off with some regret but higher grades?

The multiple-choice example thus suggests another response to decision leakage of contextual factors—that rather than simply accommodating such leakage into our utility calculations, we might consider getting rid of the leakage. In short, maybe the most rational thing to do is to condition ourselves to avoid regret in situations where we would choose otherwise without it. Without the regret we could freely and rationally choose to turn off the movie and enjoy an activity that is more fulfilling than watching a boring film. Without the regret we could change to whichever grocery line looked more promising and not worry about our feelings if our predicted outcome did not occur.

Note that a decision to condition ourselves to avoid regret in the movie example would represent a more critical use of the rational principle of avoiding the honoring of sunk costs. It would reflect a use of the sunk-cost principle that was informed by a metarational critique—one that took a critical stance toward the rational principle rather than applying it blindly. A first-order use of the sunk-cost principle would apply it no matter what and—given the natural structure of human psychology—would sometimes result in lower experienced utility because the blind use of the principle fails to account for regret. A critical stance toward the principle would recognize that sometimes it leads to lower experienced utility due to the unaccounted-for regret. But, as a further step in metarational analysis, the regret itself might be critiqued. The sunk-cost principle comes into play again in reminding us that, absent the regret, turning off the movie is the better choice. If, at this point, we decide to endorse the sunk-cost principle, it is in a much more reflective way than simply blindly applying it as a rule without a consideration of human psychology. The decision to alter our psychologies in light of the rule would in a sense be a second-order use of the rule, one that represented a metarational judgment.

This aspect of metarationality is in effect asking about the appropriateness of our emotional reactions to a decision. If we deem these reactions appropriate, then they must be factored in, and sometimes they will trump a normative rule of decision making, just as the Panglossians argue. Other times, however, we will deem the emotions less important than our other goals. We will want the better grades, the better line at the grocery store, and the activity that is better than the boring movie—and we will want all of these things more than we value avoiding regret. In this case, we revert to the traditional normative rule championed by the Meliorist—but only after having engaged in metarational reflection.

Keys and Schwartz (2007) discuss how situations that are repeated are more likely to be the ones where we might want to plug leakage and target some of our emotions for reform. Someone afraid of elevators might be perfectly rational, on a particular occasion, in taking the stairs even though the stairs are slower because they have factored in the negative utility of their fear while riding in the elevator. However, such a person living and working in New York City might well think of accepting some therapy in the service of eliminating this fear. What might look rational on a given single occasion might seem very suboptimal from the standpoint of a *life span* filled with similar activities. Financial decisions that cumulate have a similar logic. Suppose you are the type of person who is affected by friendly salespeople. You tend to buy products from those who are friendly. Furthermore, suppose that there is leakage from decision to experience regarding this factor—you actually enjoy products more when you have purchased them from friendly people. Clearly though, given the logic of our market-based society, you are going to end up paying much more for many of your consumer goods throughout your lifetime. Here, a lifetime and a single case tend to look very different. You pay 25¢ more for a coffee from the Bean People tomorrow because you like them better than the Java People. No problem. But you might answer differently if calculations were to show that buying from friendly people will cost you a compounded return of $175,667 in your retirement fund over a lifetime. With this information, you might decide to plug the leakage and stop responding to the "friendly factor" in your future decisions.

An actual consumer example comes from the "extended warranties" that are sold with many appliances. At the time of each individual purchase, these small-scale insurance contracts may give us some reassurance and comfort. But consumer magazines routinely report that, when aggregated, these are very bad products. That is, across a number of such contracts, the return to the consumer is very low—much more is spent in premiums than is actually returned by making a claim on the warranty. Of course, on one particular purchase, buying the warranty might have positive utility—not because of any money saved, but because it reduces the negative utility of the anxiety we feel at the time of purchase. Nonetheless, however comforting the warranty is in the case of *this particular* appliance, across several such appliances the warranties are a very bad deal. Thus, the consumer is better off by trying to get rid of the purchase anxiety that leads to buying the warranty each time.

These examples show the more delicate interplay between normative rules, individual decisions, and a long-term view of one's goals and desires that takes place when metarationality rather than a thin instrumental rationality is our concern. Metarationality fuses the views of the Meliorist and Panglossian by revealing the incompleteness of both views. An unreflective Meliorist is too quick to apply a blanket normative rule to a specific situation that may have alternative interpretations and subtle contextual factors that might leak into the experience of the consequences. Panglossians are of course quick to point out that there may be rational alternative interpretations of the task and that emotions at the time of decision might leak into experience. But Panglossians sometimes fail to take a broader view of life: one that would examine how certain responses may have cumulative effects over time. Panglossians often fail to see how the hostile environment of many market-based societies will exploit the "alternative interpretation" of the decision maker. A broader view of life, one that recognizes hostile environments and the cumulative effect of repeated instances, might dictate more attention to normative rules. Metarationality demands a broad view of life, a concern for task construal and the role of emotions in decision, *as well as* a concern for the expected utility of the outcome.

Summary and Conclusion

The best tools of thought are self-correcting because they critique themselves. Metarationality consists of bringing rational tools to bear in a critique of rationality itself. We have considered several important such critiques in this chapter. First, it is rational to ask whether it is enough to be satisfied with a thin theory of instrumental rationality—one that does not critique one's own first-order desires but simply treats them as given. Most people answer "no" to this question—they are able to engage in a critique of their first-order desires and goals, even to the extent of viewing a choice that efficiently pursued a first-order goal as wrong. The reason is that people evaluate their own actions and desires in terms of values that they hold. They take a second-order stance toward their desires—they often desire to desire differently. This critique of our first-order desires in terms of higher-order preferences and values is one important form of metarationality.

Another area where rationality critiques itself is in the Prisoner's Dilemma or commons-dilemma situations. In these cases a response that is narrowly rational, in that it displays dominance over other alternatives, turns out to be dysfunctional for everyone if all the people involved in a collective action respond in a way that is narrowly rational for themselves. Many dilemmas of modern life have this structure—individuals, pursuing their narrowly rational interests ruin the environment for themselves when others also act on only the thinnest rational theory. What the Prisoner's Dilemma and other commons-dilemmas show is that rationality must police itself—that there are situations where people might want to bind themselves to an agreement not to pursue their own interests so that we all might obtain a better outcome.

A thin theory of instrumental rationality requires that choices be independent of irrelevant contextual factors. A final form of metarational critique questions our judgments of what factors are irrelevant. Specifically, such a critique recognizes that seemingly irrelevant contextual and emotional factors operating at the time of decision might leak over and affect the experience of the consequence itself. If such leakage occurs, then the contextual factor is not irrelevant. Alternatively, a reconsideration of the normative principle involved might lead us undertake to recondition our psychologies so that the emotion or contextual factor does not leak into our experience of the outcome.

All of these examples of the metarational debate about rational principles illustrate that the evolution of rationality remains an open-ended process of cultural evolution.

Suggestions for Further Readings

Flanagan, O. (2007). *The really hard problem: Meaning in a material world.* Cambridge, MA: MIT Press.

Frankfurt, H. (1971). Freedom of the will and the concept of a person. *Journal of Philosophy, 68,* 5–20.

Kahneman, D., Krueger, A. B., Schkade, D., Schwarz, N., & Stone, A. (2006). Would you be happier if you were richer? A focusing illusion. *Science, 312,* 1908–1910.

Keys, D. J., & Schwartz, B. (2007). "Leaky" rationality: How research on behavioral decision making challenges normative standards of rationality. *Perspectives on Psychological Science, 2,* 162–180.

Myers, D. G. (2000). *The American paradox: Spiritual hunger in an age of plenty.* New Haven, CT: Yale University Press.

Nickerson, C., Schwarz, N., Diener, E., & Kahneman, D. (2003). Zeroing in on the dark side of the American dream: A closer look at the negative consequences of the goal for financial success. *Psychological Science, 14,* 531–536.

Nozick, R. (1989). *The examined life.* New York: Simon & Schuster.

Nozick, R. (1993). *The nature of rationality.* Princeton, NJ: Princeton University Press.

Schwartz, B. (2004). *The paradox of choice.* New York: Ecco Press.

Stanovich, K. E. (2004). *The robot's rebellion: Finding meaning in the age of Darwin.* Chicago: University of Chicago Press.

BIBLIOGRAPHY

Adler, J. E. (1984). Abstraction is uncooperative. *Journal for the Theory of Social Behaviour, 14,* 165–181.

Adler, J. E. (1991). An optimist's pessimism: Conversation and conjunctions. In E. Eells & T. Maruszewski (Eds.), *Probability and rationality: Studies on L. Jonathan Cohen's philosophy of science* (pp. 251–282). Amsterdam: Editions Rodopi.

Adler, J. E., & Rips, L. J. (Eds.). (2008). *Reasoning: Studies of human inference and Its foundations.* New York: Cambridge University Press.

Ajzen, I. (1977). Intuitive theories of events and the effects of base-rate information on prediction. *Journal of Personality and Social Psychology, 35,* 303–314.

Allais, M. (1953). Le comportement de l'homme rationnel devant le risque: Critique des postulats et axioms de l'scole americaine. [Rational man's behavior in the face of risk: Critique of the American School's postulates and axioms] *Econometrica, 21,* 503–546.

Alloy, L. B., & Tabachnik, N. (1984). Assessment of covariation by humans and animals: The joint influence of prior expectations and current situational information. *Psychological Review, 91,* 112–149.

Anderson, E. (1993). *Value in ethics and economics.* Cambridge, MA: Harvard University Press.

Anderson, J. R. (1990). *The adaptive character of thought.* Hillsdale, NJ: Erlbaum.

Anderson, J. R. (1991). Is human cognition adaptive? *Behavioral and Brain Sciences, 14,* 471–517.

Åstebro, T., Jeffrey, S. A., & Adomdza, G. K. (2007). Inventor perseverance after being told to quit: The role of cognitive biases. *Journal of Behavioral Decision Making, 20,* 253–272.

Audi, R. (2001). *The architecture of reason: The structure and substance of rationality*. Oxford: Oxford University Press.

Author. (February 14, 1998). The money in the message. *The Economist*, p. 78.

Ayton, P., & Fischer, I. (2004). The hot hand fallacy and the gambler's fallacy: Two faces of subjective randomness? *Memory & Cognition, 32,* 1369–1378.

Baranski, J. V., & Petrusic, W. M. (1994). The calibration and resolution of confidence in perceptual judgments. *Perception & Psychophysics, 55,* 412–428.

Baranski, J. V., & Petrusic, W. M. (1995). On the calibration of knowledge and perception. *Canadian Journal of Experimental Psychology, 49,* 397–407.

Barbey, A. K., & Sloman, S. A. (2007). Base-rate respect: From ecological rationality to dual processes. *Behavioral and Brain Sciences, 30,* 241–297.

Bargh, J. A., & Chartrand, T. L. (1999). The unbearable automaticity of being. *American Psychologist, 54,* 462–479.

Bar-Hillel, M. (1980). The base-rate fallacy in probability judgments. *Acta Psychologica, 44,* 211–233.

Bar-Hillel, M. (1990). Back to base rates. In R. M. Hogarth (Ed.), *Insights into decision making: A tribute to Hillel J. Einhorn* (pp. 200–216). Chicago: University of Chicago Press.

Baron, J. (1993). *Morality and rational choice*. Dordrecht: Kluwer.

Baron, J. (1998). *Judgment misguided: Intuition and error in public decision making*. New York: Oxford University Press.

Baron, J. (2008). *Thinking and deciding* (4th ed). Cambridge, MA: Cambridge University Press.

Baron, J., Bazerman, M. H., & Shonk, K. (2006). Enlarging the societal pie through wise legislation. A psychological perspective. *Perspectives on Psychological Science, 1,* 123–132.

Baron, J., & Hershey, J. C. (1988). Outcome bias in decision evaluation. *Journal of Personality and Social Psychology, 54,* 569–579.

Baron, J., & Leshner, S. (2000). How serious are expressions of protected values? *Journal of Experimental Psychology: Applied, 6,* 183–194.

Baron, J., & Spranca, M. (1997). Protected values. *Organizational Behavior and Human Decision Processes, 70,* 1–16.

Barrett, H. C., & Kurzban, R. (2006). Modularity in cognition: Framing the debate. *Psychological Review, 113,* 628–647.

Bazerman, M. (2001). Consumer research for consumers. *Journal of Consumer Research, 27,* 499–504.

Bechara, A. (2005). Decision making, impulse control and loss of willpower to resist drugs: A neurocognitive perspective. *Nature Neuroscience, 8,* 1458–1463.

Becker, G. S. (1976). *The economic approach to human behavior*. Chicago: University of Chicago Press.

Bell, D. E. (1982). Regret in decision making under uncertainty. *Operations Research, 30,* 961–981.

Bell, D., Raiffa, H., & Tversky, A. (Eds.). (1988). *Decision making: Descriptive, normative, and prescriptive interactions.* Cambridge: Cambridge University Press.

Bennett, J. (1974). The conscience of Huckleberry Finn. *Philosophy, 49,* 123–134.

Bernoulli, D. (1954). Exposition of a new theory on the measurement of risk. *Econometrica, 22,* 23–36. (Original work published 1738).

Beyth-Marom, R., & Fischhoff, B. (1983). Diagnosticity and pseudodiagnositicity. *Journal of Personality and Social Psychology, 45,* 1185–1195.

Blackmore, S. (1999). *The meme machine.* New York: Oxford University Press.

Blackmore, S. (2005). Can memes meet the challenge? In S. Hurley & N. Chater (Eds.), *Perspectives on imitation* (Vol. 2, pp. 409–411). Cambridge, MA: MIT Press.

Brainerd, C. J., & Reyna, V. F. (2001). Fuzzy-trace theory: Dual processes in memory, reasoning, and cognitive neuroscience. In H. W. Reese & R. Kail (Eds.), *Advances in child development and behavior* (Vol. 28, pp. 41–100). San Diego: Academic Press.

Brandstatter, E., Gigerenzer, G., & Hertwig, R. (2006). The priority heuristic: Making choices without trade-offs. *Psychological Review, 113,* 409–432.

Brase, G. L., Cosmides, L., & Tooby, J. (1998). Individuation, counting, and statistical inference: The role of frequency and whole-object representations in judgment under uncertainty. *Journal of Experimental Psychology: General, 127,* 3–21.

Braun, P. A., & Yaniv, I. (1992). A case study of expert judgment: Economists' probabilities versus base-rate model forecasts. *Journal of Behavioral Decision Making, 5,* 217–231.

Brenner, L. A., Koehler, D. J., Liberman, V., & Tversky, A. (1996). Overconfidence in probability and frequency judgments: A critical examination. *Organizational Behavior and Human Decision Processes, 65,* 212–219.

Broniarczyk, S., & Alba, J. W. (1994). Theory versus data in prediction and correlation tasks. *Organizational Behavior and Human Decision Processes, 57,* 117–139.

Broome, J. (1990). Should a rational agent maximize expected utility? In K. S. Cook & M. Levi (Eds.), *The limits of rationality* (pp. 132–145). Chicago: University of Chicago Press.

Broome, J. (1991). *Weighing goods: Equality, uncertainty, and time.* Oxford: Blackwell.

Bruine de Bruin, W., Parker, A. M., & Fischhoff, B. (2007). Individual differences in adult decision-making competence. *Journal of Personality and Social Psychology, 92,* 938–956.

Buckner, R. L., & Carroll, D. C. (2007). Self-projection and the brain. *Trends in Cognitive Sciences, 11,* 49–57.

Buehler, R., Griffin, D., & Ross, M. (2002). Inside the planning fallacy: The causes and consequences of optimistic time predictions. In T. Gilovich, D. Griffin, & D. Kahneman (Eds.), *Heuristics and biases: The psychology of intuitive judgment* (pp. 250–270). New York: Cambridge University Press.

Burns, B. D., & Corpus, B. (2004). Randomness and inductions from streaks: "Gambler's fallacy" versus "hot hand." *Psychonomic Bulletin & Review, 11,* 179–184.

Buss, D. M. (Ed.). (2005). *The handbook of evolutionary psychology.* Hoboken, NJ: Wiley.

Byrne, R. M. J. (2005). *The rational imagination: How people create alternatives to reality.* Cambridge, MA: MIT Press.

Camerer, C. F. (2000). Prospect theory in the wild: Evidence from the field. In D. Kahneman & A. Tversky (Eds.), *Choices, values, and frames* (pp. 288–300). Cambridge: Cambridge University Press.

Carruthers, P. (2006). *The architecture of the mind.* New York: Oxford University Press.

Casscells, W., Schoenberger, A., & Graboys, T. (1978). Interpretation by physicians of clinical laboratory results. *New England Journal of Medicine, 299,* 999–1001.

Chapman, G. B., & Elstein, A. S. (2000). Cognitive processes and biases in medical decision making. In G. B. Chapman & F. A. Sonnenberg (Eds.), *Decision making in health care: Theory, psychology, and applications* (pp. 183–210). New York: Cambridge University Press.

Cohen, L. J. (1981). Can human irrationality be experimentally demonstrated? *Behavioral and Brain Sciences, 4,* 317–370.

Colman, A. M. (1995). *Game theory and its applications.* Oxford: Butterworth-Heinemann.

Colman, A. M. (2003). Cooperation, psychological game theory, and limitations of rationality in social interaction. *Behavioral and Brain Sciences, 26,* 139–198.

Coltheart, M. (1999). Modularity and cognition. *Trends in Cognitive Sciences, 3,* 115–120.

Cooper, W. S. (1989). How evolutionary biology challenges the classical theory of rational choice. *Biology and Philosophy, 4,* 457–481.

Cooper, W. S., & Kaplan, R. H. (1982). Adaptive coin-flipping: A decision-theoretic examination of natural selection for random individual variation. *Journal of Theoretical Biology, 94,* 135–151.

Cosmides, L. (1989). The logic of social exchange: Has natural selection shaped how humans reason? Studies with the Wason selection task. *Cognition, 31,* 187–276.

Cosmides, L., & Tooby, J. (1992). Cognitive adaptations for social exchange. In J. Barkow, L. Cosmides, & J. Tooby (Eds.), *The adapted mind* (pp. 163–228). New York: Oxford University Press.

Cosmides, L., & Tooby, J. (1994). Beyond intuition and instinct blindness: Toward an evolutionarily rigorous cognitive science. *Cognition, 50,* 41–77.

Cosmides, L., & Tooby, J. (1996). Are humans good intuitive statisticians after all? Rethinking some conclusions from the literature on judgment under uncertainty. *Cognition, 58,* 1–73.

Croson, R., & Sundali, J. (2005). The gambler's fallacy and the hot hand: Empirical data from casinos. *Journal of Risk and Uncertainty, 30,* 195–209.

Cummins, D. D. (1996). Evidence for the innateness of deontic reasoning. *Mind & Language, 11,* 160–190.

Damasio, A. R. (1994). *Descartes' error.* New York: Putnam.

Davis, D., & Holt, C. (1993). *Experimental economics.* Princeton, NJ: Princeton University Press.

Dawes, R. M. (1988). *Rational choice in an uncertain world.* San Diego, CA: Harcourt Brace Jovanovich.

Dawes, R. M. (1991). Probabilistic versus causal thinking. In D. Cicchetti & W. Grove (Eds.), *Thinking clearly about psychology: Essays in honor of Paul E. Meehl* (Vol. 1, pp. 235–264). Minneapolis: University of Minnesota Press.

Dawes, R. M. (1994). *House of cards: Psychology and psychotherapy based on myth.* New York: Free Press.

Dawes, R. M. (1998). Behavioral decision making and judgment. In D. T. Gilbert, S. T. Fiske, & G. Lindzey (Eds.), *The handbook of social psychology* (Vol. 1, pp. 497–548). Boston: McGraw-Hill.

Dawes, R. M. (2001). *Everyday irrationality.* Boulder, CO: Westview Press.

Dawes, R. M., Faust, D., & Meehl, P. E. (1989). Clinical versus actuarial judgment. *Science, 243,* 1668–1673.

Dawkins, R. (1989). *The selfish gene.* New York: Oxford University Press. (Original work published 1976)

Dawkins, R. (1993). Viruses of the mind. In B. Dahlbom (Ed.), *Dennett and his critics* (pp. 13–27). Cambridge, MA: Blackwell.

De Neys, W. (2006). Dual processing in reasoning—Two systems but one reasoner. *Psychological Science, 17,* 428–433.

Dennett, D. C. (1987). *The intentional stance.* Cambridge, MA: MIT Press.

Dennett, D. C. (1991). *Consciousness explained.* Boston: Little Brown.

Dennett, D. C. (2006). From typo to thinko: When evolution graduated to semantic norms. In S. C. Levinson & P. Jaisson (Eds.), *Evolution and culture* (pp. 133–145). Cambridge, MA: MIT Press.

de Sousa, R. (2008). Logic and biology: Emotional inference and emotions in reasoning. In J. E. Adler & L. J. Rips (Eds.), *Reasoning: Studies of human inference and its foundations* (pp. 1002–1015). New York: Cambridge University Press.

Dickson, D. H., & Kelly, I. W. (1985). The "Barnum effect" in personality assessment: A review of the literature. *Psychological Reports, 57,* 367–382.

Distin, K. (2005). *The selfish meme.* Cambridge: Cambridge University Press.

Doherty, M. E., & Mynatt, C. (1990). Inattention to P(H) and to P(D/~H): A converging operation. *Acta Psychologica, 75,* 1–11.

Dominowski, R. L. (1995). Content effects in Wason's selection task. In S. E. Newstead & J. St. B. T. Evans (Eds.), *Perspectives on thinking and reasoning* (pp. 41–65). Hove, England: Erlbaum.

Dulany, D. E., & Hilton, D. J. (1991). Conversational implicature, conscious representation, and the conjunction fallacy. *Social Cognition, 9,* 85–110.

Dunbar, R. (1998). Theory of mind and the evolution of language. In J. R. Hurford, M. Studdert-Kennedy, & C. Knight (Eds.), *Approaches to the evolution of language* (pp. 92–110). Cambridge: Cambridge University Press.

Dworkin, G. (1988). *The theory and practice of autonomy.* Cambridge: Cambridge University Press.

Eddy, D. (1982). Probabilistic reasoning in clinical medicine: Problems and opportunities. In D. Kahneman, P. Slovic, & A. Tversky (Eds.), *Judgment under uncertainty: Heuristics and biases* (pp. 249–267). Cambridge: Cambridge University Press.

Edwards, K., & Smith, E. E. (1996). A disconfirmation bias in the evaluation of arguments. *Journal of Personality and Social Psychology, 71,* 5–24.

Edwards, W. (1954). The theory of decision making. *Psychological Bulletin, 51,* 380–417.

Edwards, W., & von Winterfeldt, D. (1986). On cognitive illusions and their implications. In H. R. Arkes & K. R. Hammond (Eds.), *Judgment and decision making* (pp. 642–679). Cambridge: Cambridge University Press.

Ehrlinger, J., Gilovich, T., & Ross, L. (2005). Peering into the bias blind spot: People's assessments of bias in themselves and others. *Personality and Social Psychology Bulletin, 31,* 680–692.

Einhorn, H. J. (1986). Accepting error to make less error. *Journal of Personality Assessment, 50,* 387–395.

Einhorn, H. J., & Hogarth, R. M. (1981). Behavioral decision theory: Processes of judgment and choice. *Annual Review of Psychology, 32,* 53–88.

Eisenberg, D. M., Kessler, R., Foster, C., Norlock, F., Calkins, D., & Delbanco, T. (1993). Unconventional medicine in the United States. *New England Journal of Medicine, 328,* 246–252.

Elster, J. (1983). *Sour grapes: Studies in the subversion of rationality.* Cambridge: Cambridge University Press.

Epley, N. (2008, January 31). Rebate psychology. *The New York Times,* A27.

Epley, N., Mak, D., & Chen Idson, L. (2006). Bonus or rebate? The impact of income framing on spending and saving. *Journal of Behavioral Decision Making, 19,* 213–227.

Estes, W. K. (1964). Probability learning. In A. W. Melton (Ed.), *Categories of human learning* (pp. 89–128). New York: Academic Press.

Evans, J. St. B. T. (1972). Interpretation and matching bias in a reasoning task. *Quarterly Journal of Experimental Psychology, 24,* 193–199.

Evans, J. St. B. T. (1984). Heuristic and analytic processes in reasoning. *British Journal of Psychology, 75,* 451–468.

Evans, J. St. B. T. (1989). *Bias in human reasoning: Causes and consequences.* Hove, UK: Erlbaum.

Evans, J. St. B. T. (1996). Deciding before you think: Relevance and reasoning in the selection task. *British Journal of Psychology, 87,* 223–240.

Evans, J. St. B. T. (2002). The influence of prior belief on scientific thinking. In P. Carruthers, S. Stich, & M. Siegal (Eds.), *The cognitive basis of science* (pp. 193–210). Cambridge: Cambridge University Press.

Evans, J. St. B. T. (2003). In two minds: Dual-process accounts of reasoning. *Trends in Cognitive Sciences, 7,* 454–459.

Evans, J. St. B. T. (2006). The heuristic-analytic theory of reasoning: Extension and evaluation. *Psychonomic Bulletin and Review, 13,* 378–395.

Evans, J. St. B. T. (2007). *Hypothetical thinking: Dual processes in reasoning and judgment.* New York: Psychology Press.

Evans, J. St. B. T. (2008). Dual-processing accounts of reasoning, judgment and social cognition. *Annual Review of Psychology, 59,* 255–278.

Evans, J. St. B. T., & Frankish, K. (Eds.). (2009). *In two minds: Dual processes and beyond.* Oxford: Oxford University Press.

Evans, J. St. B. T., Newstead, S. E., & Byrne, R. M. J. (1993). *Human reasoning: The psychology of deduction.* Hove, England: Erlbaum.

Evans, J. St. B. T., & Over, D. E. (1996). *Rationality and reasoning.* Hove, England: Psychology Press.

Evans, J. St. B. T., & Over, D. E. (2004). *If.* Oxford: Oxford University Press.

Evans, J. St. B. T., Over, D. E., & Manktelow, K. (1993). Reasoning, decision making and rationality. *Cognition, 49,* 165–187.

Evans, J. St. B. T., Simon, J. H., Perham, N., Over, D. E., & Thompson, V. A. (2000). Frequency versus probability formats in statistical word problems. *Cognition, 77,* 197–213.

Fantino, E., & Esfandiari, A. (2002). Probability matching: Encouraging optimal responding in humans. *Canadian Journal of Experimental Psychology, 56,* 58–63.

Feldman Barrett, L. F., Tugade, M. M., & Engle, R. W. (2004). Individual differences in working memory capacity and dual-process theories of the mind. *Psychological Bulletin, 130,* 553–573.

Fischhoff, B. (1988). Judgment and decision making. In R. J. Sternberg & E. E. Smith (Eds.), *The psychology of human thought* (pp. 153–187). Cambridge: Cambridge University Press.

Fischhoff, B. (1991). Value elicitation: Is there anything there? *American Psychologist, 46,* 835–847.

Fischhoff, B., & Beyth-Marom, R. (1983). Hypothesis evaluation from a Bayesian perspective. *Psychological Review, 90,* 239–260.

Fischhoff, B., Slovic, P., & Lichtenstein, S. (1977). Knowing with certainty: The appropriateness of extreme confidence. *Journal of Experimental Psychology: Human Perception and Performance, 3,* 552–564.

Flanagan, O. (2007). *The really hard problem: Meaning in a material world.* Cambridge, MA: MIT Press.

Fodor, J. A. (1983). *The modularity of mind.* Cambridge, MA: MIT Press.

Forer, B. R. (1949). The fallacy of personal validation: A classroom demonstration of gullibility. *Journal of Abnormal and Social Psychology, 44,* 119–123.

Frank, R. H. (1999). *Luxury fever: Why money fails to satisfy in an era of excess.* New York: Free Press.

Frankfurt, H. (1971). Freedom of the will and the concept of a person. *Journal of Philosophy, 68,* 5–20.

Frederick, S. (2002). Automated choice heuristics. In T. Gilovich, D. Griffin, & D. Kahneman (Eds.), *Heuristics and biases: The psychology of intuitive judgment* (pp. 548–558). New York: Cambridge University Press.

Frisch, D. (1993). Reasons for framing effects. *Organizational Behavior and Human Decision Processes, 54,* 399–429.

Gal, I., & Baron, J. (1996). Understanding repeated simple choices. *Thinking and Reasoning, 2,* 81–98.

Gale, M., & Ball, L. J. (2006). Dual-goal facilitation in Wason's 2–4–6 task: What mediates successful rule discovery? *The Quarterly Journal of Experimental Psychology, 59,* 873–885.

Gallistel, C. R. (1990). *The organization of learning.* Cambridge, MA: MIT Press.

Gauthier, D. (1986). *Morals by agreement.* Oxford: Oxford University Press.

Gawande, A. (1998, February 8). No mistake. *The New Yorker,* pp. 74–81.

Gigerenzer, G. (1991). How to make cognitive illusions disappear: Beyond "heuristics and biases." *European Review of Social Psychology, 2,* 83–115.

Gigerenzer, G. (1996a). On narrow norms and vague heuristics: A reply to Kahneman and Tversky (1996). *Psychological Review, 103,* 592–596.

Gigerenzer, G. (1996b). Rationality: Why social context matters. In P. B. Baltes & U. Staudinger (Eds.), *Interactive minds: Life-span perspectives on the social foundation of cognition* (pp. 319–346). Cambridge: Cambridge University Press.

Gigerenzer, G. (2002). *Calculated risks: How to know when numbers deceive you.* New York: Simon & Schuster.

Gigerenzer, G. (2007). *Gut feelings: The intelligence of the unconscious.* New York: Viking Penguin.

Gigerenzer, G., Hoffrage, U., & Kleinbolting, H. (1991). Probabilistic mental models: A Brunswikian theory of confidence. *Psychological Review, 98,* 506–528.

Gigerenzer, G., & Todd, P. M. (1999). *Simple heuristics that make us smart.* New York: Oxford University Press.

Gilovich, T. (1991). *How we know what isn't so.* New York: Free Press.

Gilovich, T., Griffin, D., & Kahneman, D. (Eds.). (2002). *Heuristics and biases: The psychology of intuitive judgment.* New York: Cambridge University Press.

Girotto, V. (2004). Task understanding. In J. P. Leighton & R. J. Sternberg (Eds.), *The nature of reasoning* (pp. 103–125). Cambridge: Cambridge University Press.

Gladwell, M. (2005). *Blink.* New York: Little, Brown.

Goel, V., & Dolan, R. J. (2003). Explaining modulation of reasoning by belief. *Cognition, 87,* B11–B22.

Goldberg, L. R. (1959). The effectiveness of clinicians' judgments: The diagnosis of organic brain damage from the Bender Gestalt Test. *Journal of Consulting Psychology, 23,* 25–33.

Goldberg, L. R. (1968). Simple models or simple processes? Some research on clinical judgments. *American Psychologist, 23,* 483–496.

Goldberg, L. R. (1991). Human mind versus regression equation: Five contrasts. In D. Cicchetti & W. Grove (Eds.), *Thinking clearly about psychology: Essays in honor of Paul E. Meehl* (Vol. 1, pp. 173–184). Minneapolis: University of Minnesota Press.

Goldstein, D. G., & Gigerenzer, G. (1999). The recognition heuristic: How ignorance makes us smart. In G. Gigerenzer & P. M. Todd (Eds.), *Simple heuristics that make us smart* (pp. 37–58). New York: Oxford University Press.

Goldstein, D. G., & Gigerenzer, G. (2002). Models of ecological rationality: The recognition heuristic. *Psychological Review, 109,* 75–90.

Goldstein, W. M. (2004). Social judgment theory: Applying and extending Brunswik's probabilistic functionalism. In D. J. Koehler & N. Harvey (Eds.), *Blackwell handbook of judgment and decision making* (pp. 37–61). Malden, MA: Blackwell Publishing.

Grether, D. M., & Plott, C. R. (1979). Economic theory of choice and the preference reversal phenomenon. *American Economic Review, 69,* 623–638.

Grice, H. P. (1975). Logic and conversation. In P. Cole & J. Morgan (Eds.), *Syntax and semantics: Vol. 3. Speech acts* (pp. 41–58). New York: Academic Press.

Griffin, D., & Tversky, A. (1992). The weighing of evidence and the determinants of confidence. *Cognitive Psychology, 24,* 411–435.

Griggs, R. A., & Cox, J. R. (1982). The elusive thematic-materials effect in Wason's selection task. *British Journal of Psychology, 73,* 407–420.

Groopman, J. (2007). *How doctors think.* Boston: Houghton Mifflin.

Hacking, I. (2001). *An introduction to probability and inductive logic.* Cambridge: Cambridge University Press.

Haidt, J. (2001). The emotional dog and its rational tail: A social intuitionist approach to moral judgment. *Psychological Review, 108,* 814–834.

Hammond, K. R. (1996). *Human judgment and social policy.* New York: Oxford University Press.

Hammond, K. R. (2007). *Beyond rationality: The search for wisdom in a troubled time.* Oxford: Oxford University Press.

Handley, S. J., Capon, A., Beveridge, M., Dennis, I., & Evans, J. S. B. T. (2004). Working memory, inhibitory control and the development of children's reasoning. *Thinking and Reasoning, 10,* 175–195.

Hardin, G. (1968). The tragedy of the commons. *Science, 162,* 1243–1248.

Hargreaves Heap, S. P., & Varoufakis, Y. (1995). *Game theory: A critical introduction.* London: Routledge.

Harman, G. (1995). Rationality. In E. E. Smith & D. N. Osherson (Eds.), *Thinking* (Vol. 3, pp. 175–211). Cambridge, MA: MIT Press.

Hartman, R. S., Doane, M. J., & Woo, C. (1991). Consumer rationality and the status quo. *Quarterly Journal of Economics, 106,* 141–162.

Hasher, L., Lustig, C., & Zacks, R. (2007). Inhibitory mechanisms and the control of attention. In A. Conway, C. Jarrold, M. Kane, A. Miyake, & J. Towse (Eds.), *Variation in working memory* (pp. 227–249). New York: Oxford University Press.

Hasher, L., & Zacks, R. T. (1979). Automatic processing of fundamental information: The case of frequency of occurrence. *Journal of Experimental Psychology: General, 39,* 1372–1388.

Hastie, R., & Dawes, R. M. (2001). *Rational choice in an uncertain world.* Thousand Oaks, CA: Sage.

Hertwig, R., & Gigerenzer, G. (1999). The 'conjunction fallacy' revisited: How intelligent inferences look like reasoning errors. *Journal of Behavioral Decision Making, 12,* 275–305.

Hilton, D. J. (1995). The social context of reasoning: Conversational inference and rational judgment. *Psychological Bulletin, 118,* 248–271.

Hilton, D. J. (2003). Psychology and the financial markets: Applications to understanding and remedying irrational decision-making. In I. Brocas & J. D. Carrillo (Eds.), *The psychology of economic decisions: Vol. 1. Rationality and well-being* (pp. 273–297). Oxford: Oxford University Press.

Hines, T. M. (2003). *Pseudoscience and the paranormal* (2nd ed.). Buffalo, NY: Prometheus Books.

Hirschman, A. O. (1986). *Rival views of market society and other recent essays.* New York: Viking.

Hoch, S. J. (1985). Counterfactual reasoning and accuracy in predicting personal events. *Journal of Experimental Psychology: Learning, Memory, and Cognition, 11,* 719–731.

Hollis, M. (1992). Ethical preferences. In S. Hargreaves Heap, M. Hollis, B. Lyons, R. Sugden, & A. Weale (Eds.), *The theory of choice: A critical guide* (pp. 308–310). Oxford: Blackwell.

Huber, J., & Puto, C. (1983). Market boundaries and product choice: Illustrating attraction and substitution effects. *Journal of Consumer Research, 10,* 31–44.

Humphrey, N. (1976). The social function of intellect. In P. P. G. Bateson & R. A. Hinde (Eds.), *Growing points in ethology* (pp. 303–317). London: Faber & Faber.

Hurley, S. L. (1989). *Natural reasons: Personality and polity.* New York: Oxford University Press.

Jacobs, J. E., & Potenza, M. (1991). The use of judgment heuristics to make social and object decisions: A developmental perspective. *Child Development, 62,* 166–178.

Jeffrey, R. (1974). Preferences among preferences. *Journal of Philosophy, 71,* 377–391.

Jeffrey, R. C. (1983). *The logic of decision* (2nd ed.). Chicago: University of Chicago Press.

Jensen, K., Call, J., & Tomasello, M. (2007). Chimpanzees are rational meximizers in an ultimatum game. *Science, 318,* 107–109.

Johnson, E. J., & Goldstein, D. G. (2006). Do defaults save lives? In S. Lichtenstein & P. Slovic (Eds.), *The construction of preference* (pp. 682–688). Cambridge: Cambridge University Press.

Johnson, E. J., Hershey, J., Meszaros, J., & Kunreuther, H. (2000). Framing, probability distortions, and insurance decisions. In D. Kahneman & A. Tversky (Eds.), *Choices, values, and frames* (pp. 224–240). Cambridge: Cambridge University Press.

Johnson-Laird, P. N. (1999). Deductive reasoning. *Annual Review of Psychology, 50,* 109–135.

Johnson-Laird, P. N. (2006). *How we reason.* Oxford: Oxford University Press.

Johnson-Laird, P. N., & Oatley, K. (1992). Basic emotions, rationality, and folk theory. *Cognition and Emotion, 6,* 201–223.

Jungermann, H. (1986). The two camps on rationality. In H. R. Arkes & K. R. Hammond (Eds.), *Judgment and decision making* (pp. 627–641). Cambridge: Cambridge University Press.

Juslin, P. (1994). The overconfidence phenomenon as a consequence of informal experimenter-guided selection of almanac items. *Organizational Behavior and Human Decision Processes, 57,* 226–246.

Juslin, P., Winman, A., & Persson, T. (1994). Can overconfidence be used as an indicator of reconstructive rather than retrieval processes? *Cognition, 54,* 99–130.

Kahneman, D. (1991). Judgment and decision making: A personal view. *Psychological Science, 2,* 142–145.

Kahneman, D. (1994). New challenges to the rationality assumption. *Journal of Institutional and Theoretical Economics, 150,* 18–36.

Kahneman, D. (2000). A psychological point of view: Violations of rational rules as a diagnostic of mental processes. *Behavioral and Brain Sciences, 23,* 681–683.

Kahneman, D. (2003). A perspective on judgment and choice: Mapping bounded rationality. *American Psychologist, 58,* 697–720.

Kahneman, D., & Frederick, S. (2002). Representativeness revisited: Attribute substitution in intuitive judgment. In T. Gilovich, D. Griffin, & D. Kahneman (Eds.), *Heuristics and biases: The psychology of intuitive judgment* (49–81). New York: Cambridge University Press.

Kahneman, D., & Frederick, S. (2005). A model of heuristic judgment. In K. J. Holyoak & R. G. Morrison (Eds.), *The Cambridge handbook of thinking and reasoning* (pp. 267–293). New York: Cambridge University Press.

Kahneman, D., Knetsch, J. L., & Thaler, R. (1991). The endowment effect, loss aversion, and status quo bias. *Journal of Economic Perspectives, 5,* 193–206.

Kahneman, D., Krueger, A. B., Schkade, D., Schwarz, N., & Stone, A. (2006). Would you be happier if you were richer? A focusing illusion. *Science, 312,* 1908–1910.

Kahneman, D., & Tversky, A. (1972). Subjective probability: A judgment of representativeness. *Cognitive Psychology, 3,* 430–454.

Kahneman, D., & Tversky, A. (1973). On the psychology of prediction. *Psychological Review, 80,* 237–251.

Kahneman, D., & Tversky, A. (1979). Prospect theory: An analysis of decision under risk. *Econometrica, 47,* 263–291.

Kahneman, D., & Tversky, A. (1984). Choices, values, and frames. *American Psychologist, 39,* 341–350.

Kahneman, D., & Tversky, A. (1996). On the reality of cognitive illusions. *Psychological Review, 103,* 582–591.

Kahneman, D., & Tversky, A. (Eds.). (2000). *Choices, values, and frames.* Cambridge: Cambridge University Press.

Kane, M. J., & Engle, R. W. (2003). Working-memory capacity and the control of attention: The contributions of goal neglect, response competition, and task set to Stroop interference. *Journal of Experimental Psychology: General, 132,* 47–70.

Kern, L., & Doherty, M. E. (1982). "Pseudodiagnosticity" in an idealized medical problem-solving environment. *Journal of Medical Education, 57,* 100–104.

Keys, D. J., & Schwartz, B. (2007). "Leaky" rationality: How research on behavioral decision making challenges normative standards of rationality. *Perspectives on Psychological Science, 2,* 162–180.

King, R. N., & Koehler, D. J. (2000). Illusory correlations in graphological inference. *Journal of Experimental Psychology: Applied, 6,* 336–348.

Klaczynski, P. A. (2000). Motivated scientific reasoning biases, epistemological beliefs, and theory polarization: A two-process approach to adolescent cognition. *Child Development, 71,* 1347–1366.

Klaczynski, P. A. (2001). Analytic and heuristic processing influences on adolescent reasoning and decision making. *Child Development, 72,* 844–861.

Klaczynski, P. A., & Lavallee, K. L. (2005). Domain-specific identity, epistemic regulation, and intellectual ability as predictors of belief-based reasoning: A dual-process perspective. *Journal of Experimental Child Psychology, 92,* 1–24.

Klaczynski, P. A., & Narasimham, G. (1998). Development of scientific reasoning biases: Cognitive versus ego-protective explanations. *Developmental Psychology, 34,* 175–187.

Klauer, K. C., Stahl, C., & Erdfelder, E. (2007). The abstract selection task: New data and an almost comprehensive model. *Journal of Experimental Psychology: Learning, Memory, and Cognition, 33,* 688–703.

Klayman, J., & Ha, Y. (1987). Confirmation, disconfirmation, and information in hypothesis testing. *Psychological Review, 94,* 211–228.

Koehler, D. J., & Harvey, N. (Eds.). (2004). *Blackwell handbook of judgment and decision making.* Oxford, England: Blackwell.

Koehler, J. J. (1996). The base rate fallacy reconsidered: Descriptive, normative and methodological challenges. *Behavioral and Brain Sciences, 19,* 1–53.

Kohler, W. (1927). *The mentality of apes* (2nd ed.). London: Routledge and Kegan Paul.

Kokis, J., Macpherson, R., Toplak, M., West, R. F., & Stanovich, K. E. (2002). Heuristic and analytic processing: Age trends and associations with cognitive ability and cognitive styles. *Journal of Experimental Child Psychology, 83,* 26–52.

Komorita, S. S., & Parks, C. D. (1994). *Social dilemmas.* Boulder, CO: Westview Press.

Koriat, A., Lichtenstein, S., & Fischhoff, B. (1980). Reasons for confidence. *Journal of Experimental Psychology: Human Learning and Memory, 6,* 107–118.

Kornblith, H. (1993). *Inductive inference and its natural ground.* Cambridge, MA: MIT Press.

Krantz, D. H. (1991). From indices to mappings: The representational approach to measurement. In D. R. Brown & J. E. K. Smith (Eds.), *Frontiers of mathematical psychology* (pp. 1–52). New York: Springer-Verlag.

Laland, K. N., & Brown, G. R. (2002). *Sense and nonsense: Evolutionary perspectives on human behaviour.* Oxford: Oxford University Press.

LeBoeuf, R. A., & Shafir, E. (2003). Deep thoughts and shallow frames: On the susceptibility to framing effects. *Journal of Behavioral Decision Making, 16,* 77–92.

Levin, I. P., & Hart, S. S. (2003). Risk preferences in young children: Early evidence of individual differences in reaction to potential gains and losses. *Journal of Behavioral Decision Making, 16,* 397–413.

Levin, I. P., Hart, S. S., Weller, J. A., & Harshman, L. A. (2007). Stability of choices in a risky decision-making task: A 3-year longitudinal study with children and adults. *Journal of Behavioral Decision Making, 20,* 241–252.

Levin, I. P., Wasserman, E. A., & Kao, S. F. (1993). Multiple methods of examining biased information use in contingency judgments. *Organizational Behavior and Human Decision Processes, 55,* 228–250.

Levinson, S. C. (1995). Interactional biases in human thinking. In E. Goody (Eds.), *Social intelligence and interaction* (pp. 221–260). Cambridge: Cambridge University Press.

Levy, S. (2005, January 31). Does your iPod play favorites? *Newsweek,* p. 10.

Lichtenstein, S., & Slovic, P. (1971). Reversal of preferences between bids and choices in gambling decisions. *Journal of Experimental Psychology, 89,* 46–55.

Lichtenstein, S., & Slovic, P. (1973). Response-induced reversals of preference in gambling: An extended replication in Las Vegas. *Journal of Experimental Psychology, 101,* 16–20.

Lichtenstein, S., & Slovic, P. (Ed.). (2006). *The construction of preference.* Cambridge: Cambridge University Press.

Lieberman, M. D. (2000). Intuition: A social cognitive neuroscience approach. *Psychological Bulletin, 126,* 109–137.

Lieberman, M. D. (2003). Reflexive and reflective judgment processes: A social cognitive neuroscience approach. In J. P. Forgas, K. R. Williams, & W. von Hippel (Eds.), *Social judgments: Implicit and explicit processes* (pp. 44–67). New York: Cambridge University Press.

Lilienfeld, S. O. (1999). Projective measures of personality and psychopathology: How well do they work? *Skeptical Inquirer, 23,* 32–39.

Loomes, G., & Sugden, R. (1982). Regret theory: An alternative theory of rational choice under uncertainty. *Economic Journal, 92,* 805–824.

Luce, R. D., & Raiffa, H. (1957). *Games and decisions.* New York: Wiley.

Lyon, D., & Slovic, P. (1976). Dominance of accuracy information and neglect of base rates in probability estimation. *Acta Psychologica, 40,* 287–298.

Macchi, L. (1995). Pragmatic aspects of the base-rate fallacy. *Quarterly Journal of Experimental Psychology, 48A,* 188–207.

MacErlean, N. (2002, August 4). Do the sums—it's in your interest. *The Observer* (London), Cash 2–3.

Maher, P. (1993). *Betting on theories.* Cambridge: Cambridge University Press.

Mamassian, P. (2008). Overconfidence in an objective anticipatory motor task. *Psychological Science, 19,* 601–606.

Manktelow, K. I. (1999). *Reasoning and thinking.* Hove, England: Psychology Press.

Manktelow, K. I. (2004). Reasoning and rationality: The pure and the practical. In K. I. Manktelow & M. C. Chung (Eds.), *Psychology of reasoning: Theoretical and historical perspectives* (pp. 157–177). Hove, England: Psychology Press.

Manktelow, K. I., & Evans, J. St. B. T. (1979). Facilitation of reasoning by realism: Effect or non-effect? *British Journal of Psychology, 70,* 477–488.

Manktelow, K. I., & Over, D. E. (1991). Social roles and utilities in reasoning with deontic conditionals. *Cognition, 39,* 85–105.

Margolis, H. (1987). *Patterns, thinking, and cognition.* Chicago: University of Chicago Press.

Markovits, H., & Nantel, G. (1989). The belief-bias effect in the production and evaluation of logical conclusions. *Memory & Cognition, 17,* 11–17.

Markowitz, H. M. (1952). The utility of wealth. *Journal of Political Economy, 60,* 151–158.

Marks, D. F. (2001). *The psychology of the psychic.* Buffalo, NY: Prometheus.

McClure, S. M., Laibson, D. I., Loewenstein, G., & Cohen, J. D. (2004). Separate neural systems value immediate and delayed monetary rewards. *Science, 306,* 503–507.

McEvoy, S. P., Stevenson, M. R., McCartt, A. T., Woodword, M., Haworth, C., Palamara, P., & Cercarelli, R. (2005, August 20). Role of mobile phones in motor vehicle crashes resulting in hospital attendance: A case-crossover study. *British Medical Journal, 331,* 428.

McIntyre, A. (1990). Is akratic action always irrational? In O. Flanagan & A. O. Rorty (Eds.), *Identity, character, and morality* (pp. 379–400). Cambridge, MA: MIT Press.

McKenzie, C. R. M. (2003). Rational models as theories—not standards—of behavior. *Trends in Cognitive Sciences, 7,* 403–406.

McKenzie, C. R. M., & Nelson, J. D. (2003). What a speaker's choice of frame reveals: Reference points, frame selection, and framing effects. *Psychonomic Bulletin and Review, 10,* 596–602.

McNeil, B., Pauker, S., Sox, H., & Tversky, A. (1982). On the elicitation of preferences for alternative therapies. *New England Journal of Medicine, 306,* 1259–1262.

Medin, D. L., & Bazerman, M. H. (1999). Broadening behavioral decision research: Multiple levels of cognitive processing. *Psychonomic Bulletin & Review, 6,* 533–546.

Medin, D. L., Schwartz, H. C., Blok, S. V., & Birnbaum, L. A. (1999). The semantic side of decision making. *Psychonomic Bulletin & Review, 6,* 562–569.

Meehl, P. E. (1954). *Clinical versus statistical prediction: A theoretical analysis and review of the literature.* Minneapolis: University of Minnesota Press.

Mele, A. R., & Rawling, P. (Eds.). (2004). *The Oxford handbook of rationality.* Oxford: Oxford University Press.

Mellers, B., Hertwig, R., & Kahneman, D. (2001). Do frequency representations eliminate conjunction effects? An exercise in adversarial collaboration. *Psychological Science, 12,* 269–275.

Mesoudi, A., Whiten, A., & Laland, K. N. (2006). Towards a unified science of cultural evolution. *Behavioral and Brain Sciences, 29,* 329–383.

Metcalfe, J., & Mischel, W. (1999). A hot/cool-system analysis of delay of gratification: Dynamics of will power. *Psychological Review, 106,* 3–19.

Mithen, S. (1996). *The prehistory of mind: The cognitive origins of art and science.* London: Thames and Hudson.

Miyake, A., Friedman, N., Emerson, M. J., & Witzki, A. H. (2000). The utility and diversity of executive functions and their contributions to complex "frontal lobe" tasks: A latent variable analysis. *Cognitive Psychology, 41,* 49–100.

Myers, D. G. (2000). *The American paradox: Spiritual hunger in an age of plenty.* New Haven, CT: Yale University Press.

Mynatt, C. R., Doherty, M. E., & Dragan, W. (1993). Information relevance, working memory, and the consideration of alternatives. *Quarterly Journal of Experimental Psychology, 46A,* 759–778.

Nathanson, S. (1994). *The ideal of rationality.* Chicago: Open Court.

Neumann, P. J., & Politser, P. E. (1992). Risk and optimality. In J. F. Yates (Ed.), *Risk-taking behavior* (pp. 27–47). Chichester, England: John Wiley.

Neurath, O. (1932/1933). Protokollsatze. *Erkenntis, 3,* 204–214.

Newstead, S. E., & Evans, J. St. B. T. (Eds.). (1995). *Perspectives on thinking and reasoning.* Hove, England: Erlbaum.

Newstead, S. E., Handley, S. J., Harley, C., Wright, H., & Farrelly, D. (2004). Individual differences in deductive reasoning. *Quarterly Journal of Experimental Psychology, 57A,* 33–60.

Nickerson, C., Schwarz, N., Diener, E., & Kahneman, D. (2003). Zeroing in on the dark side of the American dream: A closer look at the negative consequences of the goal for financial success. *Psychological Science, 14,* 531–536.

Nickerson, R. S. (1998). Confirmation bias: A ubiquitous phenomenon in many guises. *Review of General Psychology, 2,* 175–220.

Nickerson, R. S. (2002). The production and perception of randomness. *Psychological Review, 109,* 330–357.

Nickerson, R. S. (2004). *Cognition and chance: The psychology of probabilistic reasoning.* Mahwah, NJ: Erlbaum.

Nisbett, R. E., & Ross, L. (1980). *Human inference: Strategies and shortcomings of social judgment.* Englewood Cliffs, NJ: Prentice Hall.

Nozick, R. (1989). *The examined life.* New York: Simon & Schuster.

Nozick, R. (1993). *The nature of rationality.* Princeton, NJ: Princeton University Press.

Oaksford, M., & Chater, N. (1994). A rational analysis of the selection task as optimal data selection. *Psychological Review, 101,* 608–631.

Oaksford, M., & Chater, N. (2001). The probabilistic approach to human reasoning. *Trends in Cognitive Sciences, 5,* 349–357.

Oaksford, M., & Chater, N. (2007). *Bayesian rationality: The probabilistic approach to human reasoning.* Oxford: Oxford University Press.

Oatley, K. (1992). *Best laid schemes: The psychology of emotions.* Cambridge: Cambridge University Press.

Oatley, K. (1999). Why fiction may be twice as true as fact: Fiction as cognitive and emotional simulation. *Review of General Psychology, 3,* 101–117.

Ohman, A., & Mineka, S. (2001). Fears, phobias, and preparedness: Toward an evolved module of fear and fear learning. *Psychological Review, 108,* 483–522.

Over, D. E. (2004). Rationality and the normative/descriptive distinction. In D. J. Koehler & N. Harvey (Eds.), *Blackwell handbook of judgment and decision making* (pp. 3–18). Malden, MA: Blackwell.

Overton, W. F., Byrnes, J. P., & O'Brien, D. P. (1985). Developmental and individual differences in conditional reasoning: The role of contradiction training and cognitive style. *Developmental Psychology, 21,* 692–701.

Parker, A. M., & Fischhoff, B. (2005). Decision-making competence: External validation through an individual differences approach. *Journal of Behavioral Decision Making, 18,* 1–27.

Payne, J. W., Bettman, J. R., & Johnson, E. J. (1992). Behavioral decision research: A constructive processing perspective. *Annual Review of Psychology, 43,* 87–131.

Perreaux, L. (2001, May 17). Drivers all edgy: Survey. *National Post* (Toronto), p. A7.

Petry, N. M. (2005). *Pathological gambling: Etiology, comorbidity, and treatment.* Washington, DC: American Psychological Association.

Petry, N. M., Bickel, W. K., & Arnett, M. (1998). Shortened time horizons and insensitivity to future consequences in heroin addicts. *Addiction, 93,* 729–738.

Pinker, S. (1994). *The language instinct.* New York: William Morrow.

Pinker, S. (1997). *How the mind works.* New York: Norton.

Plous, S. (1993). *The psychology of judgment and decision making.* New York: McGraw-Hill.

Pohl, R. (Ed.). (2004). *Cognitive illusions: A handbook on fallacies and biases in thinking, judgment and memory.* Hove, England: Psychology Press.

Poletiek, F. H. (2001). *Hypothesis testing behaviour.* Hove, England: Psychology Press.

Politzer, G., & Macchi, L. (2000). Reasoning and pragmatics. *Mind & Society, 1,* 73–93.

Politzer, G., & Noveck, I. A. (1991). Are conjunction rule violations the result of conversational rule violations? *Journal of Psycholinguistic Research, 20,* 83–103.

Pollard, P., & Evans, J. St. B. T. (1987). Content and context effects in reasoning. *American Journal of Psychology, 100,* 41–60.

Prado, J., & Noveck, I. A. (2007). Overcoming perceptual features in logical reasoning: A parametric functional magnetic resonance imaging study. *Journal of Cognitive Neuroscience, 19,* 642–657.

Quattrone, G., & Tversky, A. (1984). Causal versus diagnostic contingencies: On self-deception and on the voter's illusion. *Journal of Personality and Social Psychology, 46,* 237–248.

Quine, W. (1960). *Word and object.* Cambridge, MA: MIT Press.

Reber, A. S. (1992). An evolutionary context for the cognitive unconscious. *Philosophical Psychology, 5,* 33–51.

Reber, A. S. (1993). *Implicit learning and tacit knowledge.* New York: Oxford University Press.

Redelmeier, D. A., & Shafir, E. (1995). Medical decision making in situations that offer multiple alternatives. *JAMA, 273,* 302–305.

Resnik, M. D. (1987). *Choices: An introduction to decision theory.* Minneapolis: University of Minnesota Press.

Reyna, V. F. (2004). How people make decisions that involve risk. *Current Directions in Psychological Science, 13,* 60–66.

Reyna, V. F., & Ellis, S. (1994). Fuzzy-trace theory and framing effects in children's risky decision making. *Psychological Science, 5,* 275–279.

Rode, C., Cosmides, L., Hell, W., & Tooby, J. (1999). When and why do people avoid unknown probabilities in decisions under uncertainty? Testing some predictions from optimal foraging theory. *Cognition, 72,* 269–304.

Ronis, D. L., & Yates, J. F. (1987). Components of probability judgment accuracy: Individual consistency and effects of subject matter and assessment method. *Organizational Behavior and Human Decision Processes, 40,* 193–218.

Royal Swedish Academy of Sciences, The. (2002b). *The Bank of Sweden Prize in Economic Sciences in Memory of Alfred Nobel 2002: Information for the public* [Press release]. Retrieved August 6, 2007, from http://www.nobel.se/economics/laureates/2002/press.html

Russo, J. E., & Schoemaker, P. (1989). *Decision traps: Ten barriers to brilliant decision making and how to overcome them.* New York: Simon & Schuster.

Sá, W., West, R. F., & Stanovich, K. E. (1999). The domain specificity and generality of belief bias: Searching for a generalizable critical thinking skill. *Journal of Educational Psychology, 91,* 497–510.

Salthouse, T. A., Atkinson, T. M., & Berish, D. E. (2003). Executive functioning as a potential mediator of age-related cognitive decline in normal adults. *Journal of Experimental Psychology: General, 132,* 566–594.

Samuels, R. (2005). The complexity of cognition: Tractability arguments for massive modularity. In P. Carruthers, S. Laurence, & S. Stich (Eds.), *The innate mind* (pp. 107–121). Oxford: Oxford University Press.

Samuels, R. (2009). The magical number two, plus or minus: Dual process theory as a theory of cognitive kinds. In J. Evans & K. Frankish (Eds.), *In two minds: Dual processes and beyond* (pp. 129–148). Oxford: Oxford University Press.

Samuels, R., & Stich, S. P. (2004). Rationality and psychology. In A. R. Mele & P. Rawling (Eds.), *The Oxford handbook of rationality* (pp. 279–300). Oxford: Oxford University Press.

Samuelson, W., & Zeckhauser, R. J. (1988). Status quo bias in decision making. *Journal of Risk and Uncertainty, 1,* 7–59.

Savage, L. J. (1954). *The foundations of statistics.* New York: Wiley.

Schick, F. (1987). Rationality: A third dimension. *Economics and Philosophy, 3,* 49–66.

Schwartz, B. (2004). *The paradox of choice.* New York: Ecco Press.

Schwartz, S., & Griffin, T. (Eds.). (1986). *Medical thinking: The psychology of medical judgment and decision making.* New York: Springer-Verlag.

Searle, J. R. (2001). *The rationality of action.* Cambridge, MA: MIT Press.

Sen, A. K. (1977). Rational fools: A critique of the behavioral foundations of economic theory. *Philosophy and Public Affairs, 6,* 317–344.

Sen, A. K. (1982). Choices, orderings and morality. In A. Sen, *Choice, welfare and measurement* (pp. 74–83*).* Cambridge, MA: Harvard University Press.

Sen, A. K. (1993). Internal consistency of choice. *Econometrica, 61,* 495–521.

Shafer, G. (1988). Savage revisited. In D. Bell, H. Raiffa, & A. Tversky (Eds.), *Decision making: Descriptive, normative, and prescriptive interactions* (pp. 193–234). Cambridge: Cambridge University Press.

Shafir, E. (1994). Uncertainty and the difficulty of thinking through disjunctions. *Cognition, 50,* 403–430.

Shafir, E., & LeBoeuf, R. A. (2002). Rationality. *Annual Review of Psychology, 53,* 491–517.

Shafir, E., Simonson, I., & Tversky, A. (1993). Reason-based choice. *Cognition, 49,* 11–36.

Shafir, E., & Tversky, A. (1995). Decision making. In E. E. Smith & D. N. Osherson (Eds.), *Thinking* (Vol. 3, pp. 77–100). Cambridge, MA: MIT Press.

Shanks, D. R. (1995). Is human learning rational? *Quarterly Journal of Experimental Psychology, 48A,* 257–279.

Shiffrin, R. M., & Schneider, W. (1977). Controlled and automatic human information processing: II. Perceptual learning, automatic attending, and a general theory. *Psychological Review, 84,* 127–190.

Sieck, W. R., & Arkes, H. R. (2005). The recalcitrance of overconfidence and its contribution to decision aid neglect. *Journal of Behavioral Decision Making, 18,* 29–53.

Sieck, W., & Yates, J. F. (1997). Exposition effects on decision making: Choice and confidence in choice. *Organizational Behavior and Human Decision Processes, 70,* 207–219.

Simon, H. A. (1956). Rational choice and the structure of the environment. *Psychological Review, 63,* 129–138.

Simon, H. A. (1957). *Models of man.* New York: Wiley.

Sinaceur, M., Heath, C., & Cole, S. (2005). Emotional and deliberative reactions to a public crisis: Mad cow disease in France. *Psychological Science, 16,* 247–254.

Skyrms, B. (1996). *The evolution of the social contract.* Cambridge: Cambridge University Press.

Sloman, S. A. (1996). The empirical case for two systems of reasoning. *Psychological Bulletin, 119,* 3–22.

Sloman, S. A. (2002). Two systems of reasoning. In T. Gilovich, D. Griffin, & D. Kahneman (Eds.), *Heuristics and biases: The psychology of intuitive judgment* (pp. 379–396). New York: Cambridge University Press.

Sloman, S. A., & Over, D. E. (2003). Probability judgement from the inside out. In D. E. Over (Ed.), *Evolution and the psychology of thinking* (pp. 145–169). Hove, UK: Psychology Press.

Sloman, S. A., Over, D., Slovak, L., & Stibel, J. M. (2003). Frequency illusions and other fallacies. *Organizational Behavior and Human Decision Processes, 91,* 296–309.

Slovic, P. (1995). The construction of preference. *American Psychologist, 50,* 364–371.

Slovic, P., & Tversky, A. (1974). Who accepts Savage's axiom? *Behavioral Science, 19,* 368–373.

Smith, E. R., & DeCoster, J. (2000). Dual-process models in social and cognitive psychology: Conceptual integration and links to underlying memory systems. *Personality and Social Psychology Review, 4,* 108–131.

Smith, S. M., & Levin, I. P. (1996). Need for cognition and choice framing effects. *Journal of Behavioral Decision Making, 9,* 283–290.

Sperber, D. (1994). The modularity of thought and the epidemiology of representations. In L. A. Hirschfeld & S. A. Gelman (Eds.), *Mapping the mind: Domain specificity in cognition and culture* (pp. 39–67). Cambridge: Cambridge University Press.

Sperber, D., Cara, F., & Girotto, V. (1995). Relevance theory explains the selection task. *Cognition, 57,* 31–95.

Sperber, D., & Wilson, D. (1995). *Relevance: Communication and cognition* (2nd ed.). Cambridge, MA: Blackwell.

Stanovich, K. E. (1999). *Who is rational? Studies of individual differences in reasoning.* Mahwah, NJ: Erlbaum.

Stanovich, K. E. (2004). *The robot's rebellion: Finding meaning in the age of Darwin.* Chicago: University of Chicago Press.

Stanovich, K. E. (2009). *What intelligence tests miss: The psychology of rational thought.* New Haven, CT: Yale University Press.

Stanovich, K. E., Toplak, M. E., & West, R. F. (2008). The development of rational thought: A taxonomy of heuristics and biases. *Advances in Child Development and Behavior, 36,* 251–285.

Stanovich, K. E., & West, R. F. (1998a). Cognitive ability and variation in selection task performance. *Thinking and Reasoning, 4,* 193–230.

Stanovich, K. E., & West, R. F. (1998b). Individual differences in framing and conjunction effects. *Thinking and Reasoning, 4,* 289–317.

Stanovich, K. E., & West, R. F. (1998c). Individual differences in rational thought. *Journal of Experimental Psychology: General, 127,* 161–188.

Stanovich, K. E., & West, R. F. (1998d). Who uses base rates and P(D/~H)? An analysis of individual differences. *Memory & Cognition, 26,* 161–179.

Stanovich, K. E., & West, R. F. (1999). Discrepancies between normative and descriptive models of decision making and the understanding/acceptance principle. *Cognitive Psychology, 38,* 349–385.

Stanovich, K. E., & West, R. F. (2000). Individual differences in reasoning: Implications for the rationality debate? *Behavioral and Brain Sciences, 23,* 645–726.

Stanovich, K. E., & West, R. F. (2008). On the relative independence of thinking biases and cognitive ability. *Journal of Personality and Social Psychology, 94,* 672–695.

Stein, E. (1996). *Without good reason: The rationality debate in philosophy and cognitive science.* Oxford: Oxford University Press.

Stenning, K., & van Lambalgen, M. (2004). The natural history of hypotheses about the selection task. In K. I. Manktelow & M. C. Chung (Eds.), *Psychology of reasoning* (pp. 127–156). Hove, England: Psychology Press.

Sternberg, R. J. (2003). *Wisdom, intelligence, and creativity synthesized.* Cambridge: Cambridge University Press.

Stich, S. P. (1990). *The fragmentation of reason.* Cambridge: MIT Press.

Stigler, S. M. (1983). Who discovered Bayes's theorem? *American Statistician, 37,* 290–296.

Stigler, S. M. (1986). *The history of statistics: The measurement of uncertainty before 1900.* Cambridge, MA: Harvard University Press.

Strayer, D. L., & Drews, F. A. (2007). Cell-phone-induced driver distraction. *Current Directions in Psychological Science, 16,* 128–131.

Strayer, D. L., & Johnston, W. A. (2001). Driven to distraction: Dual-task studies of simulated driving and conversing on a cellular telephone. *Psychological Science, 12,* 462–466.

Suddendorf, T., & Corballis, M. C. (2007). The evolution of foresight: What is mental time travel and is it unique to humans? *Behavioral and Brain Sciences, 30,* 299–351.

Sunstein, C. R. (2002). *Risk and reason: Safety, law, and the environment.* Cambridge: Cambridge University Press.

Svenson, O. (1981). Are we all less risky and more skillful than our fellow drivers? *Acta Psychologica, 47,* 143–148.

Swartz, R. J., & Perkins, D. N. (1989). *Teaching thinking: Issues and approaches.* Pacific Grove, CA: Midwest Publications.

Swets, J. A., Dawes, R. M., & Monahan, J. (2000). Psychological science can improve diagnostic decisions. *Psychological Science in the Public Interest, 1,* 1–26.

Tan, H., & Yates, J. F. (1995). Sunk cost effects: The influences of instruction and future return estimates. *Organizational Behavior and Human Decision Processes, 63,* 311–319.

Tentori, K., Osherson, D., Hasher, L., & May, C. (2001). Wisdom and aging: Irrational preferences in college students but not older adults. *Cognition, 81,* B87–B96.

Tetlock, P. E. (2005). *Expert political judgment.* Princeton, NJ: Princeton University Press.

Tetlock, P. E., & Mellers, B. A. (2002). The great rationality debate. *Psychological Science, 13,* 94–99.

Thaler, R. H. (1980). Toward a positive theory of consumer choice. *Journal of Economic Behavior and Organization, 1,* 39–60.

Thaler, R. H. (1992). *The winner's curse: Paradoxes and anomalies of economic life.* New York: Free Press.

Thaler, R. H., & Sunstein, C. R. (2008). *Nudge: Improving decisions about health, wealth, and happiness.* New Haven, CT: Yale University Press.

Todd, P. M., & Gigerenzer, G. (2000). Précis of simple heuristics that make us smart. *Behavioral and Brain Sciences, 23,* 727–780.

Todd, P. M., & Gigerenzer, G. (2007). Environments that make us smart: Ecological rationality. *Current Directions in Psychological Science, 16,* 167–171.

Toplak, M., Liu, E., Macpherson, R., Toneatto, T., & Stanovich, K. E. (2007). The reasoning skills and thinking dispositions of problem gamblers: A dual-process taxonomy. *Journal of Behavioral Decision Making, 20,* 103–124.

Toplak, M. E., & Stanovich, K. E. (2002). The domain specificity and generality of disjunctive reasoning: Searching for a generalizable critical thinking skill. *Journal of Educational Psychology, 94,* 197–209.

Towse, J. N., & Neil, D. (1998). Analyzing human random generation behavior: A review of methods used and a computer program for describing performance. *Behavior Research Methods, Instruments & Computers, 30,* 583–591.

Tversky, A. (1975). A critique of expected utility theory: Descriptive and normative considerations. *Erkenntnis, 9,* 163–173.

Tversky, A. (2003). *Preference, belief, and similarity: Selected writings of Amos Tversky* (E. Shafir, Ed.). Cambridge, MA: MIT Press.

Tversky, A., & Edwards, W. (1966). Information versus reward in binary choice. *Journal of Experimental Psychology, 71,* 680–683.

Tversky, A., & Kahneman, D. (1974). Judgment under uncertainty: Heuristics and biases. *Science, 185,* 1124–1131.

Tversky, A., & Kahneman, D. (1981). The framing of decisions and the psychology of choice. *Science, 211,* 453–458.

Tversky, A., & Kahneman, D. (1982). Evidential impact of base rates. In D. Kahneman, P. Slovic, & A. Tversky (Eds.), *Judgment under uncertainty: Heuristics and biases* (pp. 153–160). Cambridge: Cambridge University Press.

Tversky, A., & Kahneman, D. (1983). Extensional versus intuitive reasoning: The conjunction fallacy in probability judgment. *Psychological Review, 90,* 293–315.

Tversky, A., & Kahneman, D. (1986). Rational choice and the framing of decisions. *Journal of Business, 59,* 251–278.

Tversky, A., & Koehler, D. J. (1994). Support theory: A nonextensional representation of subjective probability. *Psychological Review, 101,* 547–567.

Tversky, A., & Shafir, E. (1992). The disjunction effect in choice under uncertainty. *Psychological Science, 3,* 305–309.

Tversky, A., & Simonson, I. (1993). Context-dependent preferences. *Management Science, 3929,* 1179–1189.

Tversky, A., Slovic, P., & Kahneman, D. (1990). The causes of preference reversal. *American Economic Review, 80,* 204–217.

Twachtman-Cullen, D. (1997). *A passion to believe.* Boulder, CO: Westview.

Tweney, R. D., Doherty, M. E., Warner, W. J., & Pliske, D. (1980). Strategies of rule discovery in an inference task. *Quarterly Journal of Experimental Psychology, 32,* 109–124.

Uchitelle, L. (2002, January, 13). Why it takes psychology to make people save. *New York Times,* section 3, p. 4.

Vallone, R., Griffin, D. W., Lin, S., & Ross, L. (1990). Overconfident prediction of future actions and outcomes by self and others. *Journal of Personality and Social Psychology, 58,* 582–592.

von Neumann, J., & Morgenstern, O. (1944). *The theory of games and economic behavior.* Princeton: Princeton University Press.

Wagenaar, W. A. (1988). *Paradoxes of gambling behavior.* Hove, England: Erlbaum.

Wagenaar, W. A., & Keren, G. (1986). The seat belt paradox: Effect of adopted roles on information seeking. *Organizational Behavior and Human Decision Processes, 38,* 1–6.

Wason, P. C. (1960). On the failure to eliminate hypotheses in a conceptual task. *Quarterly Journal of Experimental Psychology, 12,* 129–140.

Wason, P. C. (1966). Reasoning. In B. Foss (Ed.), *New horizons in psychology* (pp. 135–151). Harmonsworth, England: Penguin:

Wason, P. C. (1968). Reasoning about a rule. *Quarterly Journal of Experimental Psychology, 20,* 273–281.

Wasserman, E. A., Dorner, W. W., & Kao, S. F. (1990). Contributions of specific cell information to judgments of interevent contingency. *Journal of Experimental Psychology: Learning, Memory, and Cognition, 16,* 509–521.

West, R. F., & Stanovich, K. E. (1997). The domain specificity and generality of overconfidence: Individual differences in performance estimation bias. *Psychonomic Bulletin & Review, 4,* 387–392.

West, R. F., Toplak, M., & Stanovich, K. E. (2008). Heuristics and biases as measures of critical thinking: Associations with cognitive ability and thinking dispositions. *Journal of Educational Psychology, 100,* 930–941.

Willingham, D. T. (1998). A neuropsychological theory of motor-skill learning. *Psychological Review, 105,* 558–584.

Willingham, D. T. (1999). The neural basis of motor-skill learning. *Current Directions in Psychological Science, 8,* 178–182.

ilson, T. D. (2002). *Strangers to ourselves.* Cambridge, MA: Harvard University Press.

n, T. D., & Brekke, N. (1994). Mental contamination and mental rrection: Unwanted influences on judgments and evaluations. hological Bulletin, 116, 117–142.

, Gruppen, L. D., & Billi, J. E. (1985). Differential diagnosis and the ing hypothesis heuristic—a practical approach to judgment under uncertainty and Bayesian probability. *Journal of the American Medical Association, 253,* 2858–2862.

Wood, J. M., Nezworski, M. T., Lilienfeld, S. O., & Garb, H. N. (2003). *What's wrong with the Rorschach?* San Francisco: Jossey-Bass.

Yates, J. F., Lee, J., & Bush, J. G. (1997). General knowledge overconfidence: Cross-national variations, response style, and "reality." *Organizational Behavior and Human Decision Processes, 70,* 87–94.

Zelazo, P. D. (2004). The development of conscious control in childhood. *Trends in Cognitive Sciences, 8,* 12–17.

AUTHOR INDEX

Adler, J. E., 6, 34, 102, 117, 142
Adomdza, G. K., 71
Ajzen, I., 59
Alba, J. W., 110
Allais, M., 21, 77
Alloy, L. B., 111
Anderson, E., 146
Anderson, J. R., 94, 131
Arkes, H. R., 69
Åstebro, T., 71
Atkinson, T. M., 130
Audi, R., 2, 6
Author, 96
Ayton, P., 79

Ball, L. J., 89
Baranski, J. V., 71
Barbey, A. K., 59, 104, 142
Bargh, J. A., 128
Bar-Hillel, M., 55
Baron, J., 3, 8, 21, 28, 45, 46, 49, 71, 82, 93, 106, 133, 145, 146, 154
Barrett, H. C., 128
Bazerman, M. H., 28, 137, 145
Bechara, A., 127
Becker, G. S., 15
Bell, D. E., 22, 133
Bennett, J., 151
Berish, D. E., 130
Bernoulli, D., 12
Bettman, J. R., 43
Beveridge, M., 123

Beyth-Marom, R., 61, 63
Billi, J. E., 67
Birnbaum, L. A., 145
Blackmore, S., 151
Blok, S. V., 145
Brainerd, C. J., 127
Brandstatter, E., 136
Brase, G. L., 133
Braun, P. A., 71
Brekke, N., 31
Brenner, L. A., 105
Broniarczyk, S., 110
Broome, J., 21, 22
Brown, G. R., 151
Buehler, R., 71
Burns, B. D., 79
Bush, J. G., 20, 69
Buss, D. M., 128
Byrne, R. M. J., 87, 130
Byrnes, J. P., 124

Call, J., 145
Camerer, C. F., 46
Capon, A., 123
Cara, F., 88
Carruthers, P., 128, 141
Casscells, W., 56
Chapman, G. B., 67
Chartrand, T. L., 128
Chater, N., 87, 88, 94, 97, 98, 124
Chen Idson, L., 47
Cohen, J. D., 128

Cohen, L. J., 95, 124
Cole, S., 139
Colman, A. M., 119, 144, 152, 155
Coltheart, M., 128
Cooper, W. S., 107
Corballis, M. C., 130
Corpus, B., 79
Cosmides, L., 56, 88, 94, 100, 101, 103, 104, 118, 124, 133, 134
Cox, J. R., 99
Croson, R., 79
Cummins, D. D., 99, 100, 102

Damasio, A. R., 4
Davis, D., 95
Dawes, R. M., 8, 14, 18, 23, 31, 49, 50, 74, 75, 82, 84, 85, 111
Dawkins, R., 60, 151
De Neys, W., 132
DeCoster, J., 127
Dennett, D. C., 100
Dennis, I., 123
Dickson, D. H., 67
Diener, E., 161
Distin, K., 151
Doane, M. J., 37
Doherty, M. E., 61, 62, 64, 66, 90
Dolan, R. J., 127
Dominowski, R. L., 99
Dorner, W. W., 66
Dragan, W., 64
Drews, F. A., 72
Dulany, D. E., 72
Dunbar, R., 102
Dworkin, G., 150

Eddy, D., 75
Edwards, K., 112
Edwards, W., 14, 50, 95, 106
Einhorn, H. J., 82, 135
Ellis, S., 124
Elstein, A. S., 67
Elster, J., 5, 143, 145
'merson, M. J., 41, 130
  ·le, R. W., 127, 130
   v, N., 47, 48
    'der, E., 87
      ·ri, A., 82
      K., 106
      B. T., 87, 88, 89, 93, 98, 99, 100, '09, 111, 112, 121, 123, 127, '2

Fantino, E., 82
Farrelly, D., 123
Faust, D., 85
Feldman Barrett, L. F., 127
Fischer, I., 79
Fischhoff, B., 23, 43, 61, 63, 69, 123
Flanagan, O., 161
Fodor, J. A., 128
Forer, B. R., 67
Frank, R. H., 154
Frankfurt, H., 147, 148, 151, 161
Frankish, K., 141, 142
Frederick, S., 35, 73, 78, 127, 128, 142
Friedman, N., 130
Frisch, D., 114, 115

Gal, I., 82, 106
Gale, M., 89
Gallistel, C. R., 106
Garb, H. N., 111
Gauthier, D., 149
Gawande, A., 86
Gigerenzer, G., 35, 73, 91, 94, 95, 102, 103, 104, 105, 106, 107, 124, 125, 136, 137
Gilovich, T., 23, 46, 91, 142
Girotto, V., 72, 88
Gladwell, M., 4
Goel, V., 127
Goldberg, L. R., 85
Goldstein, D. G., 48, 49, 137
Goldstein, W. M., 2, 14
Graboys, T., 56
Grether, D. M., 42
Grice, H. P., 102
Griffin, D. W., 69, 71, 91
Griffin, T., 75
Griggs, R. A., 99
Groopman, J., 46, 67, 72, 75
Gruppen, L. D., 67

Ha, Y., 89
Hacking, I., 92
Haidt, J., 127
Hammond, K. R., 2, 14
Handley, S. J., 123
Hardin, G., 120, 144, 153
Hargreaves Heap, S. P., 152
Harley, C., 123
Harman, G., 2, 6, 133
Harshman, L. A., 124
Hart, S. S., 124
Hartman, R. S., 37

Harvey, N., 7, 50, 92
Hasher, L., 40, 130
Hastie, R., 8, 50
Heath, C., 139
Hell, W., 134
Hershey, J. C., 35, 45
Hertwig, R., 72, 102, 136
Hilton, D. J., 46, 72, 101, 102
Hirschman, A. O., 146
Hoch, S. J., 71
Hoffrage, U., 104
Hogarth, R. M., 135
Hollis, M., 146
Holt, C., 95
Huber, J., 40

Jacobs, J. E., 124
Jeffrey, R. C., 147
Jensen, K., 145
Johnson, E. J., 35, 43, 48, 49, 87
Johnson-Laird, P. N., 3, 88, 98, 107
Johnston, W. A., 72
Jungermann, H., 95
Juslin, P., 104

Kahneman, D., 21, 23, 25, 26, 28, 30, 31,
    32, 33, 35, 38, 39, 43, 50, 52, 55, 59, 72,
    73, 76, 77, 78, 91, 92, 93, 95, 101, 106,
    127, 128, 130, 142, 149, 161
Kane, M. J., 130
Kao, S. F., 66
Kaplan, R. H., 107
Kelly, I. W., 67
Keren, G., 86
Kern, L., 66
Keys, D. J., 115, 124, 155, 156, 157, 158, 161
King, R. N., 67, 69, 110
Klaczynski, P. A., 123, 124
Klauer, K. C., 87, 88, 98
Klayman, J., 89
Kleinbolting, H., 104
Knetsch, J. L., 35
Koehler, D. J., 7, 50, 67, 78, 92, 110
Koehler, J. J., 55, 59, 103, 105
Kohler, W., 144, 145
Kokis, J., 123, 124
Komorita, S. S., 120, 144, 152
Kornblith, H., 111
Krantz, D. H., 43
Krueger, A. B., 161
Kunreuther, H., 35
Kurzban, R., 128

Laibson, D. I., 128
Laland, K. N., 151
Lavallee, K. L., 123
LeBoeuf, R. A., 123, 142
Lee, J., 69
Leshner, S., 145
Levin, I. P., 66, 110, 123, 124
Levinson, S. C., 118
Levy, S., 81
Liberman, V., 105
Lichtenstein, S., 23, 33, 38, 39, 43, 50, 69
Lieberman, M. D., 128
Lilienfeld, S. O., 111
Lin, S., 71
Liu, E., 79
Loewenstein, G., 128
Loomes, G., 22
Luce, R. D., 14, 21, 50
Lustig, C., 130
Lyon, D., 55

Macchi, L., 55, 72
MacErlean, N., 138
Macpherson, R., 79, 123
Maher, P., 22
Mak, D., 47
Mamassian, P., 71
Manktelow, K. I., 2, 6, 99, 100, 111
Margolis, H., 88
Markowitz, H. M., 26
Marks, D. F., 67
May, C., 40
McClure, S. M., 128
McEvoy, S. P., 72
McIntyre, A., 151
McKenzie, C. R. M., 113, 114, 124
McNeil, D., 29
Medin, D. L., 145
Meehl, P. E., 84, 85
Mele, A. R., 2, 6, 7, 125, 142
Mellers, B. A., 72, 95
Mesoudi, A., 151
Meszaros, J., 35
Metcalfe, J., 127
Mineka, S., 128
Mischel, W., 127
Mithen, S., 102
Miyake, A., 130
Monahan, J., 85
Morgenstern, O., 14, 50
Myers, D. G., 154, 161
Mynatt, C. R., 61, 62, 64, 65, 66

Nantel, G., 108
Narasimham, G., 124
Nathanson, S., 2, 7
Neil, D., 80
Nelson, J. D., 113, 114
Neumann, P. J., 21, 138
Neurath, O., 150
Newstead, S. E., 87, 99, 123
Nezworski, M. T., 111
Nickerson, C., 161
Nickerson, R. S., 7, 80, 92
Nisbett, R. E., 110
Noveck, I. A., 102, 128
Nozick, R., 145, 149, 152, 161

Oaksford, M., 87, 88, 94, 97, 98, 124
Oatley, K., 3, 130
Ohman, A., 128
Osherson, D., 6, 40
Over, D. E., 2, 7, 56, 89, 94, 100, 104, 111,
    127, 130
Overton, W. F., 124

Parker, A. M., 123
Parks, C. D., 120, 144, 152
Pauker, S., 29
Payne, J. W., 43
Perham, N., 104
Perreaux, L., 72
Persson, T., 104
Petrusic, W. M., 71
Petry, N. M., 79
Pinker, S., 118, 128, 140
Pliske, D., 90
Plott, C. R., 42
Plous, S., 91
Pohl, R., 92
Poletiek, F. H., 89
Politser, P. E., 21, 138
Politzer, G., 72, 102
Pollard, P., 99
Potenza, M., 124
Prado, J., 128
    ito, C., 40

    'rone, G., 146
    W., 150

    14, 50, 133
    2, 6, 7, 125, 142
    '32
    A., 40, 41

Resnik, M. D., 11
Reyna, V. F., 21, 124, 127
Rips, L. J., 6, 142
Rode, C., 134
Ronis, D. L., 71
Ross, L., 71, 110
Royal Swedish Academy of Sciences, The., 52
Russo, J. E., 91

Sá, W., 108, 109
Salthouse, T. A., 130
Samuels, R., 7, 125, 128, 142
Samuelson, W., 37
Savage, L. J., 14, 18, 21
Schick, F., 21, 22
Schkade, D., 161
Schneider, W., 128
Schoemaker, P., 91
Schoenberger, A., 56
Schwartz, B., 40, 115, 124, 155, 156, 157,
    158, 161
Schwartz, H. C., 145
Schwartz, S., 75
Schwarz, N., 161
Searle, J. R., 144, 145
Sen, A. K., 17, 146, 152
Shafer, G., 21, 23, 31, 43
Shafir, E., 19, 20, 23, 34, 35, 40, 41, 43, 44,
    92, 123, 142
Shanks, D. R., 66
Shonk, K., 28
Sieck, W. R., 69, 114
Simon, H. A., 133
Simon, J. H., 104
Simonson, I., 19, 40
Sinaceur, M., 139
Skyrms, B., 107, 131, 132
Sloman, S. A., 56, 59, 104, 127, 142
Slovak, L., 56
Slovic, P., 21, 22, 23, 33, 38, 39, 43, 50, 55,
    69, 149
Smith, E. E., 6, 112
Smith, E. R., 127
Smith, S. M., 123
Sox, H., 29
Sperber, D., 88, 102, 128
Spranca, M., 145
Stahl, C., 87
Stanovich, K. E., 44, 45, 56, 63, 64, 71, 79,
    93, 94, 95, 99, 100, 108, 109, 110, 115,
    121, 122, 123, 127, 132, 142, 149, 161
Stein, E., 95, 125

Stenning, K., 87, 98
Sternberg, R. J., 122
Stibel, J. M., 56
Stich, S. P., 7, 125, 131, 133, 142
Stigler, S. M., 54
Stone, A., 161
Strayer, D. L., 72
Suddendorf, T., 130
Sugden, R., 22
Sundali, J., 79
Sunstein, C. R., 28, 46, 49, 94
Svenson, O., 86
Swets, J. A., 85

Tabachnik, N., 111
Tan, H., 21
Tentori, K., 40
Tetlock, P. E., 69, 71, 85, 95
Thaler, R. H., 28, 33, 34, 35, 36, 46, 49, 96
Todd, P. M., 35, 94, 125, 136, 137
Tomasello, M., 145
Toneatto, T., 79
Tooby, J., 56, 94, 100, 103, 104, 118, 124, 133, 134
Toplak, M. E., 79, 123
Towse, J. N., 80
Tugade, M. M., 127
Tversky, A., 19, 21, 22, 23, 25, 26, 29, 30, 31, 32, 33, 38, 39, 40, 43, 44, 50, 52, 55, 59, 69, 72, 76, 77, 78, 92, 93, 95, 101, 105, 106, 127, 130, 133, 146, 149
Tweney, R. D., 90

Uchitelle, L., 96

Vallone, R., 71
van Lambalgen, M., 87, 98
Varoufakis, Y., 152
von Neumann, J., 14, 50
von Winterfeldt, D., 95

Wagenaar, W. A., 79, 86
Warner, W. J., 90
Wason, P. C., 87, 89, 97, 100
Wasserman, E. A., 66
Weller, J. A., 124
West, R. F., 44, 45, 56, 63, 64, 71, 99, 108, 110, 115, 121, 123
Whiten, A., 151
Willingham, D. T., 128
Wilson, D., 102
Wilson, T. D., 31, 128
Winman, A., 104
Witzki, A. H., 130
Wolf, F. M., 67
Woo, C., 37
Wood, J. M., 111
Wright, H., 123

Yaniv, I., 71
Yates, J. F., 21, 69, 71, 114

Zacks, R. T., 130
Zeckhauser, R. J., 37
Zelazo, P. D., 130

SUBJECT INDEX

....

Abstraction, 33–34
Actuarial prediction, 82–86
Allais paradox, 21–22, 76–77
Alternative hypothesis, 87–90
  ignoring of, 60–68
Attention, 129
Attribute substitution, 73, 128

Base-rate neglect, 55–60
  alternative interpretations of, 103–104
Bayes' theorem, 52–55, 60–61
Belief bias, 107–112
Belief projection, 109–112
Between-subjects designs, 24

Cell phone use
  in automobiles, 72
Certainty effect, 76–77
Chance, 79–82
Choice axioms, 14–22, 44
  context and, 16–18, 46, 155–160
Clinical prediction, 82–86
Collective action, 152–155
  commons dilemma, 152–155
  conditional probabilities, 53, 73–76
  confirmation bias, 87–90
  conjunction fallacy, 72–73
  alternative interpretations of, 101–103
  constructed choice, 40–41
  constructed preference
  choice, 42–44

Controlled processing, 129
Covariation detection, 66–67, 109–110

Decisions
  experienced consequences of, 155–159
  "leakage" in, 155–159
  meaning and, 144–146
  symbolic nature of, 145–146
  values and, 144–146
Decontextualization, 33–34
Default heuristic, 35–36
Deontic reasoning, 100–101
Descriptive invariance, 22–36
Descriptive models, 9, 132–133
Desires
  first order, 146–152
  second order, 146–152
  evaluation of, 146–152
Developmental research, 122–124
Disjunctions
  "unpacking" of, 78
Disjunctive reasoning, 20
Dominance, 18–20, 30–33
Dual-process theory, 127–131

Economics
  "rational man" and, 15, 22–23, 38, 42–43
  rationality assumption in, 95–96
Emotions, 3–4, 158
Endowment effect, 36–38
Ethical preferences, 146

Expected utility, 8–13
    axiomatic approach to, 14–15, 46
Expected value, 11–12
Evolutionary psychology, 94–95, 98–100,
    106–107, 131–136, 140

Falsifiability, 87–90
Four-card selection task, 87–88
    alternative interpretations of, 97–101
Framing effects, 22–36, 155–157
    alternative interpretations of, 113–116
    practical examples of, 46–48
Frequency formats, 103–104

Gambler's fallacy, 78–81
Gambling, 79, 86
Gricean communication norms, 102–103

Heuristic processing, 128–129
    hostile and benign environments for,
        135–141
Heuristics and biases, 52, 90–91, 93–94
Hypothesis testing, 87–90

Independence axiom, 21–22
Independence of irrelevant alternatives,
    16–17, 39–40
Intelligence, 122–124
Irrationality
    practical examples, 46–48

Judgment
    decision making and, 51–52
Justification, 34–35

Knowledge calibration, 69–72, 104–106

Libertarian paternalism, 48–49
Likelihood ratio, 60–68
Loss aversion, 26–28, 36–37

Medical decision making, 29–30, 56–57, 75
Metarationality, 143–144, 155–159
Money pump, 14–15, 38–39

Normative model, 8–9, 44, 52–53,
    132–133

Opposite
    thinking of, 61–68
Outcome bias, 44–45

Overconfidence, 69–72
    alternative interpretations of, 104–106
Override
    of Type 1 processing, 129–130, 1
        36, 139

P(D/~H), 60–68
Personal finance, 137–138
Pragmatic inferences, 102–103, 113–114
Prediction
    clinical versus actuarial, 82–86
Preferences, 15, 22–23, 25, 31
    as constructed, 42–44
    second order, 146–152
Preference reversals, 38–39
Prescriptive models, 133
Prior probability, 55–58
Prisoner's dilemma, 152–155
Probability
    calibration, 51–52, 69–72
    conditional probability, 53, 73–76
    conjunction, 72–73
    disjunctions and, 78
    judgment and, 51–52, 55–60
    rules of, 52–55
Probability matching, 82–83
    alternative interpretations of, 106–107
Procedural invariance, 38–39
Prospect theory, 26–28, 47–48, 76–77
P. T. Barnum effect, 67–68

Randomness, 79–81
Rationality, 1–5
    beliefs and, 51–52
    bounded, 133
    broad theory of, 5–6, 143–144,
        146–152
    economics and, 15, 22–23
    emotions and, 3–5
    epistemic, 2, 51–52
    folk psychology and, 4–5
    Great Debate, 93–97, 126–127
    individual differences, 120–124
    instrumental, 1–2, 8–9, 14, 31, 46,
        131–132
    integration of preferences, 149–152
    intelligence and, 4
    logic and, 3
    Meliorist position in Great Debate,
        93–94, 116–120, 132–135
    narrow view of, 5–6, 143–144

Rationality (*continued*)
  Panglossian position in Great Debate,
    94–95, 116–120, 132–135
  personal autonomy and, 46–48
  practical examples, 46–48
  thin theory of, 5–6, 143–144, 146
  utility theory and, 8–9, 46
Reason-based decisions, 34–35, 40–41
Regret, 21–22, 115–116, 156–157
Regularity principle, 39–42
Risky choice, 18
Rorschach test, 110–111

Self assessment, 72
Social intelligence, 102–103
Status-quo bias, 36–38

Subjective expected utility, 9, 13–14
Sunk-cost fallacy, 114–116, 155–157
Sure-thing principle, 18–20
Syllogistic reasoning, 107–109

Thinking dispositions, 122–124
Transitivity, 14–15

Utility theory, 8–14

Ventromedial prefrontal cortex, 4–5
Vividness, 129–130, 139
Voting
  symbolic utility of, 145–146

Within-subjects designs, 24